PRAISE FOR *ROAR LIKE A GODDESS*

"Acharya Shunya, the first female head of an ancient Vedic lineage, brings the powerful Hindu goddesses Durga, Lakshmi, and Saraswati alive for our modern context with her vivid pre-patriarchal interpretations of their qualities and activities. She offers direct practices to locate these goddess energies within ourselves. The book provides an ongoing point of reference to refresh our goddess connections in the face of everyday challenges. Her personal stories and those of other women offer inspiration and guidance for readers to strengthen personal agency, dedication to self-care, and care of others based on wisdom, self-respect, and respect for all life."

RACHAEL WOOTEN, PhD

Diplomate Jungian analyst and author of *Tara: The Liberating Power of the Female Buddha*

"What Acharya Shunya has accomplished in this book is nothing short of a reinterpretation of the Hindu tradition, harnessing its mythic power for the empowerment of women of all faiths (or none). Her command of a vast and varied tradition is unmistakable, her wisdom is evident, and her enthusiasm is infectious. This is a book destined to be life-changing for anyone bold enough to enter into its symbolic world. It not only rocks—it roars."

REV. DR. JOHN R. MABRY

author of *Spiritual Guidance across Traditions*

"One of the gifts we receive from the Indian tradition is the recognition of the Divine Feminine as Shakti, the nondual energy of life. The goddesses of India are faces of the one great Shakti, and each of them has her own nature—which is a facet of our nature. When we know how to internalize and contemplate these goddess energies, their Shakti can transform us from within. Acharya Shunya beautifully reveals how understanding and practicing with these goddesses can empower a woman to experience her own deep power, beauty, and wisdom."

SALLY KEMPTON

author of *Awakening Shakti* and *Meditation for the Love of It*

"*Roar Like a Goddess* is a portal to the power of the three wisdom goddesses that lie within each of us. This book is a transmission that will awaken and empower you."

TRACEE STANLEY

author of *Radiant Rest* and *Empowered Life Self-Inquiry Oracle Deck*

"Through my work as a yoga advocate and spiritual activist, I've found it increasingly important to turn to ancient spiritual texts as a blueprint for modern living. In her newest book, Acharya Shunya does just this: through discussion of goddess legends and theory, she provides actionable information for empowerment and establishes herself as a unique voice in the field of yogic and feminist studies. Unafraid to speak truth to power, Acharya Shunya's voice is powerful and resonant like a channeled message for us from the divine goddesses of Vedic culture. There are many messages and practices that all will find useful, regardless of gender identity. I love the meditations and affirmation practices particularly as a foundation for self-development, as well as a powerful addition to my personal practice. *Roar Like a Goddess* is a timeless book so needed right now, in our times. It is a resource and a delight to read that I will be turning to again and again."

SUSANNA BARKATAKI

author of *Embrace Yoga's Roots*

"*Roar Like a Goddess* is a much-needed clarion call for every woman (and man) to stand up and exclaim: 'I'm willing to be seen. I'm willing for my voice to be heard. I'm willing to be fully connected to myself. I'm willing to own and express my place of value, purpose, and belonging within myself and in the world around me.' Shunya's is not an ego-centric petition. Hers is one that also exclaims: 'I'm willing to see you, hear you, stay connected to you, and welcome you as equally empowered as I am.' Shunya's words are not a request but a clear-hearted demand that this modern era asks of all of us—all women and all men: to stand up and affirm our interconnectedness and express our full potential as human beings. Filled with keen insight, inspiring stories, and potent exercises, *Roar Like a Goddess* is a treasure and pleasure to read—a seminal work for all of us who wish to embrace a clear path to knowing and standing up in who we truly are."

RICHARD MILLER, PHD

founder of iRest Institute, developer of iRest Meditation (iRest.org), and author of *iRest Meditation: Restorative Practices for Health, Resiliency, and Well-Being* and *The iRest Program for Healing PTSD*

"In this modern compendium of ancient Hindu goddess mythology, Archarya Shunya teaches us how to harness our divine rage with power and precision—like focused fury from the forehead of the goddess! Thank you, Archarya, for this potent gift. The aim of divine rage is not vengeance, but to reorder the world."

VALARIE KAUR

author of *See No Stranger* and founder of the Revolutionary Love Project

"*Roar Like a Goddess* is my favorite kind of mythological book, as it demands the contemporary reinterpretation of the stories and archetypes we encounter and acknowledges their evolutionary nature. Acharya Shunya skillfully shows how *we* are the ones who must keep the Goddess energies evolving and alive within us, which will ultimately lead us to becoming the fully sovereign, authentic beings that we were born to be."

MEGHAN DON

author of *Feminine Courage: Remembering Your Voice and Vision Through a Retelling of our Myths and Inner Stories*

"*Roar Like a Goddess* is not a book *about* the Goddess; it is the voice of the Goddess, bold and clear, with a message ancient and ever new: *You are That.* Drawing from her life experience, the inspired wisdom of the Vedas, and a fearless commitment to support spiritual awakening for all, Acharya Shunya has gifted us with a revolutionary guidebook for living truthfully, compassionately, and fully. Nothing less will bring forth the healing necessary for our families, nations, and our planet. Gift this book to yourself, your mother, daughters, friends, and allies. It's time."

YOGACHARYA ELLEN GRACE O'BRIAN

spiritual director of Center for Spiritual Enlightenment and author of *The Jewel of Abundance: Finding Prosperity through the Ancient Wisdom of Yoga*

"*Roar Like a Goddess* is one of the most introspective, thought-provoking works in the true spirit of 'know thyself' in current times. Who is a true goddess? What does it take to become one? Acharya Shunya takes us to an astute journey merging the ancient and the modern, guiding each one of us to rise to our Highest Self. A must-read for every woman out there, and perhaps men too!"

SOMANJANA CHATTERJEE

board member of Silicon Valley Interreligious Council

"In this timely and transformational book, Acharya Shunya offers spiritual seekers a much-needed gift: a rational, sensible, and eminently practical understanding of the Divine Feminine in all its diverse expressions. With engaging storytelling and a treasure trove of practices, *Roar Like a Goddess* shows the way to communion with the Goddess within all of us, regardless of our gender or belief system."

PHILIP GOLDBERG

author of *American Veda, The Life of Yogananda*, and *Spiritual Practice for Crazy Times*

"Tuning in to the archetypal and symbolic energies of Durga, Lakshmi, and Saraswati offers us a way to embody our inner power and self-agency at a time when we are all being called upon to wake up in the world. If you need to find or refine your voice and would like to encourage others in your life to do so too, please gift yourself and everyone you know a copy of *Roar Like a Goddess*."

FELICIA TOMASKO

editor in chief of LA YOGA Ayurveda and Health and faculty at Loyola Marymount University's Center for Religion and Spirituality

"*Roar Like a Goddess* is radical permission to embrace our holy wrath, highest pleasure, and deepest authority for the benefit of all beings. The Goddess herself pours forth and transforms our consciousness directly through the stories in these pages. Acharya Shunya shows us how to let our own lives become the very vehicle of the Divine Feminine. If our world has a path forward, this is the map."

VERA DE CHALAMBERT

public theologian, spiritual storyteller, and Harvard-educated scholar

"*Roar Like a Goddess* explains the unique and complex theology of Shakti in an accessible manner . . . to all who seek an understanding of reality that views the body, mind, and consciousness as inhabited fully and without limit by the Divine. Acharya Shunya opens up the possibility of self-transformation and self-affirmation through the practice and path of the Divine Feminine—to all who have known oppression."

RITA D. SHERMA, PHD

author of *Radical Immanence: An Ecological, Emancipatory, Hindu Theology of the Divine Feminine* and director and associate professor, Graduate Theological Union Center for Dharma Studies

ROAR
LIKE A
GODDESS

Also by Acharya Shunya

Ayurveda Lifestyle Wisdom: A Complete Prescription to Optimize Your Health, Prevent Disease, and Live with Vitality and Joy

Sovereign Self: Claim Your Inner Joy and Freedom with the Empowering Wisdom of the Vedas, Upanishads, and Bhagavad Gita

ROAR
LIKE A
GODDESS

EVERY WOMAN'S GUIDE TO
BECOMING UNAPOLOGETICALLY
POWERFUL, PROSPEROUS & PEACEFUL

ACHARYA SHUNYA

sounds true
BOULDER, COLORADO

Sounds True
Boulder, CO 80306

Published 2022

Cover and book design by Karen Polaski
Cover and interior illustrations © 2022 Ekabhumi Charles Ellik

FSC
www.fsc.org
MIX
Paper | Supporting
responsible forestry
FSC® C103098

Printed in the United States of America

BK06356

Library of Congress Cataloging-in-Publication Data

Names: Acharya Shunya, author.
Title: Roar like a goddess : every woman's guide to becoming unapologetically
    powerful, prosperous, and peaceful / by Acharya Shunya.
Description: Boulder, CO : Sounds True, 2022. | Includes bibliographical references.
Identifiers: LCCN 2021047975 (print) | LCCN 2021047976 (ebook) | ISBN
    9781683648826 (paperback) | ISBN 9781683648833 (ebook)
Subjects: LCSH: Goddess religion.--India.
Classification: LCC BL473.5 .A24 2022 (print) | LCC BL473.5
    (ebook) | DDC 201/.43--dc23/eng/20220118
LC record available at https://lccn.loc.gov/2021047975
LC ebook record available at https://lccn.loc.gov/2021047976

10 9 8 7 6 5 4 3 2 1

I dedicate this book to the roaring memory of my mother.

Full of Power, as Power is Your Body O Goddess,
You are the Time-honored One, Supreme Mistress of the Universe;
You are the Shakti, Imperceptible Divine Power of All Conscious Beings,
Both the Visible and the Invisible are Your Forms O Goddess!

LALITA SAHASRANAMA STOTRAM, TRANSLATED BY AUTHOR

CONTENTS

IT IS TIME TO ROAR
LIKE A GODDESS

T he authority and dominance associated with the act of *roaring* are not typically associated with the human female on our patriarchy-ruled planet today. Vocal expressions generally attributed to womankind usually fall into several categories: First there are the submissive, soft, melodious, sing-song, wispy, out-of-breath, cute-as-hell, daddy's-little-princess voices; next are the always-questioning, never-decisive voices, placating and overly persuasive, begging and imploring, "Can you help me? I am a damsel in distress"; then there are the nagging and whiny voices, and—*how dare women enter male territory*—the shrill, strident, bossy, and bitchy voices; and last but not least, there are the "come hither," foxy, sexy siren voices. Of course, these voices are not the real, fundamental representation of womankind. They have emerged from the internalization of a cluster of self-lessening beliefs collectively known as "patriarchy."

Patriarchy is a system of beliefs that put men first. It promotes a society dominated by men: sexually, emotionally, economically, religiously, and of course, politically. Patriarchy is not simply a phenomenon that invades individual minds, specific families, or isolated feudal cultures. It is a ubiquitous, insidious social disease, difficult for most women to ignore and still harder to uproot because patriarchal beliefs morph, adapt, and reappear in every era and every society, ancient or modern.

In a climate of patriarchy, the most difficult leap a woman will ever take is to trust her true voice—the one I compare to a roar. Despite the difficulty, it is time for all women to discover who they really are, to claim their true status in the human jungle and roar with their innate, lioness-like power.

Through spiritual knowledge that awakens and liberates us from stereotypical scripts, women can begin trusting themselves and learn to roar against the facades of conformity and other self-diminishing habits they have become accustomed to over time. As simply being human is not yet enough for women to feel safe and celebrated on our planet, it is time for women worldwide to look inward and roar with bold, goddess-like self-recognition!

If you are feeling skeptical about or unfamiliar with the concept of roaring like a goddess, it may be due to the way the term *goddess* has been defined to you, perhaps as some angelic entity in a faraway land. Let me reassure you that the *goddess* I am referring to is the same as your higher *Self*. She is not far away geographically, but near you. She *is* you. This goddess represents wholeness and alignment with your hidden spiritual Self and its power and true potential.

I grew up in the Hindu culture worshipping Divine Feminine as multiple goddesses, all representing different facets of One Supreme Goddess known as Shakti. What began as devotion to a divine entity situated somewhere far beyond me has culminated into a deeply affirmative "friendship" with the goddess who dwells very close to me, in fact right inside my heart as my own Self.

This single recognition, that the goddess is none other than my higher Self, helped me experience empowerment in my different roles as a teacher, daughter, mother, wife, and conscious citizen of our planet. I am not simply a devotee anxiously waiting to be redeemed by goddess grace, but rather a roaring goddess-woman herself, who has found her true voice and who could actively help herself by exploring and unearthing latent goddess attitudes and strengths from within!

That is why throughout the book, I will keep gently reminding you that while you can certainly access divine grace by connecting to a goddess outside you, it is also important to recognize the goddess powers lying latent within you. Your true Self is a direct portal to the goddess dimension of this universe. This means you're not limited to seeking aid from an otherworldly feminine divinity; you can unearth goddess-like strength buried within your very being, here and now. In fact, every goddess power is available to you.

Goddess power is:

- **Divinely sourced from within**, not obtained from the world externally
- **Self-existing**, not created unnaturally
- **Self-celebrating** rather than self-effacing
- **Self-validating** rather than externally validated
- **Infinite and grows with expression**, not in limited supply
- **Bold** rather than fearful
- **Equal** rather than superior/inferior
- **Self-aware** rather than self-conscious
- **Vulnerable** rather than defensive
- **Sharing** rather than hoarding
- **Creative** rather than copying
- **Generating flow** rather than struggling
- **Peaceful** rather than worrying
- **Flexible** rather than rigid
- **Abundant** rather than scarce
- **Unifying** rather than divisive
- **Adorned** rather than garish
- **Critiquing** rather than criticizing
- **Direct** rather than harsh
- **Enjoying wellness** rather than illness

- **Joyful** rather than sorrowful
- **Roaring** rather than meowing!

In the chapters to come, you will meet the Supreme Hindu/Vedic Goddess Shakti and her chief goddess manifestations:

- Durga, the goddess of power and self-determination
- Lakshmi, the goddess of abundance and inner contentment
- Saraswati, the goddess of wisdom, peace, and self-actualization

In addition to sharing timeless goddess mythology, I also share a revolutionary revisioning of the Divine Feminine, bringing the archetype, personality, and behavioral traits of these three goddesses into a modern context, which I hope will help you discover these traits within yourself and lead an emotionally liberated life, in the here and now.

I have personally found great solace in these three goddesses. Durga models how to embody courage in the face of challenges and how to enjoy healthy goddess-like rage when that rage is necessary to discover our true voice. Lakshmi teaches us how to love ourselves, value ourselves, and *be* ourselves. Saraswati demonstrates the way to finding lasting peace within by expressing our goddess roar at last.

Their stories and teachings will help you free yourself from the invisible prisons of patriarchal control and begin leading a more empowered, abundant, and enlightened life with an enhanced ability to love yourself, champion yourself, and reach the goals you set for yourself, undeterred by internalized misogyny or institutionalized patriarchy. It's true that strides have been made in gender equality—and it's important to acknowledge and celebrate those advances—but as a society and culture, we still have a long way to go.

The oppression of women is multilayered and has been upheld by cultural norms, tradition, and religions through inequalities in the workplace, the law, and even the home. Some of the glaring examples still affecting Western women, as reported by the

Guardian, are "a legal system historically designed by men; the lingering misrecognition of rape as simply an excess of male desire; a police force carrying a legacy of sexism; the cultural and religious shaming of sexually active women; the objectification of women's bodies; pornography; the fact that women in general are discouraged from speaking out."[1] This is why, despite doing all the right things in their womanly roles and "ticking all the boxes," many women—consciously or unconsciously—believe that they will never be enough. When you internalize these three goddess archetypes, however, you will embody *unapologetic power, prosperity, and inner peace!*

HOW THIS BOOK IS DIFFERENT FROM OTHER GODDESS BOOKS

In this book I offer an in-depth exploration of the Hindu goddess archetypes, for the purpose of breaking free of patriarchal conditioning and letting go of internalized misogyny. Like all books on mythology, this book also sheds light on fascinating legends that transpired "once upon a time" involving allegorical characters, humans, beasts, demons, gods, and of course the goddess herself. But I don't stop with the verbatim retelling of the tale. Since I am a scholar of Hindu scriptures, like the Vedas, Upanishads, and Bhagavad Gita, I use my expertise, collectively known as "Vedic wisdom," to decode the symbolism behind each goddess and offer insights and practices you can implement in your life, right away.

Therefore, the goddess stories in this book will not just move you or thrill you with supernatural adventures of goddesses in a bygone era, but they will also potentially transform your life forever by imparting spiritual insights and psychological tools to help you roar with your true voice, today.

Currently, you may be a *sleeping goddess*. To awaken to your goddess powers, all you need to do is embrace new goddess attitudes and a lifestyle of abundance and wisdom. Then, you will step outside the imprisoning boxes of patriarchy, transform your life through lived power, and even become a source of empowerment for countless other women.

Nothing in your life is random, not even the darkness. Nothing is an accident. All that you encounter in life are gifts of the highest order.

Acharya Shunya
Fifteenth Day of November, 2021

Note: Although I use the term "women" throughout this book, all beings who identify with the feminine gender or who have suffered any kind of oppression (no matter their sex at birth or gender identification) can benefit from this book because the desire to be truly powerful, prosperous, and peaceful is an ancient, unforgettable instinct. To roar with authenticity and inviolable self-respect is an innate human inclination.

The terms *Vedic* and *Hindu* are used interchangeably throughout the book. The word *Goddess* is capitalized only when addressing a goddess by name. Finally, I have provided my own original translations of the verses, hymns, and other chants quoted from ancient goddess texts, unless otherwise noted.

THE SEARCH FOR THE HIDDEN GODDESS

I t takes a certain emotional willingness to step beyond stereo-typed roles to access goddess consciousness, which represents total and absolute emotional and spiritual freedom. You need the defiance to belong to yourself first before others can claim you as theirs, a penchant to celebrate your true colors without resorting to trendy and approved masks to please others, and an insistence on honoring your inner flame despite the possibility of your relationships getting scorched by its intensity.

To be a real-life goddess, accumulating degrees and intellectual and professional accomplishments can be helpful and should be celebrated, but they are not enough—such achievements don't have to be a woman's ultimate accomplishment. Beauty and glamour alone, without empowered attitudes, don't do the job either. Neither does a picture-book life with a husband, children, and a dog or cat, in a house with a white picket fence. In fact, in so many cases, the workplace accomplishments, the body and its beauty, and the home and family that women yearn for—and will do anything to have and hold on to—eventually become chains, binding them tightly within the restrictive lines of the patriarchy.

There is nothing wrong with wanting and having these things, but empowering and freeing spiritual instruction is needed alongside every worldly pursuit, so we women can realize our desires and not become damaged goods in the process. I wish our planet had "goddess wisdom schools" to impart the skills that deeply empower ALL women—such a thing would create a radical paradigm shift on our planet. Until that happens, it is up to the women who understand the art of living, and are roaring like goddesses, to teach the women who are ready to follow their lead.

My mother, a true roaring one, was my first goddess teacher—caring but strong, compassionate yet fierce in her convictions, generous but not beyond her own sovereign boundaries. She raised my sister and me with a lionhearted spirit in the India of the 1960s. Even then, most of society was estranged from its spiritual roots and entrenched in institutionalized patriarchy. My mom, supported by her ultra-progressive and loving husband (my father), undeterred and unintimidated by anyone or anything, taught us how to feel good in our own skin and appreciate our feminine bodies—and to feel "enough" in who we are, as we are. On her deathbed, she said, "Don't forget, goddess is with you, always looking out for you. She lives within you; you will never be alone. When you have no one else, not even me . . . you will have the goddess in your heart! Just call out to her!"

For many years after Mom's transition, which was shortly after my tenth birthday, something was missing in my life . . . a living and breathing feminine role model in whose heart great storms and greater stillness coexisted. Someone whose self-awareness was so vast that she could hold all my growing feminine angst. Someone with ancient soul wisdom, who would help me break down my doubts and apply goddess wisdom to my own life.

That is why even though I was quite the little goddess myself as a kid, self-assured and self-shining under my mother's care, I started losing some of that fire after she died. And my goddess flame was all but wiped out when I got married for the first time and left my progressive-minded family to join my husband's more conventional family with their entrenched values. My partner back then at least made a pretense to meet me where I was, but his immediate and extended family explicitly rejected my power and challenged my right to be who I was at every step. Subconsciously, without even being aware of it, I began to allow their patriarchal voices to grow strong in my head. Their voices suppressed my voice. Slowly, my inner goddess became concealed by the dust of false, self-limiting, societally imposed beliefs that I had bought into—*hook, line, and sinker!*

When we become forgetful of our spiritual truth, we abandon ourselves, suppress our needs, lose our true voice, neglect the goals we set out for ourselves, and never really undertake the journey to wholeness and self-acceptance we yearn for deep inside. Habituation, powerlessness, and fear conceal our divine potential from us. That is what happened to me.

Because I knew that "light" intimately in my own heart (if only a short time as a young girl), I did not stay in darkness for long. I questioned my "conformity" every time I said yes to stereotypical expectations, and I pushed against the "compromising" walls of my own mind incessantly. When enough was enough—a point that arrived sooner than later, thankfully—I embarked on an outward journey, leading my way out of a suffocating and unequal relationship.

Remembering the goddess training I received from my family, I quietly undertook a second, even more important journey within to uncover and reclaim my true Self . . . the hidden goddess. Deep down, I knew how liberating it feels to *roar like a goddess!* I was fortunate that my grandfather, Baba Ayodhya Nath, whom I simply refer to as "Baba," was a renowned yogi, Vedic Guru, and Ayurvedic healer. He was a champion of women's rights even before I was born, which was somewhat unusual for a man born in 1900. Baba was a devotee of the Divine Feminine, and through his male body, truth-telling speech, and truth-evoking eyes, I found a different kind of mother talking to me, guiding me—the Mother of the Universe, whom we Hindus know as Divine Mother, *Maa* (mother) *Shakti*, and her divine incarnations as Durga, Lakshmi, and Saraswati.

I remember Baba telling me about the Divine Feminine with words loaded with meaning:

> *Shunya, goddess is the creative power surging through*
> *every atom of your body. She is the essence of your living*
> *body, mind, and soul. She is not far from you. She dwells*
> *not only in the realm of cosmic consciousness; she dwells*
> *inside you, too, as your own true Self. A wave is small,*
> *fleeting, short-lived, while the ocean is infinitely large*
> *and permanent. But the reality is that the nature of both,*
> *the wave and ocean, are water, and from that viewpoint,*
> *there is no difference between consciousness as goddess*
> *and expressions of that consciousness as us humans.*

The search for my inner goddess was, I am happy to report, fruitful. It helped me understand my true worth at last, and as a result, I became inwardly powerful as well as peaceful. I don't need to be a super woman or an accommodating woman. I simply need to remain an awakened woman, no longer asleep to my own goddess capacities. That is enough.

Now I share what I discovered with you.

VEDIC WISDOM ON DIVINE FEMININE AND EMPOWERED WOMANHOOD

> *O Goddess, you are known through the path of the Vedas.*
> *You are the very essence of the Vedas.*
>
> SRI KAMALA STOTRAM, VERSE 2

The wisdom Baba was referring to when he gave me such empowering and freeing teachings comes from the Vedas, which are the oldest scriptures of Hinduism and which also gave birth to the spiritual lineage I have belonged to from birth. Once exclusively transmitted orally from a guru to a trusted disciple in Vedic spiritual lineages, the great wisdom of the Vedas can be found easily today, published as four big books called the *Rig Veda, Sama Veda, Yajur Veda,* and *Atharva Veda.* They are rare among sacred texts in that they have contributions not only from male seers, known as *rishis*, but from twenty-seven female seers, known as *rishikas*. Both the men and woman seers have contributed their channeled wisdom in the form of hymns and knowledge-packed verses.

Goddesses Durga, Lakshmi, and Saraswati are first and foremost introduced in the Vedas. The Vedas gift us forward-thinking, holistic guidance on how to be empowered and live harmoniously despite differences. The Vedas call for an inclusive society that values all genders and classes of people. In fact, we need no greater proof of their pro-feminine stance than the fact that they are the only sacred literature in the world that has been extensively authored by women seers, not just men.

The Vedas proclaimed equal opportunity for men and women in education, profession, marriage, and spiritual choices. They called for equality in everything from leadership to inheritance. They made no social prohibitions on women's secular and spiritual advancement, as that would go against their very spirit.

Below is a list of twenty-five Sanskrit feminine terms that appear in the Vedas, along with their English translations. This is how women are viewed in the Vedas:

- Aditi, because she is never dependent (in the sense of being boundless, limitless in her consciousness)
- Aghnya, for she is not to be hurt and should be treated with utmost respect
- Brihati, for she is large-hearted
- Chandra, because she is luminous like the moon
- Devi, since she is a goddess herself
- Havya, because she is worthy of invocation
- Ida, for she is venerable like the Earth
- Jyota, because she is the brilliant one
- Kamya, because she is lovable, desirable
- Mahi, since she is great, she represents the union of heaven and earth
- Mena, because she is knowledgeable
- Nari, for she is not (unnecessarily) inimical to anyone

- Purandhih, for she is liberal minded and possesses a plentiful nature
- Rtavari, for she is the preserver of truth
- Sanjaya, since she is victorious
- Saraswati, since she is learned, she possesses the essence of the Vedas
- Simhi, since she is courageous, protector of those who depend upon her
- Subhaga, because she is blessed, perfectly blissful
- Shubhada, for she is the bringer of goodness, good fortune, and luck
- Sumangali, since she is auspicious
- Suvarcha, since she is splendid
- Suyama, since she is self-disciplined, well guided, teachable
- Syona, for she is beautiful, pleasing, auspicious, propitious
- Vishruta, since she is famous
- Yashasvati, for she is glorious

The Divine Feminine has been long overlooked, overshadowed, or suppressed by concepts of an exclusive masculine god, patriarchal religions, and sexist societies. However, we are now in an age of revival for the goddess, as well as *goddess-like women* representing empowered womanhood. To my immense satisfaction, I found the Vedic vision of divinity to be truly outside the patriarchal conception of an exclusive masculine divinity. The Vedas, and by extension Hinduism (because the Vedas are the theoretical bedrock of Hinduism), celebrate divinity in all colors and genders, in mixed gender, and ultimately, beyond gender as formless, nameless, boundless, pure magical consciousness, as indicated in this ancient verse from Vedic scripture: "Ultimate Reality is not female, male, or mixed gender. Whatever form this formless Great Reality assumes, it becomes identified with that."[1]

Most Hindus revere the Divine Feminine as Durga, Lakshmi, and Saraswati and the Divine Masculine as Brahma, Vishnu, and Shiva. Ardhanarishwara is half masculine and half feminine and symbolizes the inseparability of the sacred feminine and the sacred masculine.

Here is a random selection of verses from the Sri Ardhanarishwara Stotram, a hymn composed in the eighth century by a revered master deeply respected inside my lineage, Sri Adi Shankaracharya:

My salutations to both Shakti and Shiva,

To Shakti whose body shines like molten gold,
To Shiva whose body shines like the burning camphor,
To Shakti who has a well-made-up hair with flowers and
ornaments studded,
To Shiva who has the indifferent matted locks . . .

To Shakti whose dance creates the world,
To Shiva whose dance annihilates the world.
Salutations to Shakti, the World Mother,
Salutations to Shiva, the World Father . . .

To Shakti who is divinely merged with Shiva,
And to Shiva who is divinely merged with Shakti.

MEET THE SUPREME HINDU GODDESS: SHAKTI

Creation, Sustenance, and Destruction are Your Powers,
O Eternal Goddess.

DEVI MAHATMYA 11.11

A unique all-encompassing Supreme Goddess known as Shakti is described in myriad scriptures as the embodiment of ultimate power. The word "Shakti" is derived from the Sanskrit word *shakt*, which means "capable of," "to be able," or "able to perform." Shakti reflects the nature of Cosmic Feminine Being, which is the creative, generative, dynamic power behind this universe.

Shakti powers the entire universe and all her creatures by her sheer dynamic presence. As queen of the universe, Shakti represents the one and the many, the immanent and the transcendent at the same time. She is ultimately inseparable from the universe itself. Just as the tree, the flower, and the fruit emerge from the seed, so do the different goddesses emerge from Shakti, the seed of divine power.

While Shakti is all-powerful, what she ultimately represents is *power itself*. In her book *Awakening Shakti*, philosophy and meditation teacher Sally Kempton explains how Shakti is essentially opposite of the ingrained, cultural view of women: "To recognize power as feminine is game changing. In the West, we are used to regarding the feminine as essentially receptive, even passive."[2] In considering Shakti as power, it might also be useful to think of power itself as the mother of existence, personified in the figure of a goddess. Therefore, whatever name or form she takes on, she is unambiguously omnipotent. Shakti is that beyond which no greater power can exist. Thus, Shakti elevates the goddess to the highest degree and, by association, us women.

There are hundreds of goddess expressions of Shakti, including the Goddesses Ambika, Parvati, Kali, Sita, Radha, and Usha. But our focus in this book is on three goddesses: Durga, Lakshmi, and Saraswati, who are often considered the holy trinity of Supreme Goddesses.

Durga teaches how to embody fearlessness in order to release the previously locked-up personal courage to be who you are and accept yourself, despite your learning curves and mistakes. Lakshmi's insistence on embodying dharma, or higher values, before acting ensures that this freed-up power is utilized for connecting with abundance, or personal and universal good—and not lost in chasing outer ephemeral wealth. Saraswati bestows the spiritual wisdom of who you are deep inside you, making you at last immensely peaceful in your own divine light.

Bear in mind that the hundreds of diverse goddesses are not separate but are really all expressions of the same One Shakti, the un-manifest, formless, nondual unity. The Vedas, and by extension Hinduism, don't teach worshipping innumerable goddesses and gods. The Vedas simply invite infinite ways of beholding the same One Divine Presence who is cooperating and housekeeping our cosmos via infinite forms . . . since what is Supreme is ultimately a trans-body intelligence, formless, and all-pervading.

INDIAN MYTHOLOGY: AN INTRODUCTION
TO TWO ENDURING CHARACTERS

Mythology is always timeless and beyond culture, religion, gender, and era. Myths are tales of characters who never existed, and yet the characters, who variously embody shades of light and darkness, are eternal.

In all goddess myths from India, we regularly meet two types of characters, which are called *devas* and *asuras*. Each is a broad category representing *mythical existence*. What is common between them is that they both enjoy having power; where they differ is how and to what ends they use that power. The asuras allow power to go to their heads, while devas respectfully use power from their hearts. In my opinion, self-serving and self-absorbed *asuric attitudes* are the seed of patriarchal beliefs. Such attitudes—on the parts of both men and women—result in prejudice, gender discrimination, homophobia, racism, and sexism.

The devas, on the other hand, also enjoy power, but they do not compulsively mark their egoic territory with it. They are not focused on dividing up the world based upon who looks like them, prays like them, eats like them, and mates like them; rather, they use their power to understand, accommodate, and appreciate differences. Naturally, in mythological tales you will find that the goddesses support, protect, and reward the devas, and teach hard lessons to the asuras. In fact, the term "deva" is aligned with the root sound in Sanskrit *div*, which means "divine light."

You, too, can find devas and asuras walking around in your own personal myth today, and I will teach you how to recognize and protect yourself from the asuras and how to embody trust and generosity toward the devas. Here's how to begin to recognize them in your life.

- **Asuras:** The asuras in your life story are people who gossip about you, stab you in the back, or who pull or hold you down professionally or personally (perhaps just because you are a woman).
- **Devas:** The devas of your life are the people who stand by you, who have always supported you and

see something special (perhaps a goddess) inside
you, no matter your gender, class, or religion.

Remember, asuras and devas can be of any gender—not just masculine or feminine, but gender fluid too. And in the Vedic worldview, no one is permanently sinful or "asuric." Evil dwells in our mind only until we become illumined. Everyone has an equal chance to evolve through introspection and course correction—even the so-called asuras! So, the ultimate goal of all mythological tales that are intertwined with the Vedic-Hindu tradition is encouragement toward embodiment of dharma.

Devas are not perfect either. Who is? Yet unlike the asuras, who gaslight and deflect blame, devas admit their mistakes, course correct, and adopt progressive attitudes. Thus, rather than creating black-and-white characters, all good and all bad, Hindu mythology creates characters in shades of grey.

Devas and asuras are everywhere—in mythology, in corporate meeting rooms, inside legislative assemblies, inside bedrooms and intimate relationships, and finally inside your own mind as your own forces of darkness and light. We are typically half-devas and half-asuras—half the time our mind is drawn toward higher ideals and mutual respect, and half the time toward blinding prejudice and self-betrayal by meekly accepting that prejudice.

In the coming chapters, you will learn from goddess archetypes about how to thrive in life despite attempts from inner and outer asuras to pull you down! You'll also learn to appreciate the devas in your life and hold on to them, by absorbing lessons from the lives of goddesses.

THE SOURCE OF MY STORYTELLING

In India, there exists a timeless tradition of dramatic storytelling, called *Katha Vachan*, where the teller of the story would be an elder of the family, a professional storyteller in the community, the village bard, or a temple priest. My childhood was filled with wonder and awe, when goddess legends would come alive through the art of theatrical storytelling, often dramatically accompanied with musical instruments like the Indian drums and flute. My mother, too, shared these stories at bedtime with me, until they settled in my heart; I would often enact the goddess tales with my friends for an audience consisting of our parents and siblings.

Orally transmitted since the beginning of time, the same tales take on different shades and details in different lineages and geographical areas of India, while the main elements remain the same. Several legends (not all) did get written down at some point between the third and tenth centuries in eighteen major and eighteen minor texts collectively called the Puranas,[3] which themselves underwent more iterations over the succeeding centuries thereafter.

Since several versions of the same myth exist across different written and oral iterations, rather than adhering to a strict textual, chronological, or historical discussion, I have returned to the stories told to me in my childhood and how listening to them inspired something timeless and powerful within my heart. More than anything, it is my mother's bedtime storytelling of the goddess tales that is the source of the myths I share in this book.

That is why my interpretation of the tales will be deliberately different from the "classic" versions, even nontraditional at times, and explained through a present-day lens, one that takes into account the #MeToo and #TimesUp movements. Clearly, equality and the empowerment of women and anyone who identifies with the feminine gender are important conversations. I hope my retelling the goddess myths will conjure liberated archetypes and help all people identified with the feminine gender reclaim goddess-like power from within.

From my perspective, awareness about the inherently progressive nature of the Vedas has declined with the march of time in India.[4] Superstition and, at times, patriarchal stains surrounding the myths are emerging here and there. Therefore, a revolutionary revisioning of the goddess myths and activation of the original Vedic heritage surrounding the Divine Feminine are not only important but critical—because the myths in their true form can support a pro-equality movement. This is why I have deliberately returned to the original teachings in this book. I question the more indoctrinated, "colonized" versions of goddess myths that subtly endorse patriarchy, and offer my own truth, freedom, and wisdom-evoking reinterpretations.

IT'S TIME TO REINTERPRET
THE GODDESSES

In this book, I share my own insights about the goddesses based on years of contemplative study and meditation, both with my grandfather (Baba) and on my own, with my inner Self guiding me every step of the way. My aim is not to disparage religious sentiments but to present updated interpretations. Both as an *Acharya*—the preceptor of my Vedic lineage—and as a teacher of the path of soul ascension through embodying Divine Feminine wisdom, it is my duty to shine the light on the empowering and liberating wisdom that has become clouded by the patriarchal sentiment over time.

In part 1, I present Goddess Durga as a role model who vanquishes internalized misogyny. You can use her archetype to take back your feminine power—power that you may have given away due to institutionalized patriarchy.

In part 2, we'll explore the Goddess Lakshmi archetype, who models living with internally sourced satisfaction. Lakshmi teaches that contentment is power unto itself. It makes us non-grasping, self-valuing, self-celebrating women.

In part 3, Goddess Saraswati is our guide for reclaiming the goddess from within. She is the ultimate teacher of our deepest journey to our higher Self. She reminds us who we are beyond the body—the ultimate knowledge, imparting lasting peace.

Also, at the end of each chapter I have provided contemplations for you to incorporate and internalize the goddess wisdom, to make it your own. I suggest you start a companion journal and write your free-flow responses to my questions. You could even set aside a few minutes a day to open to contemplation and meditate on any words and phrases that resonate with you, that you want to embody, or that are affirmations for you. You may even wish to speak these sentences aloud or use them as inspiration for an artistic expression through drawing or painting. I have used and continue to use these contemplations to connect with the goddess and embody a goddess-like state of being. These sections are yours to use in whatever way works best for you to help you embody the goddess wisdom. There is no wrong way to approach the goddess! You may also find it enriching to go back and read the thoughts you captured in the future after your inner goddess is activated.

When I dared to activate my inner goddess and embody these bold and beautiful archetypes, I walked away restored, whole, and sovereign! And when you tune in to the timeless mythological goddess dimension, you, too, will walk the subtle path of transformation from lesser awareness to greater awareness, from fear to fearlessness, from existential confusion to a life of powerful self-determination. Collectively and individually, the goddesses teach us not to live from the scripts of others, but to redefine and reclaim ourselves and our lives.

Now more than ever, the myths and teachings of the Vedic goddesses, the archetypes of unashamed and unapologetic womanhood, are needed.

Enjoy roaring once again, like the goddess that you are!

PART I

DURGA

CHAPTER 1

DURGA

The Power Inherent in Every Power

*By your power this universe emerges into existence,
is protected, and annihilated too, O Durga.*

DEVI MAHATMYA 1.75

When I was eight, I was bullied by a twelve-year-old girl who picked on younger children. One day, I resolved to put an end to the situation. I had grown up seeing the deity of Durga, a gorgeous goddess, astride a lion. To gather my courage and face the bully, I imagined going to school not on foot but on a lion. That single mental image gave me the courage to walk down the corridor where the bully lurked each day at lunchtime, waiting for me. I remembered my mother reminding me that Goddess Durga dwells inside me, in all her intensity, ferocity, authority, and divinity, even if I could not "see" her. That day as I imagined myself as Durga on her lion, I noticed the bully would not look me in the eyes. And after that, while she might make a snide comment, she would quickly skulk away, as if she were afraid of me. Gradually, she stopped picking on me altogether.

When we become aware of our sleeping powers, everyone around us becomes aware of them too. Bullies show up only as long as we remain unaware of our powers or think we are unworthy of acting powerfully.

I can say that together, Durga, her lion, and little Shunya, operating from her core of Shakti, managed to win a few important battles at school some forty-five years ago. Baba told me that if we don't quash the inner asuras, the outer asuras will keep showing up, and so this battle was not only with the bully outside me but also with the fear inside me—all mine—that was blocking my power.

DURGA'S DIVINE ANIMAL: A LION

In Hinduism, many gods and goddesses have a divine creature, called a *vahana*, that supports them in their work and transports them all over the universe. Durga is often depicted astride a lion. Lakshmi's vahana is the owl, and Saraswati's is the swan.

The sacred birds, reptiles, and animals associated with Hindu deities as envoys and emissaries are essentially divine entities themselves. They are much more evolved than humans, and they share the divine powers, strengths, and wisdom of the deities they serve. These beings have taken nonhuman forms as required to spread divine light.

Therefore, the vahanas—along with their assigned gods or goddesses—are treated with great respect and devotion. In no way should we regard them as "beasts of burden." In fact, they are a continuation of a deity's divine consciousness and an expression of the Divine Feminine in animal form.

Is it any surprise that a lion transports Durga as she attends to emerging and collapsing universes? The lion symbolizes that *she* rides the instinct for domination, it does not ride her. The goddess is in control. In modern parlance, *she's got it together*.

This image makes me love Durga wholeheartedly, and we can emulate her in all our life battles. Durga is forceful, striding through the dark forces of misogyny, male ego, and patriarchy, defiant and invincible. Imagine working at a cutthroat company where everybody is out to get you, but today you ride in on your lion. Imagine not giving in on an issue concerning your child the next time your in-laws raise their voices or eyebrows because you are riding your lion. Imagine someone coming out of the closet finally, but they're not alone and tentative as they reveal their sexuality. Their Shakti lion, which they straddle in pride of how their inner Durga made them, accompanies them.

Durga helps those who possess great values win every battle. She reminds us that we never need to people-please, avoid conflict, just go along with the crowd, or be chronically overlooked, overbooked, and overcompensating. We don't need to deny our own truth. She reminds us that engaging in anything that smacks of codependence or self-abandonment, whether physical or verbal, ultimately takes away our power.

When the lion kills, it does so dharmically—not to score points or harm anyone, and certainly never because it is having a tantrum. Steady and majestic, the lion neither apologizes for its power nor attacks unnecessarily. It only hunts to satiate biological hunger and to protect its territory. Abiding by its own rules, the lion is victorious in its habitat, every time.

When the lion shows up, the hyenas run for cover. In the same way, lionhearted women don't give up and don't back down. Durga's message is be who you are deep inside you—a goddess:

Be bold.
Be fearless.
Be shameless.
Be the heroine of your life.

Believe me, when you show up channeling your Durga, astride your lion, *roaring like a goddess*, your faultfinders, mockers, critics, deflators, and backbiters will run, sometimes for good!

DURGA IS POWER INCARNATE

If Shakti is the Ultimate Power, then she could have no truer representation than Goddess Durga. That is why Shakti and Durga are considered one and the same. *As power incarnate, Durga represents both the power that is cosmically supreme and the power that is resident within all beings.* Like her original nature as

Mother Shakti, Durga fulfills three crucial roles in the universe: creator, preserver, and destroyer. She is sometimes called a warrior goddess because she takes up great battles for the restoration of dharma, since dharma refers to activities and ideas that support the universe in a positive manner. Durga quashes the power of non-righteous or non-dharmic beings (asuras) and enhances the power of the righteous ones (devas).

Durga is all-powerful. She ultimately represents *power itself*. As powerful as any given deity might be, he or she can only ever contain a portion of that totality of cosmic power Durga represents. As I've mentioned before, it's useful to think of power as the mother of existence, personified in the figure of Durga, instead of considering Durga as powerful.

DURGA'S EMERGENCE: A MYTHICAL MEMORY

Once upon a time, the devas, headed by their king Indra, faced a battle for their homeland. The asuras—under the leadership of their king Mahishasura, who was a half-buffalo, half-humanlike grotesque entity—had forcefully entered their lands and taken over. The devas tried to protect their celestial home, but lost bitterly to Mahishasura and his army, because Mahishasura had received a boon—a boon that no male entity could kill him. Knowing that no masculine force could be victorious over him and assuming that no woman could imagine contending with him, he did not fear Yama himself, the god of death. He was as good as immortal.

Aimlessly wandering the earth, the homeless devas decided to discuss the matter with the masculine versions of Shakti: Brahma, Vishnu, and Shiva. Naturally, the holy trinity were angered about what had happened. From their anger, which was no ordinary anger but wrath of God, a blessed light emerged and coalesced. This same spiritual light emerged from the bodies of all the assembled devas, and gradually, the radiant light spread so high and so wide that all three worlds—heaven, hell, and earth—were shining from its radiance.

As that happened, the light transformed into a divine female form, so beautiful and so majestic, the likes of which the devas had never seen before. Tears started flowing from their eyes as they simply gasped at the brilliant, blessing power they beheld. Before them, to protect them, Shakti emerged, as Goddess Durga.

By conjoining and collaborating their respective powers—rage and righteousness in this case—the devas accessed the supreme field of power, which is one and the same as Durga.

Some storytellers present an interpretation of this myth suggesting that Durga was created by the power of the devas. But I feel it is the opposite. The power inherent in all beings—godly, human, and animal—emerges from Durga or Shakti. This theme is repeatedly emphasized in the myths chronicled in the goddess literature of yore. The male trinity—Brahma, Vishnu, and Shiva—say to Shakti incarnated as Durga, "I have been made to assume bodily form by you."[1] Durga is also seen to emerge from Goddess Parvati's body in another myth. And in yet another, she emerges from the body of the sleeping God Vishnu.

But, while Durga emerges from the bodies of gods, Durga is not the creation of those entities. She is the original, uncaused power (Shakti) that pervades our entire existence and dwells in all living bodies. In fact, as a hymn suggests, "She is the goddess by whom this world was spread out through her own power, whose body is comprised of the powers of all the hosts of gods."[2] Therefore, Durga is a sovereign goddess, and her power is what makes the gods sovereign. That is why the assembled gods bow to her, recognizing that their own individual powers are only aspects of her supreme power.

In a myth popular across several Puranas, the masculine trinity of Gods Shiva, Vishnu, and Brahma, as well as other minor gods and assembled devas, are seen giving Durga gifts of gratitude and joy.

Shiva, who is the god of cosmic dissolution or sacred endings, presented her with a trident from his own trident (*Trishula*)—a three-pointed weapon that is said to annihilate all darkness and illusions, the greatest illusion being the ego itself.

Vishnu, who is the preserver and maintainer of cosmic order and purveyor of dharma in the universe, brought forth a spinning discus out of his own discus (*Sudarshan Chakra*) and gave it to Durga. When the discus spins, it warps time itself, bringing the life story of evil doers to an immediate end—literally, by chopping off the head, and figuratively, by halting the perpetuation of ignorance, which lies at the root of sinful action.

Brahma, the god of creation and father of all sentient beings, gave a string of prayer beads and a pot of holy water to Durga, representing her ability to focus her mind and remain blemishless and ever-pure through recreating herself in the light of truth, in every situation.

Samudra-deva, the ocean god, gave her a massive conch shell, through which Durga could blow air and make the most vivid "OM" sound, reverberating across galaxies. The sound from the conch was reassuring to the dharmic ones, but would ignite fear in the non-dharmic ones. He also gave her garlands made of never-fading flowers to wear over her head and neck. The milk-white sea—known in the Hindu lore as Kshirsagar and featured in another important myth that I relate later in this book—gifted Durga a most spectacular garland made of pearls white as moonlight, and an ever-fresh and incorruptible set of splendid garments, befitting of a goddess.

Agni, the fire god, gifted her a fiery spear. Vayu-deva, the air god, gifted her a bow, as well as two inexhaustible quivers full of arrows. Indra, king of devas, brought forth a diamond thunderbolt and a bell from his elephant. The god of death, Yama, gave her a staff from his own staff; a single blow from it would spell instant death for any foe. Varuna, the god of water, gave her a noose (since the incessant whirlpools in a body of water can act quite like a deadly noose) and a very beautiful lotus to hold in her hand.

Surya-deva, the sun god who radiates light and warmth through every pore of his skin, now shone his radiance through every pore of Durga's skin, while Kala-deva, the god of time, gave Durga his own sword and a sparkling shield against death, representing her immortality. Vishwakarma, the celestial architect, gave her various ornaments and a brilliant axe, missiles, and an unbreakable armor. Himavat, the mountain god and personification of the great Himalayas, gave her gems and the lion as her vehicle. Kubera, the god of wealth, gave her a drinking cup always full of celestial nectar-like wine.

Sharing these gifts is representative of what can happen when our more masculine minds, which often like to go it alone, choose to collaborate instead. When this happens, no less than a feminine divine power, Shakti, emerges. The presenting of gifts to Durga for her to wield, which are quintessential "weapons" (or strength or strategy) owned by each male god, represents the recognition that to be truly successful against our own unconscious ego, or against forces of darkness in society, we must bring together our own conflicted and individuated powers—mental, emotional, intellectual, social, political, and material—to win the battle at a spiritual level, involving our own Durga, our Self.

In the myth, Durga spoke up and addressed the awed holy trinity. Her voice boomed with a power that stirred the entire universe. "Fear not. I am Shakti. I have manifested as Durga to avenge you and relieve you from the suffering caused by the asuras. I will defeat the asuras and destroy the monstrous Mahishasura." Then, she proceeded to where the asuras were assembled, enjoying their ill-begotten hegemony over the realm of the devas!

Decorated with ornaments, honored with weapons, and self-assured in her invincibility, Durga single-handedly faced an entire army of millions of asuras. She roared with laughter again and again. The entire sky was filled with her inestimable, astounding goddess roar, and its echo reverberated throughout the universe and millions of galaxies still unseen by human eyes. Durga's roar is the goddess war cry.

Naturally, the half-demon half-buffalo Mahishasura, who represents arrogance and stubbornness, gave a tough fight, surrounded as he was with his millions of demonic cronies. He transmuted himself into many forms during the battle with Goddess Durga, becoming a killer lion; a mad, trampling elephant; a man wielding a sword; a buffalo; and finally, himself again. The demon's multiple transformations remind us of the many ways evil lurks, both in our minds and in our society. He uprooted entire mountains and launched them at Durga. But she was unstoppable.

All this was little more than play for Durga, the power of this universe. When she'd had enough, she simply threw a noose around Mahishasura's neck and pulled it tight. He tried to free himself, but the more he struggled, the tighter she made the rope. At last, he lay flat on the ground gasping for breath, and Durga stood erect on his prostrate body. With her foot on his neck, she thrust her trident into his chest. With this final blow, he was dead. When the Mahishasura lay slain with his armies annihilated, justice and truth were restored in the three worlds, and the hosts of devas, headed by Indra their king, rejoiced with joy and relief.

DURGA: THE POWER THAT OVERCOMES EVERY CHALLENGE

Durga is depicted as supreme Shakti and creator of the universe. She fights and defeats various violent, greedy, repulsive demons who are also sexual predators. She attains victory over even the most horrific ones, who are symbolic of lust and greed of every kind.

Remember that Durga becomes fierce, violent, and cruel only toward evil forces. She does not hesitate to destroy ignorance, ego, and the darkness that surrounds the minds of stubborn beings. She has great discernment of action. She can also be tranquil and sweet, and gently protect dharmic beings of all genders. She knows when to roar like a cosmic lioness as big as the entire universe and instantly spring to self-protective and dharma-protective action. She is Divine Mother, after all.

Durga is an archetype of dharmic power in service of greater good. Power is not a bad thing; context is important, and sometimes the willingness to confront injustice and inequality requires the activation of goddess-like power. In my imagination, Durga's club smashes false notions, like the feeling that women must hide their power to avoid making men uncomfortable. Dharmic or righteous use of power can lead to personal transformation, such as finally leaving an abusive situation. Mass movements born out of a sense of injustice are also indicative of a greater power being channeled for positive social change for the entire planet.

Indeed, Durga can be an archetype of unprecedented power, courage, and strength, showing us the way to live with self-respecting boundaries despite a whole planet reeling under bigotry and gender inequality. Her archetype can help us cleanse, deconstruct, and reconstruct our minds that have been brainwashed with patriarchal beliefs. Perhaps your inner goddess, too, does not want you to "keep the peace at any cost." Rather than staying stuck in anxiety, over-analysis, and self-judgment, it is time to think, act, mate, and *roar* like a goddess!

A MODERN-DAY DURGA FACES FEAR IN THE FACE OF RACIAL DISCRIMINATION

We can see Durga in the story of a seamstress who went beyond the fear of being unfairly imprisoned to change the world as we know it today for all of us.

In 1955, a seamstress named Rosa Parks, who was the grand-daughter of enslaved African Americans and grew up in a deeply segregated America, was returning home from a hard day at work in a department store in Montgomery, Alabama. She sat quietly on the bus, in an area marked for "colored folks." But when the bus continued to fill with White folks, the driver asked Rosa to give up her seat and stand so a White passenger could take her seat. This happened routinely: White bodies were given preferential treatment over Black bodies. There was no law or official ordinance giving drivers the authority to demand a passenger give up a seat to anyone, regardless of color. However, the bus drivers of Montgomery were shaped by convention and supported by the police force in separating Black and White passengers at any cost, and gave the latter preferential treatment over the former. They could ask Black passengers at any time to stand up and give up their seats to White passengers. Clearly White passengers enjoyed privilege over Black.

That fated day when the bus driver asked Rosa and a few of her fellow Black passengers to move to the back of the bus, the others complied with the driver, but Parks refused and remained seated. The driver was livid. He demanded to know why she didn't stand up, to which Parks replied, "I don't think I should have to stand up." The indignant driver called the police and had her arrested. Rosa later recalled that her refusal wasn't because she was physically tired, but that she was tired of giving in.

Despite an entire race and its discriminatory law and police force drilling down upon men and women like Rosa, despite institutional guilt and fear for sheer survival from racial backlash, this woman's firm and simple NO eventually led to the abolishment of racial segregation laws. Events that transpired in protest of her arrest, such as the boycotting of public transport by people of color, known as the Montgomery Bus Boycott, continued for several months, severely crippling finances for its transit company.

With the boycott's progress, however, came strong resistance to the resistance. Black citizens were randomly rounded up and thrown into jail for violating an antiquated law prohibiting boycotts. In response to the ensuing events, members of the African American community took legal action. Parks's biography states, "In June 1956, the district court declared racial segregation laws (also known as 'Jim Crow laws') unconstitutional. The city of Montgomery appealed the court's decision shortly thereafter, but on November 13, 1956, the U.S. Supreme Court upheld the lower court's ruling, declaring segregation on public transport to be unconstitutional."[3]

The combination of legal action, backed by the unrelenting determination of the African American community, made the Montgomery Bus Boycott one of the largest and most successful mass movements against racial segregation in history.

For many years, Rosa Parks sat demurely in the bus, confined to the area demarcated for Blacks. And later, the same Rosa Parks shed all her inhibitions to announce a plain and simple NO in the face of racism. In my interpretation, *the goddess inside Rosa was asleep* for some years *until the goddess woke up with a roar* on that fateful day, which happily altered the course of history for all Black people in America. You, too, can become a whole new person, unrecognizable from the former you, when Durga awakens within you and roars with spiritual determination: Enough! No More! I am done with unfairness and inequality NOW!

RUNNING INTO THE ARMS OF FEARLESSNESS

"Women from around the world have been wearing the number 261 on their outfits, bibs, and body because it makes them feel fearless in the face of adversity, whether it is a tough marathon, a difficult business presentation, or coping with the many challenges of life." These are words from iconic athlete, sports and social advocate, author, and Emmy award–winning television commentator Kathrine Switzer's website.[4] What does the number 261 have to do with Kathrine's life and her message to women worldwide to become fearless? Everything.

In 1967, women were not allowed to compete in the Boston Marathon, yet another male-only event driven by patriarchal ideals. But at twenty years old, registering as K. V. Switzer instead of using her first name, Kathrine managed to get an official bib, number 261. And when the time came to run, she ran as fast as she could despite an angry official trying to pull her off the course! The photo of this historic moment—when a woman, through her sheer grit, showed the whole world women can run, too, as good as any man—made it to *Life* magazine's 100 *Photographs that Changed the World*. Kathrine went on to create and direct the Avon International Women's Running Circuit, a program of four hundred women's-only races in twenty-seven countries that eventually reached over one million women and led to the inclusion of the women's marathon in the Olympic Games in 1984.

Now in her seventies, Kathrine is still running, and a few years ago she founded a nonprofit called 261 Fearless. This organization, with chapters all over the world, helps women beat their fears and break boundaries through running.

How can we do anything but applaud such women, who demonstrate the goddess-like courage to question set patterns and change the course of history, for all women?

In conclusion, when you begin connecting with your own goddess power in daily life, the Durga inside you shall laugh as she roars—not with arrogance, but with confidence and ease. You have nothing to fear. Durga is the Divine Mother, protecting and guiding you with wisdom and compassion always.

A DURGA CONTEMPLATION FOR YOU

I ASK: Where am I holding back, stuck, or afraid?
I RECOGNIZE: I am Durga, Shakti, Power itself!

I CONNECT: Looking into a mirror, I see
   the fire of courage in my eyes.
I DECIDE: I arm myself with "weapons": intellect,
   clarity, integrity, persistence.
I ACT: I get on my lion and do what needs
   doing, say what needs saying.
I REMEMBER: There is nothing to fear in righteous action.
   Durga laughs as she roars, with confidence and ease.

CHAPTER 2

WHEN RAGING IS A GODDESS THING TO DO

The Goddess destroys adversity and suffering with her blessed anger.

DEVI MAHATMYA 9.31

A ll humans do not view anger with the same lens. Society does not allow for everyone to embody anger equally, even when the reason is the same.

If people of a certain color or class express anger, for example, they are considered heroes of humanity, harbingers of positive change, leaders of human revolutions. But if people of another color or class or gender embody anger, they are painted in one stroke as "dangerous" to society and themselves.

For countless centuries, women in both Eastern and Western societies have been warned universally about anger. Not only is its expression considered unwomanly, but we have been conditioned to block out anger entirely from our collective awareness.

Oh, how the pundits, the so-called intellectuals, professors, teachers, and media personalities go on about women's power of nurturance, their ability to soothe raging hearts, harmonize conflicted ideas and relationships, sacrifice for peace, suffer for good reasons, and forge a whole new path for humanity through the sheer power of placation, pacification, appeasement, overcompensation—and ultimately, their super-woman ability to keep their silence. This is all rhetoric from patriarchal institutions and those raised and bred in patriarchy, and from time immemorial religion, too, has been one of patriarchy's greatest assets.

Dr. Harriet Lerner, author of *The Dance of Anger*, observes,

> *Even our language condemns [angry] women as "shrews,"*
> *"witches," "bitches," "hags," "nags," "man-haters,"*
> *and "castrators." They are unloving and un-lovable.*
> *They are devoid of femininity. Certainly, you do*
> *not wish to become one of them. No wonder it takes*
> *courage to define oneself as a feminist, to risk being*
> *viewed as "one of those angry women."*
>
> *It is an interesting sidelight that our language—*
> *created and codified by men—does not*
> *have one unflattering term to describe men*
> *who vent their anger at women. Even such*
> *epithets as "bastard" and "son of a bitch" do not*
> *condemn the man, but place the blame on a woman—*
> *his mother![1]*

The wise, gender-neutral Vedas nurture no such false qualms about anger. Anger, known as *krodha* in Sanskrit, is considered a divine emotion, much like joy, peace, and tranquility. It has a spiritual purpose and is meant to help us determine when our boundaries or sense of safety is being violated—physically, verbally, sexually, or emotionally. Anger is a sign that you are not satisfied with your present situation.

Healthy anger is an expression of Shakti, an empowering, activating spiritual force that rouses us from our comfort zone to renegotiate agreements and redefine expectations. Anger helps us overcome false guilt and irrational fear by unleashing momentum, strength, passion, energy, intensity, and driven behavior to move toward restoration of our sovereignty, respect, or boundaries. Anger can provide the motivation to constructively correct an injustice. It urges us to act on our inborn sense of justice.

Therefore, a short-lived experience of timely, healthy anger goes a long way. Even animals display anger when they are threatened or encroached upon. Clearly, anger has an alerting and protective function in the divine scheme of things, and rather than giving anger itself a bad rap (especially if women embody it), it is better to learn to discern between healthy and unhealthy versions of anger and to express or retrain it accordingly.

This scientifically valid approach, more than ten thousand years old, exists in Hinduism, because the Vedas teach judiciousness, never absolutism. No wonder all Hindu goddesses and gods are depicted in art and mythology as having several hands (as a symbol of their supernatural abilities). While in some hands, they hold symbols of peace, prosperity, and spiritual awakening—like the lotus flower, *japa mala* (prayer beads), or hold their hand raised in a "fear not, I am protecting you" gesture (*mudra*)—in other hands they hold weapons, like a mace, bow and arrow, or discus. They are ready to experience righteous rage and set out for battle to protect dharma. They are both constructive and destructive, able to enhance light or destroy darkness, proactively. That is why in goddess myths and hymns, Durga is often fuming and roaring with anger, like her spirit animal, the lion.

We must stop listening to the voices that say all anger is bad or evil or that it does not become women. Let go of such foolish teachings that arise from fear of women recognizing their true power.

WHAT IS YOUR RAGE ASKING OF YOU?

Anger suggests a correction is needed. When we become angry with our poor health or sedentary ways, we begin exercising and eating right. Or, if our boss or colleague is making uninvited sexual advances, we get angry and report them to human resources. If we don't feel our anger, we won't take the actions we must take. Sometimes, if we were abused as children and our feelings got suppressed, we must get in touch with the anger many years later and only then return to balance.

Naturally, anger can arise in the face of upcoming difficulty, too, since it may help us meet the root of the challenge with vigor and set it right. For example, an impending foreclosure may make us angry with our own fiscal situation and give us renewed energy to look for another job or loan. But when we don't wish to face the difficulty and get caught up in emotional resistance, the anger builds disproportionately around the difficulty itself, and energy that could be directed to correcting the fiscal situation is wasted. Then there is a danger of implosion, potentially causing disease, or an explosion, causing damage to relationships.

Sometimes, others cause us grievances that cannot be overlooked. In a worldly, day-to-day realm, it may be important to finally call out such a person. You can initiate a correction process by opening a dialogue on what can be done to make amends, such as an apology. You can correct repressed anger only by speaking up, expressing what is true to your true Self.

Also, if you find yourself on the other side of the equation and are the person who has angered another, and if you truly want to reclaim your goddess purity and lightness, you shall take steps to correct what was incorrect: come clean, apologize, and submit yourself to a course of justice if that's what it takes.

EXPERIENCE ANGER LIKE A GODDESS

When we think of anger, we almost always think of an emotion that leads to violent actions. But there is a difference between experiencing anger as a pure emotion and what you then decide to do with the anger, what action you take because of it—which is a secondary decision of your ego.

Durga's anger deserves reverence because it quells the destructive forces that endanger dharma. In her battles with unconscious beings, she models a perfect relationship with anger. Instead of blinding her, anger opens her eyes, expanding her perception and awareness. During what appears to be thunderous rage, she is, in fact, composed and focused with single-mindedness. Her every move is conscious and tactical to uphold dharma. So, healthy anger must be experienced and appreciated consciously, rather than suppressed or swallowed.

The goddess experiences anger "for an instant" as it arises, informs, and guides. It does not stick around to color her entire personality red, making her unconscious. When we remain conscious, we will neither suppress anger nor fly off the handle. We work with it.

I feel anger as flash, almost like electricity all over my body and mind, and then seek to know why it flashed. This is the beautiful relationship I have with anger today. It is as if I have a private valet that screams "Red alert!" in every cell when my boundaries are violated by sleepwalkers, and I can always find a correct way to address the situation—for example, by walking out on a disrespectful conversation, or addressing it in depth at a later point, calmly, with discernment and detachment.

Before I act, I also ask myself: "Why am I angry? Is my anger coming from egoic entitlement, or is this something else, deeper or bigger, that deserves my attention? What are the actions that will most likely get me what I need? Will raising my voice help? Will a dialogue help? Will understanding help? Will firmness and compassion help? Will an all-out courtroom battle help?" As I see it, there are three types of anger: unconscious anger (asura), conscious anger (deva), and superconscious anger (Durga).

Unconscious Anger: Asura

Unconscious anger has no connection with dharma. It emerges exclusively from selfish entitlement. When we are unconscious, our mind is often steeped in desires and a sense of entitlement to get those desires met at any cost. We get angry when our wishes are thwarted. We rage at any living or non-living obstacle that we imagine is keeping us from our desire fulfillment. We get mad when we must deal with loss of whatever we are attached to (a lover or a promotion). We also cannot handle change or transience (aging, disease, death) because we have no greater philosophy or perspective to cope with life's changeability. So, we rage, pull, push, and control with increasing frustration. Anger from entitlement, attachments, control, and ignorance is unconscious anger.

Over time, if this pattern continues, the mind becomes vindictive, delusory, sleepless, bitter, projecting scenarios that don't necessarily match reality, anxious. Irritation and other negative emotions dominate the mind. My suggestion is to see through this anger every time—don't suppress it but don't indulge it either; try to restrain it, transform it; understand it and ultimately illumine it with self-knowledge.

Conscious Anger: Deva

Conscious anger is connected to dharmic desire to correct personal situations and is entirely healthy. It keeps us safe. It informs us of our boundary violations—physical, mental, emotional, or sexual. When this anger comes up, it informs us and then it dissolves, fades away, or retires from our dominant mind in due course. It does not simmer forever, and it does not distort our perception or permanently affect us in any way, which is what unconscious anger does. We can retain our ability to make judicious choices, forgive, and move on, if that is a reasonable option, or we can battle further, if that is the best option. Ultimately, what we do with our anger comes from a more discerned place in our mind, not our gut impulses.

Conscious anger feels non-vindictive but correctional. It stays proportional to reality and yields some restlessness, but not of an unmanageable nature. In fact, one may feel more empowered and peaceful in due course, due to clarity and sense of dharma. This anger will help you make corrections to your own habits or in setting new boundaries and expectations with others. How you express your new expectations will change, case by case, depending on who you are talking to. You will make conscious choices and grow from this anger.

Superconscious Anger: Durga

Superconscious anger is rare to experience. It has no personal agenda. It protects dharma and boundaries of all sentient beings. It arises solely to reinstitute dharma. This is divine anger. Whoever experiences superconscious anger has gone beyond their own ego to feel the pain and suffering of all beings who are being unfairly victimized by asuras. They act from anger to lead correctional movements, missions, and battles to restore dharma in this universe. This anger is a force of good, and positive change, every single time. One feels blessed from within! You are fortunate if you can be a conduit or supporter of the superconscious anger.

Superconscious anger is the way of the goddess, and here's how to convert your anger to goddess anger: Don't take your anger lightly. Don't dismiss it or suppress it. Go deeper. Listen to it. What is it trying to tell you? Try to transform your raw emotion by making your engagement with it more deliberate. Be willing to feel your anger somatically (how it expresses itself in your body), breathe with it, pause mentally, and reflect upon why it has arisen, why it lingers, why it burns your heart.

This way, through mindfulness, you can convert any unconscious emotion of anger into a conscious experience that is no longer "blinding" you with fury. In fact, it shall open your eyes to what you had been failing to see all along. Instead of staying stuck in unconscious iterations of anger, like resentment, victim consciousness, or irritability, you can begin using your conscious anger to your advantage, helping you solve problems, make decisions, and heal challenging situations.

As you tune in to your inner Durga more and more, you will channel your conscious anger for the greater good, for a larger number of people—as superconscious anger. The goddess-like anger I have experienced from injustices of patriarchy and misogyny in my own life, for example, have ultimately led to the manifestation of this book—a book that will inspire positive change and hope for all women and suppressed beings worldwide.

Superconscious anger becomes an expression of inner guidance and soul inspiration. It is the most powerful type of anger—one you can learn to understand, befriend, and draw upon from your inner Durga. Learning to contact your superconscious anger and bring it into life's daily challenges will bring you unexpected solutions and help make your life more fulfilling. You will become an instrument of positive change, and the world will be glad that you channeled your rage like Durga, for the sake of all of us!

THE RELATIONSHIP BETWEEN DHARMA, NONVIOLENCE, AND RIGHTEOUS RAGE

The concept of dharma is discussed at length in the Vedas. Dharma is a set of non-religious universal practices of self-restraint, as well as a lifestyle of embodying ethical values to help our forgetful egos remain cognizant of the boundaries of all sentient creatures (physical, sexual, verbal, emotional, intellectual, and social boundaries) and to not transgress them with an abuse of power, nor to become the victim of others.

Dharma asks that we be more sensitive to others' pain and live by higher humane values like nonviolence, compassion, truthfulness, and honesty. Dharma also asks that we never abandon ourselves or our self-respect. Without dharma contextualizing our strength and boldness, we may get lost in the world of ego battles and justify our abuse and exploitation of others. We may feel deeply inadequate, remind others of their inadequacy, or occasionally become foolishly violent while defending positions we were never meant to defend.

One of the central dharma values is nonviolence, or *ahimsa*. Ahimsa can be, in a simple way, translated as "harmlessness"—to not wish or do harm to any living creature. The commonly used English equivalent "nonviolence" is inadequate as it gives a false impression that ahimsa is just a negative virtue. Ahimsa is not mere abstention from the use of force, not just abstention from killing and injuring; it also implies the positive virtues of compassion and benevolence because not killing and not injuring a living being implicitly amounts to protecting and preserving it and treating it with humaneness, respect, and love.

From a goddess perspective, we have to ask: Does practicing ahimsa put us in direct contrast with practicing conscious and superconscious anger?

It is true that the holy books of the Hindus—the Vedas and the Bhagavad Gita—extol the value of ahimsa. Here's but one example: "Ahimsa is the highest dharma. Ahimsa is the best austerity. Ahimsa is the greatest gift. Ahimsa is the highest self-control. Ahimsa is the highest self-sacrifice. Ahimsa is the highest power. Ahimsa is the highest friend. Ahimsa is the highest teaching."[2] But you may be surprised to learn that the same sacred texts do not advocate a blind upholding of ahimsa (like some religions and leaders encourage): certainly not over justice, equality, self-respect, and righteousness—and if these are threatened, even *himsa* (violence) is permissible, albeit with judiciousness.

Absolute values may represent an awe-inspiring ideal, but in my opinion, the ideal falls flat for worldly seekers like you and me.

There is no denying the fact that we live in a society made up of a few awakened (Durga-like) and some semi-awake (deva-like) citizens, but unfortunately, a majority are sleepwalking (asura-like) egos, out to destroy dharma. Durga does not battle because she is an inherently angry person who delights in violence! Durga's anger and violence are anchored in dharma, of compassion and care—nonviolence—for the greater good.

Of the four main religions emanating from India, Buddhism and Jainism teach absolute implementation of nonviolence, while Hinduism and Sikhism offer a much more judicious application of the implementation of ahimsa. Therefore, to the Hindus and Sikhs, it is perfectly dharmic to use carefully measured violence in order to stop greater violence.

Personally, I am no advocate of violence. But violence, too, has its rightful place in life; life does not preclude death, does it? We are asked to fight against evil and injustice at both a personal and a collective level, rather than simply to close our eyes and pretend all is well. We cannot deny there are certain dire moments in the lives of individuals, as of communities and nations, when we will have to meet force with force in order that justice be done. That is why in both Hinduism and Sikhism, dharmic battles, called *Dharma Yuddha*, are those in which a dharmic one fights in the battlefields of life, lifting the sword with peace in their heart and truth in their speech, not under the influence of unconscious anger. However, even an iota of unconscious anger makes one liable for committing the sin of unrighteous violence.

In different words, both traditions rightfully advise the same message:

- Ahimsa should be upheld with great reverence, but it must not make you emotionally and intellectually impotent and unable to fight unfair aggression.

- Ahimsa should not enable spiritual bypassing or make you tolerant of atrocities against innocent animals, men, women, or children of our planet (of any religion, creed, or gender).

- Ahimsa should not result in making you
  a meek slave of your aggressor.

- Your vow of ahimsa should not empower your aggressor
  to inflict atrocities on you or your loved ones.

Therefore, if someone were to force their way into your house and harm you or your child, you must not sit back and take it in the name of practicing ahimsa. You may need to resort to himsa, or violence, for self-defense in such a circumstance. And this is dharma, in the same way a soldier cannot put down her arms when at war and a police force must use violence at times for greater good. Not doing so would go against dharma.

Therefore, as discussed in the list above, we must all eschew "unconscious anger," the mere indulgence of mindless rage or vindictive, petty animosity; expressing hatred, dislike, and egotism; and deriving pleasure from a show of personal power. But we must not hesitate to embody our "conscious anger" to protect dharma in our individual myths. We may be chosen to also embody what I call "superconscious anger," which brings about restoration of dharma at a collective level. Then, like Durga, we may become dharmically angry for the sake of universal evolution of consciousness.

Indeed, Durga protects dharma. She does not battle because she delights in violent bloodshed! The pulverizing and destroying Durga depicted in the myths is always ultimately kindhearted. Her savage side is shown to the enemies of dharma—those who oppose goodness, righteousness, ethics, law, cosmic duty—while her compassionate form is shown to the adherents of dharma. Her violence is divine, born of necessity, reserved for the destruction of destructive forces, and thus constitutes an aspect of preservation of dharma, and not its destruction. Like the nursing tigress, her fangs are bared only toward those who endanger her cubs, while the cubs themselves may lie at ease in her protective underbelly, enjoying her nourishing milk.

We, too, must turn away from unconscious anger. Our job is to cultivate a Durga-like clarity of our own dharma—the ethical imperative—in a given situation, and essentially work toward peace, but remain prepared for any necessary battle at the same time. Because this planet still contains asuric beings who see women as no more than objects of pleasure, treat people of color as dirt, and don't hesitate to harm fellow humans only for having a different sexual preference. Clearly, anger against such injustices is part of a divine dharmic order.

ROARING DURGAS EXISTED IN EVERY CULTURE

In eighteenth-century India, a twenty-two-year-old royal widow, Queen Lakshmibai of Jhansi, was unfairly dethroned by the colonial rulers of India. However, Lakshmibai did not take this meekly. She fought many battles with the British with an army in which she inducted women and taught them sword fighting. She even organized guerilla attacks on her usurpers, until at last, Lakshmibai was shot down from her horse and killed. But before dying, according to eyewitness accounts, while she sat bleeding on the battleground, she picked up her pistol and shot her killer. In the British report of this battle, the British General Hugh Rose commented that Queen Lakshmibai was "personable, clever, and beautiful," and she was "the most dangerous of all Indian leaders."[3] Lakshmibai is not alone. There are dozens more *roaring goddesses* from India's history, from as early as the first century CE, from the southernmost tip of India to the Himalayas, India's northernmost tip.

And that is not all; here are just a few of the many stories of warrior women across history and around the world:

- Archaeologists have discovered the skeletons of "badass" warrior women in Mongolia, dating back to the period of Mulan. Artnet News reports, "Close study of the skeletons suggests that the women, one about twenty, the other over fifty, were skilled at archery and had extensive experience on horseback. . . . It may have been that women were needed to defend home and country alongside the men."[4]

- In Russia, the bones, weapons, and headdresses of four real-life Amazon warriors were discovered.[5]

- Yaa Asantewaa was the queen mother of the Ejisuhene in what is now modern Ghana. She raised and led an army of five thousand against the British colonial forces who had captured the previous king and sought to completely subjugate her people.[6]

- The Mino were an all-female military regiment of the present-day Republic of Benin from the seventeenth to nineteenth centuries. They had a ferocious reputation, and were famous for decapitating colonial soldiers during combat, as well as those whom they took captive.[7]

- Queen Nzinga Mbande was a powerful seventeenth-century ruler of the Ambundu kingdoms of Ndongo and Matamba in modern-day Angola. She fearlessly and cleverly fought against the Portuguese Empire, who were colonizing the Central African coast in an attempt to control the slave trade in the area at the time.[8]

- Harriet Tubman was an African American abolitionist and humanitarian, who worked as a Union spy during the American Civil War. Born a slave, she escaped and went on to lead rescue missions using the Underground Railroad that saved at least seventy enslaved people. In 1863, Tubman guided the Combahee Ferry Raid, which liberated more than seven hundred enslaved Blacks in South Carolina and made her the first woman to lead an armed expedition in the Civil War.[9]

I have not even covered all the continents, but suffice to say, the Durga archetype is alive and well across the annals of time. It is only more recently—with the spread of false "feel-good" spiritual notions like absolute pacifism alongside the puritanical values preached by patriarchal interpretations of all religions—that we women seem to need reminders of our warrior goddess heritage.

Wake up, Durga! Don't take abuse and discrimination based on gender, color, or anything else lying down. If you have been unfairly treated, wrongly blamed, victimized, or marginalized, just call out to Mother Durga. She will rise from the depths of your own soul to protect you by reminding you of your own dharmic rage. She will manifest as a helper, a friend, a teacher, or a book from out of the blue that reminds you of your own buried power. You will become Durga herself when you rise in shining self-respect and self-defense, fearlessly setting wrongs to right for yourself, the planet, and all innocent beings.

I AM THE DAUGHTER OF A DURGA: MY JOURNEY WITH ANGER

I witnessed my mother openly express her conscious anger toward wrongdoers, reprimanding her boundary violators. At the same time, she respected others' boundaries. And she was equally trusting, vulnerable, and kindhearted with people who showed her that they were worthy of her trust. She told me that I must embody my Shakti like a living flame; everyone should get light and radiance from me, but the same people should be cautious about poking a finger through me or my business because then they would get burnt. Slowly, but surely, I have become that flame.

Finger-pokers don't like your flaming boundaries. They shame you for having them. For a while, I let everybody make me feel guilty for being powerful. But not for too long; I was eventually able to see through it. Now, my flame is brighter, bigger, more radiant. It appears formidable to the asuras, yet as a friend and source of light to the devas.

It is heartbreaking to see all the pretense that goes on in the name of being anger-less—and as a result, optionless, passionless, goddess-less. Equally sad is the sheer unconsciousness that is embodied behind false pacifism—all the anger we humans must collectively suppress to "prove" our worthiness to divinity!

Thank Goddess, we women do have divine role models who roar instead. That is why my anger today is not merely directed toward men who seemingly abuse us women, but toward our own spiritual ignorance as sleeping goddesses, which can make us easy targets.

Furthermore, it is one thing to protect ourselves; it is a whole other thing to rise and speak up for the protection and celebration of all beings. Perhaps this book—which has emerged from channeling my superconscious anger—will be a gift for women worldwide.

A DURGA CONTEMPLATION FOR YOU

I ASK: What makes me angry? Which of the
three forms of anger is this?

I RECOGNIZE: Anger is a messenger. What is
it telling me or asking of me?

I CONNECT: Where in my body do I feel anger?
Does it change with my awareness?

I DECIDE: I can react unconsciously or respond with discernment.

I ACT: What dharmic action will I take? What are my next steps?

I REMEMBER: I am Durga, composed power, warrior goddess!

CHAPTER 3

ROAR LIKE A GODDESS WHEN ACCOSTED SEXUALLY

O Durga, who dare behold thy enraged face of death and still live?
DEVI MAHATMYA 4.13

According to my interpretation of a legend narrated in the Puranas, Durga, too, was objectified in her womanly incarnation. She, being a goddess, reacted not with shame but fury. She roared so loud that the ominous sound rocked the world and pulverized entire galaxies into dust.

This story begins when two asura brothers, Shumbha and Nishumbha, conquer the human world as well as the celestial realms, where the devas are said to reside. With their evil minds and non-dharmic deeds, the asuras managed to dispossess the noble-minded devas of their wealth, snatch their powers, and appropriate their women-partners, children, and privileges. The brothers were the most influential asuras in the world at that time, especially when it came to ill-gotten power and riches! The devas and gods once again appealed to Durga to save them from the plight of the asuras. Durga agreed.

Soon enough, two servants of the asuric brothers named Chanda and Munda happened upon Durga in her womanly avatar as Ambika. They were struck by her beauty, unparalleled in the whole universe. They ran back to their masters to share the news that they'd seen a young, exquisitely beautiful damsel named Ambika. None like her dwells on this planet, they swore to one of the brother's, Shumbha, with grins that could hardly contain their own greasy lust. They fed Shumbha's pride further by asking, "O Great One, at this time, all worldly gems have been seized by you. But why has this gorgeous lady, a jewel among women, not been taken by you, yet? Surely, such a gem among women has been exclusively created by the creator for your pleasure alone?"

On hearing rather graphic descriptions of her beauty, Shumbha's desire was aroused, all right. Now, he wanted to claim her as his own, just like anyone whose senses are not under control and wants to own and derive pleasure from anything they find attractive and desirable. He had no other thought but to possess this famed beauty at any cost.

Shumbha sent a smooth-talking messenger to fetch Ambika. Shumbha told his messenger to bring her a marriage proposal with assurances of untold wealth and power. "Tell her," Shumbha told his messenger, "'Great wealth, beyond compare, will be yours by accepting me. I will be your servant. Think this over and become my wife.'"

Ambika (who was really Durga) wanted to annihilate the asuras. She said, "The one who conquers me in a battle and overcomes my pride is clearly comparable to me. He alone can be my husband."

The messenger could not believe that this wisp of a girl dared to invite his great master—currently the master of asuras, humans, and gods—to a battle. With barely restrained scorn, he told her, "Come on lady, don't play hard to get. A proposal of love should be responded to with love, not an invitation to battle. After all," he added for good measure, "love is the highest emotion! Besides, your body is too soft and too delicate. You are not made for battles. Stop all this talk of battles. Come with me to my master now. He will make you the mistress of this world."

(*Dear reader, does the messenger remind you of people who don't take you, your word, or your abilities seriously, just because you are a woman?*)

Durga refused. The messenger now spoke with considerable indignation, saying that even all the goddesses together could not defeat his master. "Who are you, but a woman without a husband?" he asked, taking a dig at Durga's still-single status. "The devas, headed by their king Indra, could not stand in battle against my masters. So how will you, a mere woman, face them all by yourself? Either you listen to me and go to him of your own volition lovingly or I will eventually take you to my master regardless, dragging you by your hair!" Apparently, according to the messenger, she had no choice, but to meekly go along to be loved!

Durga stood her ground, and her tone changed. She said, "Having rejected Vishnu, Shiva, and other gods, why should I take your asura master as my husband? Go away, I have no need for a husband, asuric, devic, or godly. I am my own mistress." In other words: "I am no desperate gal, mister!" Durga's alluring speech in the beginning and then her later defiance and disdain confused the messenger. He returned to his master empty-handed.

Shumbha sent another wicked collaborator asura with the specific orders, "Bring her kicking and screaming if necessary!"

(*Ah, we see how love can stoop to lust and violence when so-called love is not met with love in return.*)

One by one, Shumbha's asuric commanders and generals received their orders: "Bring back that vile woman by any means or in any condition!" All fought her, but not before they had reminded her of her womanly imperatives: "It is nice you are a heroic woman and all that, but remember you are a woman. Your powers of cultivating peace and harmony through loving and seducing are greater."

(*Does this turn of events remind you of when men without morals accost a woman who is immune to subtle sexual aggression, or when they cannot get their way, they shame her about her womanhood and the fact that she dares to reject them?*)

Durga, in her manifestation as Ambika, got to experience for herself what the rest of us women feel when patriarchal messages of "staying in a woman's place" fall on our ears. We are told it is our anger that causes men to become annoyed, violent, and dangerous with us and our children. But Durga did not bother responding to them, or pander to their ignorance. She annihilated them and their ignorance with her ultra-feminine rage.

KALI EMERGES FROM DURGA

It was clear to Shumbha and Nishumbha by now that this was no ordinary woman. Feeling uneasy, they nevertheless decided to continue to battle anyway (egotistical people never know when to back down). They sent several valorous commanders leading millions of asura solders to where the goddess stood her ground alone, undefeatable. And what is more, right there amid the bloodshed, Durga birthed Kali, a new expression of herself. This she did from her third eye, demonstrating how hidden spiritual strengths can emerge when we need them.

Goddess Kali is scary-looking and terrifying. She is fierce, dark as the darkest hour of the night, a disheveled-looking goddess. When I say "dark" it is not just in reference to her complexion, but her relationship with light—her body reflects zero light but absorbs it all entirely. Imagine her like a spiritual "dark hole" that can devour all the current millions of galaxies, if she wants.

Her tongue, red and protruding, represents passion and creativity, and she is naked because she is beyond illusion. Kali's nakedness also represents primal consciousness and the original expression of the Inner Being. Kali does not let us pretend we "got light" when we are merely borrowing it; she strips away our flimsy pretenses until we really turn on our own original "Inner Light." She tells us that as long as we keep wearing "clothes" and "masks" (conditioned consciousness) to conceal our light, power, and truth from ourselves, we will never defeat our inner and outer asuras. When she is present, no possible illusion can exist. Truth alone is truth—bare bone, perfection in imperfection, light within darkness. Thus, it is natural for Kali—Durga's innermost being—to be naked. Kali is free from illusory coverings because she is beyond all false conceptions. Just like the earth and sky, she can dare to face the truth, in all its nakedness. Her motto is *Bring it on!*

Kali, the One Truth Beyond Time (her name literally means "the one beyond time"), is raw power. Kali embodies the boundless nature of spirit and existential freedom to be who we are without any outer garb—unpretentious, unapologetic, fearless, indomitable, a sheer force of nature—in fact, nature incarnate! Ultimately, Kali is indifferent to opinions because she is fired up with Truth and Shakti. She isn't angry or wild; she is REAL, bare and simple.

With four arms, Kali is the original multitasker. She carries an open sword in one hand and the severed head of an asura (representing ignorance) in another. With the other two hands, she blesses her worshippers, saying, "Do not fear. I protect the righteous and only attack the unconsciousness inside you." Her red eyes, bloodstained face, and naked breasts give her added intensity and clarity of purpose.

Durga as Kali means business. As Hannah K. Griggs wrote in her essay "Indian Women's Uplift Movements and the Dangers of Cultural Imperialism," "The paradox of Kali—who is terrifying and motherly, destructive and protective, powerful and tender—reflects the paradox of womanhood and of humanity. By embracing each contradictory part of her identity, Kali transcends identity. . . . Kali is one of many manifestations of Devi [Shakti], the 'Ultimate Reality,' which surpasses all names and forms . . ."[1]

Finally, the brothers sent their most ominous commander by the name of Raktabija, who possessed a magical power. Whenever a drop of his blood fell on the ground, a duplicate asura would be born on that spot. Raktabija attacked Ambika, and in response, she hurled her bolt at the asura. Wounded, Raktabija began bleeding, and each drop of his blood gave rise to a clone of himself, each equally brutal. As more weapons were hurled by Ambika, more drops of Raktabija's blood gave rise to new demons. Soon the battlefield was full of countless demons attacking Ambika. Though Ambika stood her ground despite the millions of Raktabija clones attacking her, decisive action was needed. At that critical moment, Kali opened her mouth, as vast as this whole universe, and her tongue came out. She started gulping down every drop of blood emanating from the demons killed by Ambika, as well as devouring the demons themselves. Not one more drop of blood fell to the ground. Ambika and Kali worked together until the last drop of asuric blood had been licked clean from the battlefield.

Finally, the last clone was left standing. Ambika attacked the asura with her trident, and Kali swallowed the blood flowing from his fallen body. Raktabija was dead. Smack! Thanks to Kali's tongue, that was the end of Raktabija's pestilence forever.

Durga as Goddess Kali literally drinks the blood of asuras, which means *she devours unconsciousness* . . . gobbles it up. Goddess Kali is not a monster who selfishly or arbitrarily wreaks havoc in the universe. Her blood-dripping sword slices the bonds of ignorance and ego, which are represented by the severed heads she holds in one of her many hands. Her blood-swallowing tongue indicates her willingness to digest and process darkness, and not be overcome or overwhelmed by it. Her destructiveness and drinking of blood (blood is symbolic of egoic arrogance) are for restoring dharma, or what is right, and protecting the light bearers. Having no patience for "asuras" like lust, pride, greed, rage, and injustice, she went on a rampage, devouring every asura in her way. Continuing with the story, with Raktabija annihilated, the brothers Shumbha and Nishumbha decided to enter the battle themselves, though they had had a setback at the death of all their strong allies. The brothers were committed to either bring Ambika to her senses or die a hero's death (they had gone too far to flee). Nishumbha began combat with the goddess, but within minutes he lay slain. Now only Shumbha was left standing alone in the entire battlefield, strained and stinking with asura blood. Barely able to look the goddess in the eye as he shuddered from fear, Shumbha still managed to blurt out a taunt that Durga was relying on her helpers (Ambika, Kali, etc.). At this point, the goddess absorbed all her avatars back into herself, and Durga as Durga pierced Shumbha's body with her pointed spear. Shumbha fell, lifeless, on the ground.

With the asuric brothers now dead, and the world cleansed of millions of asuras in the process, cosmic order was once again restored on earth by the victory of dharma over non-dharma, of light over darkness, of truth over falsehoods. The devas and gods praised Durga for once again coming to their rescue.

In her myths, Durga comes to the rescue of the devas every single time because they are essentially good (dharmic). The unethical, however, those who usurp others' power, lose all agency with Durga. They not only forfeit any claim to appealing to the Divine Feminine, the higher order, but it is only a matter of time before they meet their dismal fate, because Durga, who is inseparable from the intelligence of this universe, will see to their destruction in some way or another. To protect the righteous and to punish the unrighteous is her essential nature.

Like Durga, we, too, should evaluate who deserves our help and who does not. We should not hesitate to face the enemies of goodness and dharma. As you take the teachings of the goddess to heart, your inner Durga will awaken, and you will be much more willing to encounter the asuras of your life!

WHEN YOU ARE
ACCOSTED SEXUALLY . . . ROAR

Durga becomes fierce only when the dharma stakes are super-high. Otherwise, she simply sits on her lion, composed and royal as *Maa Durga*, looking out for us. When we need her and cry out "*Maa . . .*," she runs to comfort us.

During the battle with various asuras, Durga roared again and again, with a sound half goddess and half lion that reverberated throughout the universe. The mountains shook, and the rivers changed course when Durga roared, as the great unity of the innate powers of all the gods. All the planets were agitated and quaked with fear in their orbits. Meteors shot randomly hither and thither. Stars burst spontaneously; entire galaxies shook, morphed, and mutated with that Goddess roar.

That is how a goddess sounds when she is accosted sexually or otherwise transgressed. The goddess is not all sugar and spice. She is Divine Consciousness. Reality with a capital R. *So are you*. And fury is exactly what the world needs sometimes to correct its course.

Making the earth bend with her footsteps, scraping the sky with her crown, shaking the netherworlds with the twang of a bowstring, Durga stood there covering all quarters of the universe with her goddess roar, reverberating everywhere.

Let Durga-as-Kali's story remind you to respond with your goddess roar when you have to deal with the biggest, trickiest, most obstinate asura in your life that challenges your self-respect and sexual sovereignty, whether inside or outside of you. And when necessary, never hesitate to roar like Durga!

If life situations require you to roar to protect your sexual boundaries, then that is what you do. Like never before, women are coming out and reclaiming the power they have lost, consciously or unconsciously. But many more people, not just women but even men, at times, and transgender and nonbinary-gendered souls, too, are still hiding, still survivors of sexual abuse and domestic violence, even in the twenty-first century, in which the cultural systems often fail to support and protect them.

We can look to Durga for inspiration even if we cannot outwardly reclaim our power at that time. When Durga was solicited sexually without her permission, she answered with a roar. She taught the asuras, who dared to think of violating her, a lesson they will never forget. She was really teaching us women how to value our bodies and our right to the sanctity of our bodies, like a goddess. And if life has you in a corner where you can't think or act like Durga, then even the knowledge of her archetype will give you the permission to deeply feel your anger, neither numbing it nor bypassing it, but being with it in a conscious manner.

Of course, you must always respond to the asuras in your life with your physical and emotional safety in mind, as the threats of domestic violence, sexual assault, and rape are all real. If you do not feel safe to roar publicly yet, then I suggest you roar privately inside your heart until you have planned your exit from a dangerous situation, or at the least tapped into your safety and support network. We can always roar in a way that helps us emotionally break free from the binding rhetoric of shame, fear, and self-blame, but does not endanger ourselves, our loved ones, or our livelihood.*

THEY TRIED TO SUPPRESS THEM, NOT KNOWING THEY WERE DURGAS

Activating our inner Durga is important not just for making life bearable and happy, but for making the weaker among us (of all genders) truly powerful, as well as to deal with unwanted sexual advances, first and foremost. Just because women are nurturing and emotional does not mean we are weak or powerless objects of pleasure.

---

* If you or someone you know is a survivor of sexual abuse, you can contact RAINN, the largest anti-sexual violence organization in the US, for 24/7 support, self-care tools, and information (rainn.org).

Many women in India are highly educated and technically skilled, often enjoying as much professional freedom as men. They run the government, lead corporations, and influence ideas, art, fashion, science, and culture on a world stage. But there is another India made up of women who exist in the shadow, beneath the economic boom. They are given very little autonomy by the men in their society and are forced to stay sexually submissive and emotionally submissive by a dangerously unforgiving, patriarchal society. In fact, the National Family Health Survey[2] reported that about 31 percent of married women in India have experienced physical, sexual, or emotional violence by their spouse, and this number is likely higher as most violence against women goes unreported in India. We urgently need to create a new image for these women, individually and collectively, that connects their nurturing side with their warrior side and refuses to apologize for either. And this is exactly what one group of women in India did at the grassroots level, in a rough and rustic, yet very real way.

They call themselves the Gulabi Gang (Gulabi means "pink" in Hindi) because they dress in pink, and they wield bamboo canes like weapons, ever willing to take on the villains who dare to defy the dignity of women when conventional methods fail to produce justice. The group's founder says, "Yes, we fight rapists with lathis [sticks]. If we find the culprit, we thrash him black and blue so he dares not attempt to do wrong to any girl or a woman again."[3] This gang is now four hundred thousand strong across rural India and growing.

This gang reminds me of CODEPINK, a women-led grassroots organization working to end US-funded wars and military occupations and to support peace and human rights initiatives. Women everywhere are taking the color pink and giving it an all-new hue of self-determination because we know that society will only change if we eliminate the inherent subordination of the role given to women.

Durga's battles with "outer" asuras represent the battles all women must fight with the "inner" asuras of fear and our astounding okay-ness with a lack of self-respect, which together make us silently concede to and put up with sexual abuse and assault. The #MeToo movement perhaps was the first time, thanks to online technology, that millions of educated and tech savvy women "came out" with their stories of sexual abuse and gender discrimination, leaving not a shred of doubt that sexual harassment of women knows no boundaries—rural or urban, traditional or modern, illiterate or educated. To women world-wide, united across class, cultures, and countries, the magnitude of the problem was evident. Now, many more exposing hashtags, such as #ChurchToo, #TimesUp, and #SilenceIsNotSpiritual, are acting like virtual bamboo canes!

The more you survey the battlefield of your mind as the goddess you are, the more your increasing awareness will allow you to overthrow your inner and outer enemies. You will regain your freedom to think and behave like a goddess.

A DURGA CONTEMPLATION FOR YOU

I ASK: Have I been dismissed, disrespected, or
   assaulted because of my gender?

I RECOGNIZE: Patriarchy runs deep. Do I unwittingly perpetuate it?

I CONNECT: In silence, I listen to what comes up in my body, mind,
   and consciousness as I contemplate the qualities of Kali.

I DECIDE: I will never tolerate sexual discrimination, abasement,
   or abuse.

I ACT: When sexually transgressed, I speak out (roar!)
   immediately, seek out support, and dharmically resist.

I REMEMBER: Kali is within me. Freedom and truth empower me!

CHAPTER 4

THE GODDESS PATH TO UNCONDITIONAL SELF-RESPECT

O woman! Act like none but the queen and
mistress of everyone in the family.

RIG VEDA 10.85.46

O nce upon a time, Shakti, the Great Goddess and mother of the universe, decided to take birth as a girl child in King Daksha's home. When Daksha saw his newborn daughter's face and her radiance that filled the three worlds, he knew she was no ordinary daughter. And to confirm his inkling, the newborn spoke up like a cosmic queen in a voice that reverberated across the entire universe, causing flowers to blossom instantaneously: "Daksha, I shall remain your daughter only so long as you give me respect. The moment you forget, I shall cast this human body aside and reassume my original fiery form as Pure Power."

Daksha and his wife agreed, and why would they not? They were delighted and proud beyond imagination that Divine Mother Shakti herself had come to their home as their daughter. They named her Sati, from the root word *sat*, which means the "Ultimate Truth."

Time passed, and slowly Daksha and his wife forgot that their beloved daughter with all her human traits was a Great Goddess.

Meanwhile, earth had never seen better times. All was peaceful. There were no wars or pandemics. The seasons were on time. The crops were bountiful. The fruits dripped with elixir.

Then Princess Sati came of marriageable age. While her parents suggested to her various wealthy heirs of neighboring kingdoms, Sati, because she knew she was Shakti deep inside her, yearned to unite with Shiva, her Divine Masculine counterpart. Sati had heard that Shiva the great yogi-god resided in the Himalayas.

It was not easy to convince Shiva to accept Princess Sati's proposal, but it all ended happily when Shiva saw in Princess Sati's eyes his beloved goddess partner, Shakti! Shiva and Sati were betrothed, and Sati took off her princess attire and braided wildflowers in her hair. Then she left joyfully with her divine yogi husband, Shiva, for his mountain abode.

Sati's human parents were not pleased, though they smiled politely. Many considered Shiva a god in the garb of a yogi (ascetic), but his lifestyle was so meager that Daksha was repulsed by his son-in-law. Daksha had privately hoped for a wealthy son-in-law, but his hopes were dashed by his daughter, who was mature and powerful beyond her years and always seemed to have her way.

Years passed, and then one day, Daksha organized a grand fire ritual. He decided to invite all the well-known human and godly personalities from all over the universe to this festive occasion. Daksha deliberately "forgot" to invite his daughter and her wild-looking husband, who wore snakes around his neck and only a tiger skin wrapped around his lower body.

By chance, Sati ran into the moon god, Chandra, and his wife, Goddess Rohini, all dressed up to attend the grand festive occasion. She was shocked to learn that Daksha had not invited his only daughter and son-in-law.

Sati was burning with indignation. She showed up at her father's house and demanded an explanation! Sati spoke: "You have spurned my self-respect and humiliated my partner too. Why?"

Sati's father screamed back with defiant pride, "I let you have your way when you chose Shiva as your life partner! But don't expect any more from me. Your husband roams around half naked, for goodness' sake! I will not invite him to dine with my classy guests, and I knew you would not come without him." And then as an afterthought he added, "Since you are here, you can stay if you want. I am sure your mother has some clothes for you befitting today's gathering."

Sati spoke, completely in touch with her conscious anger. "No, I will not stay. In fact, now I will leave you altogether. I told you, I will be your daughter only as long as you respect me. What you did is not acceptable. Now, right here on this festive occasion, amidst your hundreds of classy guests, I will cast off this disrespected daughter's body with the fire of my righteous rage. Don't forget I am Shakti. And Shiva, who you have called such vile names and disrespected sorely by not inviting him, is my other divine half. Daksha, you have disrespected the very gods (Shiva and Shakti) you were trying to please through your silly ritual."

Then a radiant fiery flame, which was Pure Shakti herself, erupted forth from Sati's body and headed toward the sky. The body that Shakti had once possessed as Sati was now engulfed entirely in flames. The charred body dropped to the floor.

Shakti had left, after self-immolation of her human body as Sati.

Daksha was left bitterly crying for everything he had lost, including his beloved princess.

Shakti manifested in front of Shiva and said, "I have not forgotten my promises to you, my love of you, and of the divine work we must do together. I will come back to you soon in a new body."

This tale from the Puranas invariably gets my attention, every single time. Why? For the sheer courage of conviction demonstrated by the goddess in her human avatar!

If you are feeling shocked and wondering how self-immolation is an act of courage, remember, all the elements of the myth are symbolic, not literal. If self-respect is at stake, then through the fire of our anger, we must "burn down" the very relationships that adhere to our bodies and make us appear in people's eyes as unworthy of respect.

Daksha could only see with his eyes the body of his daughter. He could not see the Shakti (original power) that was enlivening the bodies of the two beings he called daughter and son-in-law.

Every time I retell this myth, it gives me goosebumps. Shakti, in her incarnation as Sati, set the standard of self-respect for all time. She is telling humans to treat their daughters with extreme respect. And she is telling us daughters of human parents to treat ourselves with unconditional self-respect! We need reminders because, too many times, we women give our loved ones, superiors, colleagues, lovers, and friends countless chances to disrespect us. Shakti is telling you: *disrespect is never okay*. Because if you allow it once, then you are giving the signal that you are going to be okay with more disrespect in the future. The moment you see it coming your way, it is imperative that you act. At the minimum, speak up when it is safe to do so. Say you don't like it. Walk away with your head held high. As for the thread of emotional attachment that keeps making you go back to the disrespectful ones, burn it!

NUMBER ONE LESSON FROM SHAKTI: EMBODY SELF-RESPECT

It is time every woman made self-respect more important than romance, beauty, looks, domestic bliss, and securing professional achievements. If you don't stand up for yourself, be it at work or at home, chances are no one else will. It is self-respect alone that leads to healthy boundaries.

Some telltale signs of a lack of self-respect are:

- You do not stand up for yourself when others ill-treat you, walk over you, take you for granted, make you invisible, or behave like you don't exist. You justify to yourself why you are silent, and you continue engaging, despite being treated like a doormat.

- You have gotten into the habit of agreeing with people so much that now you don't know your own opinion. Or, if you have opinions, you choose to keep them private because you think agreeing will make you more likeable.

- Lack of self-respect also shows up in a sense of generalized unworthiness. You feel guilty in expressing your needs

and desires, or in taking "me time" to rest or take a
well-deserved vacation. While you give gifts, you quell
your right to receive gifts. You say yes, all the time,
when many times you should really be saying no.

- Lack of self-respect extends to every area of your life.
  You let so-called friendly souls—family, colleagues, and
  even neighbors—treat you with borderline disrespect.
  They may mock you, play pranks, or tease you while you
  put up a brave face and treat it like some big joke.

When self-respect is lacking, women who are facing a disrespectful spouse or in-laws, domestic abuse, control, or sexual violence
tend to overstay the relationship. They keep looking for a reason to
leave, as if what is happening—reason enough for any self-respecting
woman—is not enough. They allow themselves to be manipulated,
victimized, exploited, taken for granted, controlled, bullied, and
forced, all due to lack of self-respect.

Can anyone be blamed for lack of self-respect? We all possess
that magical Self that is one with Shakti, but sadly, most women are
dealing with the wrong kind of messages from childhood, and thanks
to internalizing feminine guilt, they think respect can be gained
only through proving they are worthy of respect: by holding high-
paying jobs, making sacrifices in domesticity, having a thin body, or
a happening social life.

But the Self-respect I am talking about is a sense of self-value
that is not conditional, not based upon your accomplishments, but
inherent because of who you are to begin with. It is based upon the
knowledge that you are not merely a material body trying to score
points in the material realm, but a spiritual being—Shakti incarnate as a woman. Continued contemplation on this hidden truth can
fill you with innate, fundamental, and unconditional self-respect.

Often women don't have beautiful empowering goddess myths in
their cultures, nor access to knowledge of the Self from the Vedas to
wake them up from their acquiescence to ongoing maltreatment. In
modern societies, nobody says outright, "You are a girl, so you better

stay down there!" But nevertheless, the entire society and media, even in the most advanced places on earth, reinforce the image of successful womanhood—chiefly based upon looks, popularity, weight, niceness, sweetness, and smartness, but not before the ability to snag a male partner. Self-respect is not considered a must-have trait for women.

Professionally successful women, if they are not married by a certain age, are universally considered a little less worthy of respect than the woman who not only has professional accomplishments but also a committed partner and kids to claim as her own. And as one confused student justified her stance to me, "If one must dumb down a little to make that happen, step back a little, and even overlook occasional disrespect from our partners *to have it all*, then why not?"

It is for women like this student that I am writing this book, who self-sabotage their own inner goddess by their slippery standards born of false values and who are unaware of their goddess potential to lead a truly magnificent life.

ACCEPT YOURSELF TO RESPECT YOURSELF

In a unique way, goddess archetypes can help modern women construct their own narrative about who they are and claim an identity that is not imposed or judged by a colonizing masculine mindset. They can finally be themselves as they are, rather than be "imagined" into being and becoming by others—least of all by the males around them. This is an important journey of spiritual reclamation. Ultimately, it will lead to greater self-acceptance, an end to shame, and greater integration with all aspects of the feminine experience.

Durga is not apologetic for being wise, powerful, fierce, gentle, or single. She is the mistress of her universe. She is in charge. Shakti's wide range of appearances and qualities—ferocious to compassionate, attractive to repulsive, uncommitted to wholehearted, sensual to chaste, passionate to meditative—might feel strange to cultures that view the Divine in a moral straitjacket. I invite you to welcome the extraordinary vision of the ancient Vedic seers, who did not force a limited expression of the Divine Feminine on humanity. The stunning and shocking unfamiliarity of the goddess forms, overtly powerful while simultaneously nurturing or sensual, can help free us from our predictably limited states of mind. They can propel us into the realm of the unfamiliar, unknown, and unexpected, where anything is possible because the feminine is divine.

But if we are always engaged with an illusory fictitious self—one that the world or significant others want to see—can we ever really respect our self? Such fictions are a waste of time. Your spiritual journey to your inner Durga begins when you voluntarily start peeling off masks, one after another.

Worldwide, we women have rejected our right to be who we are deep down—often unconsciously. Age-old feminine guilt ensures that we try hard to be or become what others want from us—without even fully realizing it. When I was young, I did not fully accept myself and therefore could not deeply respect myself. Despite reasons to not act in disempowered ways, many times I became "that" which others wanted me to be—the good wife, the super mom, the diligent daughter-in-law, the shoulder to cry on for other needy women, the reliable neighbor, the pious soul. All along, I was estranged from my own truth. When I ran out of steam, patriarchal society, in India and later in the US, handed me yet more well-worn scripts, and off I went again, living out a new (but ancient) narrative of feminine self-rejection.

Vulnerability is considered a sign of feminine weakness and neediness. In a male-dominated culture, with male gods, male politicians, and a male-driven economy, women are obliged to play by the rules set by males in a game chosen by males. But once you bring greater wisdom, consciousness, knowledge, and light to your vulnerability, it becomes enlightened vulnerability. And in modern times, women must find a greater acceptance of their inherent womanhood. In an internalized patriarchy, we have lost this acceptance of our feminine characteristics.

We need to stop overcompensating for our feminine vulnerability; stop hiding our feminine courage, anger, or rage; stop making excuses for our emotional nature that is truly divine. It's unsurprising that women experience depression when we don't allow ourselves to roar with righteous rage nor cry openly and express our discomfort where and when it matters. We simply cope, far too much and for too long.

You matter. It's important to give adequate attention to your needs and vulnerabilities, and take care of your inner goddess. Your needs matter. Your truth matters.

Grounded in a spiritual appreciation of your true nature, why not offer yourself radical self-acceptance? Accept yourself *as you are*, and be real. Accept that scar or wrinkle that you think is your worst enemy. Don't highlight only what you like about yourself. Bring self-acceptance to that (inner or outer) scar, too, because everything is part of a Divine Feminine order. Self-deception conceals the inner goddess and stops us cold on the journey we have yet to undertake. Truth reveals her and brings the goddess closer to you.

A woman in one of my workshops shared this about her marriage: "If I am not tough with my husband of twenty-five years—vocal, loud, rigid in my opinions, and preferences—he will just roll right over me. He does, actually! He gaslights and pretends I didn't say something clearly because it lets him get what he wants without having to discuss it with me. Yet I am learning if I say it quietly and say less, react less, and disengage, he pays more attention. But it is still difficult for me to always trust the softer approach. It brings up a lot of fear that I will not be seen. A lot of fear."

Having to be "hard" is not necessarily more self-respecting than having to be accommodating. Both are superimposed scripts on our inner goddess, embedded by patriarchy. It is simply a reactive opposite of the meek way some women embrace their humanhood.

Rebellion is not the only way to oppose patriarchy. That is why all women can learn from Durga, who is not confined to any one stereotype—meek or aggressive, strong or pliable, rebelling or docile—but rather, with inner strength and conviction, she embodies all her dimensions with ease and spontaneity, and above all, judiciousness. She is so much stronger than most of us can comprehend. It takes courage to embrace the inner Durga, who represents wisdom, balance, and intuition, not just the extremes of rebellion or passivity. With such courage, you can become not merely defiant but invincible in your divine, goddess-blessed life. You can be Durga, both nurturing and tough—become a feminine power, a feminist force, and everything in between. This combination of fierceness and softness is a great way for us women to embody our Shakti, without being either/or! When my husband is surprised by my multiple skills, strengths, and dimensions, I remind him that is a sign of my inner goddess being awake.

SELF-RESPECT IS A DHARMIC OBLIGATION

Dharma is cultivated through higher-vibration ideas, values, or attitudes that engender self-respect first and foremost, because we begin to see ourselves not merely as struggling women who have weight to lose, pimples to cover up, degrees to earn, and jobs to hold down, but as instruments of divine goodness. We recognize that a Divine Feminine force, a greater will, is moving through us, asking us to be the best possible versions of ourselves. When we show our own self-respect and form this foundation of self-value, then extend respect and kindness to others—after due discernment of who is worthy of our respect and who is not—then we become more like the goddess, who always lives with self-respect and whose life is an example to others.

Therefore, dharma inspires us to possess and practice those virtuous or valuable thoughts that make us bold and courageous in celebrating who we are as women and at the same time compassionate, sensitive, and responsible beings toward others.

When you make "respect" one of your core needs, your own value system will become more enlightened. Then, guided from within, you will only stay and interact in healthy relationships. You will not put up with disrespect a minute more than is necessary. You won't have sliding standards. And people will know better than to mess with you and your respect. Also, your practiced dharma of self-respect will elicit Divine Mother Durga's grace and protection. She will be pleased that you are trying to emulate her and live like her. Your mind will become a pure crystal, radiating your goddess power, divine abundance, and a more awakened state of being.

To engage with Durga and self-respect, read the following words slowly. Then, pause and contemplate. Feel.

The Great Self-Respecting Goddess
dwells in the very depths of your being.
Realize her through quiet contemplation.

Feel her power surge in your heart.
She is hidden in you
like fragrance lies hidden in the flower.

Adore the Self-Respecting Goddess
by ensuring no one gets away with disrespecting her
through you.

The Goddess of Power, Durga, says to you
Show me value by valuing yourself
Show me love by loving yourself
Show me care by caring for yourself
Show me wisdom by protecting yourself.

Contemplative knowledge is half the battle won. Women must realize that embodying the dharma of self-respect is as important as eating healthy, exercising, and relaxing with our supportive friends, if not the most important thing of all. When you keep valuing yourself as a bearer of Shakti, you will attract relationships worthy of your inner goddess. At the very least, you will gain your own self-approval every time. And sooner or later, you will attract mutually honoring relationships or influence your current relationships in such a way that you can dwell in them with your self-respect intact. I cannot promise you will win in all your relationships, but I can promise you that with knowledge of how to be a true self-respecting goddess, you won't lose yourself!

Below are four mandates of self-respect I made for myself and tried to live up to in my own life, many years ago. They served as my own self-respecting boundaries. Maybe they will help you too. Or, you can write your own mandates.

- Mandate 1. Here onward, to celebrate my inner goddess, I am going to respect my legitimate human needs. I will acknowledge what I need and speak up where required, and not suppress my voice, internally or externally, so I can give to others when it is my turn to give and share, without bitterness or unease.

- Mandate 2. Before I concern myself with becoming a "good" wife, daughter, mom, sister, employee, or friend, let me become a "self-valuing person" to myself. And to do that, I will value myself as a unique expression and instrument of goddess who is inherently valuable, and I need not prove this value to anyone, only live from it, with quiet, sweet self-validation.

- Mandate 3. Though my true self is a goddess, my vulnerable physical self can become fatigued. I accept that, and I will not push my body. I will gift my body ample sleep, exercise, and care so the instruments of my inner goddess (body, senses, and mind) are not merely used but also rejuvenated daily and seasonally. I will listen to my body's needs and never shame it for having limits.

- Mandate 4. I am done accepting abuse of any kind, under any belief system: societal, cultural, religious, moral, karmic, astrological, or otherwise. To strengthen my conviction of unconditional self-respect, I will be selective about the company I keep, or stay alone if required, anchored in the light and strength of my inner goddess. Now onward, all my external relationships are secondary and subservient to my cause of self-respect. It alone is paramount.

A student recently shared how her journey of self-respect healed her relationship with her in-laws.

> I met my husband at college where biochemistry was
> our common love. We come from vastly different
> backgrounds, and we were happy until it came to meeting

*each other's parents. My folks are working class. I put
myself through college by working part time and using
part scholarship. Nick's parents are old rich! Nobody
said anything, but I knew my in-laws were disappointed
in their son's choice—me! I found myself slipping into
pleasing behaviors whenever I was around them. I also
paid extra attention to what I was wearing or saying.*

*The more I tried to please Nick's parents, the more
they seemingly distanced from me. I lost my confidence.
My failed attempts at squeezing warmth from them
consequently froze my heart into coldness. Now I had
become them: the rejecter, distant, and disengaged!*

*I got filled with bitterness from the "why me"
syndrome and wondering, "How could they be so mean?"
I was swinging between being the victim or feeling like
an aggressor, until I was exposed to the nondual goddess
teachings. I learned why pleasing or rejecting behaviors
do not support the emergence of my inner goddess.*

*"I am Shakti" became my ongoing contemplation.
So, instead of smiling outwardly and resenting them
inwardly, I proactively set emotional and physical
boundaries for the first time in my life. I told them and
my partner my experienced truth in a letter, in a very
simple, non-charged, straightforward manner, using
direct yet nonviolent language. I told the in-laws that I
was feeling unwelcome, uncomfortable, and unsure, so
I will stop coming to their home or calling them on the
phone, for whatever time it takes, until either I have
bridged the gap between us emotionally and feel ready to
engage or they invite me back because they looked at their
actions and the hurt it was causing me.*

*I had no doubts. For the first time, it did not matter
if they liked me or not. I knew "I am Shakti," and I
deserve the same respect that I am willing to offer. And
this was my truth, all of it. And this is what I proceeded to
do. I stayed away.*

As I stepped back, my husband stepped up. I found
him having questioning conversations with his parents,
asking them to step up and understand how much he
loved his wife.

Then, after a hiatus of a few years, they visited us for
Thanksgiving. I found myself strangely peaceful. I did not
rush to wear makeup or don expensive clothes in their
anticipation. When I opened the door, I felt like my Shakti
was with me. My eyes met two pairs of warm eyes. I
responded with my natural warmth, no longer held back.

I am glad I respected myself and my feelings for a
change. It changed my life.

DURGA-LIKE POWER ARISES FROM SELF-RESPECT

Like my student above, all women must stop seeking validation from others. Instead, let us seek our own approval. When we fall into a habit of seeking approval, we not only lose our self-respect, we also lose our power. When our minds are burdened with a need for validation, our power becomes hidden and our self-esteem tanks. We don't like ourselves. Therefore, it is important to stop outsourcing our sense of worth to people and possessions and instead generate it from within. You must outwit the asura of wanting approval from others and become your own cheerleader.

In my case, the self-respect and personal power I embody arose not because I looked outside me for validation but because I dared to blossom into who I am meant to be—an unconventional Guru of a deeply traditional body of knowledge. Yet, through all this, I remained true to myself and followed no preexisting mold.

I am more transparent than most teachers from my tradition. I share openly about my life and challenges. My inner goddess laughs wholeheartedly in public. I teach and uplift by embracing what I call my "enlightened vulnerability." I can be the teacher I am meant to be while letting the goddess guide me.

There is no need to seek approval or try to fit in. Embody your original ideas and unique body of work and do what you were meant to do on this plane—be it raising your kid or ruling a nation. Make a habit of pausing to discern what you really live for, what you value in your life. You may not know it right away, but this habitual self-inquiry will lead to a thoughtful, deliberative, and ultimately self-respecting approach to life instead of an externally driven existence, seeking outer validation and respect and often not getting it.

Activating the timeless and universal goddess legends in your heart is an important step in this empowered direction.

A DURGA CONTEMPLATION FOR YOU

I ASK: In what way(s) do I lack self-respect?
  What would self-respect look like?
I RECOGNIZE: Self-respect is unconditional, not
  dependent on outer circumstances.
I CONNECT: Placing my hands over my heart, I close
  my eyes and remember my divinity.
I DECIDE: I will value, cultivate, and embody self-respect.
I ACT: I stand up for myself, care for myself, start the conversations,
  and make necessary changes to reclaim self-respect.
I REMEMBER: Shakti is pure fire. Burn away what no longer serves.

CHAPTER 5

ESTABLISH BOUNDARIES TO LIVE ROYALLY LIKE DURGA

Durga manifests as prosperity for
the devas, as misfortune for the asuras.

DEVI MAHATMYA 4.5

S hakti incarnated as Durga was objectified as an object of lust by countless asuras. She was told repeatedly "a woman is made for pleasuring men." Her boundaries were repeatedly crossed. She was not taken seriously. After all, she was a mere woman. What difference did her "No" make to anyone?

I love how Durga responded: "Yes, I am a woman. No, I have not taken birth as a woman to pleasure you. I have taken birth to kill you."

How many of us have such clarity of purpose, clear boundaries, and awareness of our inner power, so we can dare to be different? Of course, we must not kill. But, can we embody her killer convictions? In this chapter, we'll look at how healthy boundaries can help us reclaim our goddess birthright to write our own scripts.

Durga is invincible because her boundaries are impassable, impenetrable, and indisputable. She shows us to not take transgressions lightly. She is the ultimate feminine archetypal protector of personal boundaries.

Another mythological tale that is revered as a holy reality is captured in the Hindu epic *Ramayana*. Characters from this epic are said to be manifestations of Vishnu (Supreme Male God) and Lakshmi (Supreme Female God), and both are powered by Shakti.

When Prince Rama (who is an avatar of Vishnu) was wandering through the forest with his wife Sita (avatar of Lakshmi), an asura king named Ravana cast his lusty eyes upon Goddess Sita. Her incredible beauty enchanted him. He wanted her, but he knew she was not going to make it easy.

So, one day, when Sita was alone in their humble forest dwelling, Ravana, disguised as an aging beggar monk, asked her to come out of the safe boundaries of her home to give him alms. Though she knew better and had been warned not to go out, Sita figured she had no reason to suspect a harmless-looking monk. So, she knowingly crossed her own boundary and let her guard down. As a result, Ravana was able to capture her and forcibly carry her back to his asuric kingdom, despite her screaming protests.

In this myth, Shakti is showing us women what happens when we are misled. As a result, Sita does not stick to a firm "No." Can we trust anyone unless we know who we are dealing with, inside and out? Can we allow mere appearances to reassure us?

But Sita was Shakti after all. She did not simply cry regretfully until Rama came and rescued her. Once she realized she'd been tricked, Sita immediately reinstated her boundaries. Instead of thinking, "I have lost it, I'm a victim," she thought, "I am powerful."

Sita spent days in Ravana's kingdom, sitting under an Ashoka tree. The entire time, Ravana could not force her to enter his private chamber. Why?

Because she had remembered who she was. Her no meant no.

She placed a single blade of grass between herself and Ravana— who towered over her, entreating her to become his queen. She spoke without a thread of fear: "If you dare cross my physical boundary, this blade of grass, it will catch fire and burn your entire kingdom to ashes." More than her warning, the conviction in her voice was enough. Ravana could take no further advantage of her while she was his captive.

The blade of grass represents what boundaries are for modern women: an invisible force field that we are in charge of instituting in our life and relationships. No one will remind you. It is up to you to either forget it, like Sita did initially, or act from it, like she did when she asserted it to Ravana. Sita tells us that it is never too late to remember our inner power and reclaim our personal boundaries.

WHAT ARE PERSONAL BOUNDARIES?

I define boundaries as a protective shield based on your beliefs and values. Boundaries protect you from people—physically, sexually, socially, emotionally, intellectually, spiritually—until you deem they are safe and respectful of who you are and respectful of your nos and yeses.

Boundaries need to be in place all the time, not just when you interact with creepy or suspicious strangers. Inside intimate relationships, what is acceptable to you and what is not should be conveyed to your significant others, well before they cross those boundaries.

A bonus of having clear personal boundaries is that only the type of people you seek in your life will be there in your life. The rest will automatically be filtered out by your boundaries.

In my book *Sovereign Self*, I told the story of a bad-tempered snake who would bite for no reason. One day he heard the discourse of a saint that moved him to understand that he should practice ahimsa and not bite any more. But the next time the saint saw the snake, he was shocked to see his condition. Children had thrown stones at him, making the saint ask, "What happened to you?"

"After your discourse, I decided to not bite anyone," replied the snake.

"Oh boy," the saint said. "That's great you've stopped biting people for no reason, but did I tell you to stop hissing to keep others from biting you? Why did you choose to become so powerless that you could not even defend yourself?"

This story illustrates the necessity of keeping our personal power in place. We can assert healthy boundaries, not to be offensive, but in self-defense against the sleepwalkers that we are bound to meet sooner or later.[1]

PAY ATTENTION TO
BOUNDARY VIOLATIONS

Do you accept a handshake or a hug? If so, from whom, and when? What type of physical contact do you prefer? Even someone sitting or standing uncomfortably close to you and touching or handling things that belong to you are boundary violations.

At a verbal level, no one should get away with abusing you, talking at or down to you, not allowing you to speak or be heard, giving you unsolicited advice, sharing your secrets, saying things that are derogatory or inflammatory about your integrity or character, or gossiping about you.

At an emotional level, you should let no one play with your feelings or mock you for your beliefs, use what you've told them in confidence against you, laugh at you, or treat you like a doormat because you have feelings for them. Forcing you to feel guilty when you are not or coercing you to feel differently are also violations.

At a mental level, boundary violations include intimidation, unwarranted criticism, demeaning behavior, judgment, extortion, browbeating, demoralization, bullying, subduing, manipulation, control, and scare tactics. These are all serious boundary violations.

At a sexual level, no one has any right over your body sexually. Even your lawfully married spouse has no right over you sexually, unless you are a consenting adult and this consent is explicitly present in each act of sexuality, from casual touch to intercourse. Who can touch you, how they touch you, where they touch you, when they touch you, and who you choose to have children with, or not, is up to you—100 percent. Behaving inappropriately or being too familiar, especially sexually, is a violation, including sexual references and overtures.

At a social level, norms are often laid out by a culture. For example, it is a universal social rule, instituted for good reasons, that adults don't date minors. At a fiscal level, we don't normally let people get away with borrowing money and not returning it. Controlling joint finances to such an extent that one person becomes dependent, hiding important asset information from a partner, or cheating a partner in any way with regard to money are all boundary violations.

Once we awaken the goddess within and become more familiar with our Shakti roots, as we've been discussing throughout this book, womankind *can* step up and reclaim their goddess boundaries. We can do so despite a childhood in which we were emotionally, sexually, or physically unsafe and were not taught to cultivate boundaries, and also despite our current patriarchal society, where men—and far too many women as well—seduce us to remain unconscious objects of pleasure for mankind.

ACT IMMEDIATELY ON A BOUNDARY VIOLATION

After leaving the body of Sati (whom we read about in the last chapter), Divine Mother reincarnated again as a woman. This time she took birth as the daughter of the king and queen of the Himalayas. They gave her the name Parvati, which means the "daughter of the mountains." Parvati grew up and married Shiva again, the protector, destroyer, and regenerator of the universe, and Sati rejoined Shiva as Parvati. Together they raised a family with two divine sons and a divine goddess as a daughter.

Shakti as Parvati supports all women in their right to enjoy domesticity, motherhood, and sexual pleasures with their chosen partners. After all, love, fertility, child rearing, carnal desire, lust, passion, and infinite sexual pleasures are also very important dimensions of the goddess. Her love is all-encompassing.

In the domestic version of Divine Feminine as Parvati, the spouse of Shiva and mother of his three children, what we find is an empowered, self-respecting goddess. Parvati is not merely a domesticated goddess, relegated to the background, running the cosmic household of God Shiva. While she is his loving spouse, romantic partner, and mother of their children, she is no docile sidekick, clutching to her partner for her identity. She has opinions, and Shiva frequently consults her and at times learns from her. He depends upon her for restoring moral order to the universe. As a goddess, she is not second to Shiva but rather his complementary equal. In many texts, she is the Ultimate Reality from which gods like Shiva, Vishnu, and Brahma have emerged. In fact, Shiva cannot be Shiva without Parvati because she is Shakti, the power.

Goddess Parvati has two aspects to her. In her placid, more benevolent, and nurturing role, she is known as Goddess Kaamakshi, the goddess of love. A parrot sits near her right shoulder, symbolizing cheerful love talk, seeds, and fertility. But when the world is in peril from asuras, Parvati becomes Durga and Kali to counteract unconsciousness from non-dharmic asuric beings. Astride a lion as Durga, Goddess Parvati takes off to distant galaxies and at times to Earth to protect her devotees and destroy all evil that plagues the world. When Parvati is out saving the universe and fighting battles as Durga, Ambika, and Kali, her husband Shiva runs the domestic household and looks after their children because he knows his wife is on an important mission.

To me, this is an ancient but perfect model of the necessary cooperation and understanding—and healthy boundaries—between a modern couple with children, when both parents are creatively contributing to the world and must take turns raising the children. It is not just the wife's job. And only a woman who deeply values herself and respects her greater duties toward the universe, beyond husband and kids, will boldly embody all these dimensions of herself. The capacity to nurture as well as the capacity to contend with inner and outer darkness with formidable strength emerge from a consciousness that values itself. Self-respecting womanhood requires a hard outer shell, like Durga, in order to establish clear boundaries; and a soft, supple, selfless living core, like Parvati, in order to unselfishly protect those she loves.

Another myth I heard again and again illustrates the value of timely correction when our boundaries are crossed: One day in timelessness, the deva Kubera, who is the treasurer of wealth in the heavens, prayed for a boon from Shiva, the Great God. To get his attention, Kubera meditated rigorously, which pleased Shiva. One day, Shiva appeared miraculously from thin air to give Kubera a boon, and accompanying him was his consort Parvati. When Kubera's eyes fell on Goddess Parvati, he was overcome by her beauty. It was like all the beautiful flowers of earth had come together in her face; a billion full moons shone in her complexion and the blackness of outer space had descended into her flowing tresses, which fell in waves and swayed gently in the wind. Her simple attire could not conceal the enchantress of the universe who bewitches the whole world.

Kubera was so taken by her divine splendor, that his right eye involuntarily winked. Furious at this disrespectful and gross crossing of her physical and sexual boundaries, Goddess Parvati made that offending eye blind that very instant. Then she left.

Kubera fell at the feet of Shiva explaining how he'd had no intention of offending the Great Goddess. "Oh Lord, I did not wish to offend Mother Parvati; neither were my intentions evil or lecherous. I had simply become mesmerized by her beauty. I am unfortunate that my own body chose to show the appreciation with an act that insulted her. Please forgive me."

Shiva knew his partner's principles when it came to boundaries. "Transgressions of boundaries, even when done unconsciously, nevertheless are distasteful to the one whose boundary you crossed with your roving eye. It is disrespectful and unpardonable," Shiva told Kubera. "You are now accountable for two things: One, for the act, and two, for your state of unconsciousness that is a danger to you personally and to this universe. You are a deva; I expected you to be more vigilant about your own body and mind as you interact with others. You have offended a woman, and she has every right to give you punishment. I do not see a need for my intervention. The moment you realize that your actions were inappropriate, you should come clean and apologize. I can't promise you'll be forgiven, but it is your dharma to express sincere regret anyway and never cross boundaries again."

Kubera threw himself at the goddess's feet. He cried and begged, and when Parvati saw that his remorse was real, she said: "How miserable you are without your dirty eye, but tell me, how can I restore your eyesight when that eye is the reason you crossed my boundary?"

At this, Shiva proposed she could give him an eye smaller than the other, and yellow in color. Kubera had few options so readily agreed. When Parvati restored Kubera's eye, she said, "There! Now everyone will see your yellow-colored eye and ask what happened.

Then, you will be forced to tell them about how you leered at a goddess who represents all womankind. This is your punishment. You will bear the brunt of your action forever."

Today, Kubera, the demi-god of wealth, is walking around with one yellow eye, explaining the importance of not being unconscious, and to never ever violate boundaries of respect.

Like Parvati, make your boundaries your priority. Don't expect that just because you act decently toward others, that they will behave the same way with you. Like Kubera in the myth, people may be sleepwalking, lacking awareness or social skills; or they may be evil, dense, and dark like the asuras Durga encountered in her myths. So, you must look out for yourself, stay alert, and instantly let others know when they have crossed a line.

A goddess can gouge any eye that dares to disrespect her, blind the lechers, twist necks of haughty asuras, and drink the blood of those who don't stop their evil ways. We human goddesses will not resort to that. But can we reflect Parvati's fierceness and quickness in action when anyone dares to cross our boundaries? Can we at least growl like a goddess and say firmly, "This is entirely unacceptable"? Can we assert our true feelings or opinions or say no when we want to say no rather than go along and say yes?

SAY NO WHEN IT IS TIME TO SAY NO

Saying no is not just about being noncooperative. It is a sign of maturity, self-respect, and inner strength. Go ahead and say yes if you have the desire, energy, and time to engage with something or someone and you won't regret or resent it later. After all, we do thrive in a culture of reciprocity. But learning how to respectfully say no, too, is important, if you want to respect your inner goddess.

Here's one modern-day goddess's personal account with saying no.

I've played so many roles in my life—a wife, a daughter, a sister, a friend, a real estate agent. I've been a pleaser and a chameleon, trying to connect with whomever I meet and hope they like me, wanting people to think I was a certain way and to never disappoint them. I've felt responsible for other people's comfort and happiness and got into the habit of saying yes more than I should.

I was feeling sad for myself and resentful about the people in my life whom I said yes to a lot until I realized I needed to cultivate better inner boundaries and say no occasionally. My work began with understanding that my inner goddess supports me in being clear in my yes or no, not ambiguous.

I still want to do a good job for my real-estate clients. Yet, I am beginning to say no to potential clients that don't feel right. Recently, I said no and turned down an opportunity, though my business partner insisted we say yes to it. After speaking with the potential clients on the phone, I intuitively knew it wasn't the right fit for me for sure and said no. My business partner was angry with me and tried to guilt me into saying yes. But I stuck to my no.

The deal would have meant more houses sold and so, more money. My business partner would have been pleased for sure, but not my inner Self, because I would have had to behave like a wheeler and dealer. This knowledge that I can set a boundary and I can say no to people and to opportunities that may sound wonderful but don't serve me after all, is a game changer.

This knowledge—that my ego may be a people pleaser (a hopeless yes-sayer) but my inner Durga is always a truth teller—has been so comforting. It has taken the pressure off me. The ability to cultivate boundaries has created so much more balance and equanimity for me in all my roles, not just as a real estate agent. I believe these are goddess moments to cherish for a lifetime.

SPEAK UP IF YOU FEEL UNCOMFORTABLE

Sometimes, our significant other, partner, grown children, boss, or co-workers may embody a forceful personality and enjoy verbal dexterity over us. They may even be verbally aggressive at times, just because they are unconscious. Even if they are not the uncool guys in our life script (the asuras) but the cool guys (devas), it still can be intimidating standing up to them. More often than not, the less forceful speaker caves into a pool of suffocating silence and unexpressed misgivings. And if the person we are speaking to has a quick temper that shows up now and then unexpectedly, then rather than speaking what we must, we end up being hypervigilant, managing and preventing potential outbursts.

If staying away is not an option and these relationships are worth preserving, then it's time to find our goddess roar. Empower yourself with the idea that as a modern-day goddess, roaring with the dignity of a queen, not suffocating in silence, is your true nature.

Here is another goddess story from our modern era. It is all about how a woman learned to uphold her boundaries when it came to standing up to a verbally forceful partner.

> *I learned to be a peacekeeper very early in my life, as my mom was a very dominating person and had a quick temper. I have always struggled with articulating my feelings and standing up for myself.*
>
> *My lack of boundaries opens the door for others to determine my thoughts, feelings, and needs. I have given my power away more times than I can count. To keep the peace or for fear of driving someone away, I would choke back my true thoughts and feelings. This I've done for fear of upsetting someone, or quite frankly I just haven't been able to find the words to express myself. When put on the spot, I would become terrified, and my mind goes blank, so I ramble or say nothing. I then dwell on it for hours or days, playing it over and over in my mind and wishing I could have said something.*
>
> *Through the goddess teachings, I gained an understanding and connection with my inner Durga. I understood that being a goddess and having healthy emotional boundaries does not mean overpowering someone else by raising your voice or taking any other posture of power. It can be done quietly, too, because it is connecting with your inner SELF. Finding power*

from your heart to stand up for yourself and beliefs is what boundary setting is all about. It is finding that power in tough situations to express yourself in a kind but strong way.

My husband can be quick to get angry too. In the past when we have disagreed and I felt challenged, I would remain quiet. But now, when I'm confronted or unhappy about something, staying silent is no longer an option. I take a deep breath and reach inside my heart to connect with my inner goddess, and then speak—not loudly, but effectually and fearlessly. Despite any fear, I utter my goddess truth anyway, slowly and calmly. My truth is indeed setting me free. I have noticed my relationship has gotten more open and more real.

DROP THE GUILT TOWARD UNCONSCIOUS PEOPLE IN YOUR LIFE

Implementing boundaries can be especially confusing with parents and family. But this must be done because much emotional turmoil and distress comes from taking on what is not ours. We must become responsible for our happiness, our behavior, our choices, and our feelings. We also cannot take on responsibility for others' happiness, others' behaviors, others' choices, and others' feelings. Period.

A modern-day goddess explained how she regained her power by saying no to supporting her unconscious parents' ongoing emotional drama.

My parents could never get along. They fought constantly in my presence without any regard for my emotions or fears. The fighting would get so wild, they would end up breaking things and pieces of furniture in the house. They were so caught up in their anger, blame, and self-pity that they would forget about me and get immersed in their bursting emotions. Me, as a tiny dot, would go behind the curtains to hide and disappear from this world.

A severe feeling of loneliness landed upon me. Since I couldn't trust my family for emotional security and

comfort, I started to look for it elsewhere. I studied very
hard and tried to make myself bigger with academic
achievements. I studied abroad for a while after
university and finally left the house and got married
when I was twenty-six.

But my parents still fight and constantly involve me in
their fights, wanting me to pick sides. They expect me to
find a solution to their problems. I used to be constantly
stressed until I found the goddess teachings. I can now
find the courage to say no with straightforwardness. The
dharma of self-value has been my best companion.

I didn't know I had this power in me. For once, I
am not crying or pitying myself like a child when I talk
to them. I am telling the plain truth and drawing my
boundaries without getting caught up in the drama of
their lives. What gives me the strength, I ask myself? I
am not drawing this power from my tiny little dot self for
sure. A larger Divine Feminine presence in me speaks the
truth without crying.

I am not the small dot who cries herself to sleep
anymore. I am Durga, and I find her when I connect to
my own true Self. I am enough, pure, loveable, fearless,
and blissful. My only true ambition in life now is
awakening to my inner Durga.

The preceding stories from modern-day goddesses clearly
elucidate the role of boundaries and why they are important for
evolution of consciousness. Putting boundaries in place doesn't
make you self-centered or unwomanly. It means you're authentic. You know your limits and your values, and you listen to your
feelings. When you assert healthy boundaries, do what's right for
you, and take care of yourself, you are then freed up to be generous to others. It is simple: when you make it a priority to say yes
to what you need and say no to what drains you, you will become
more emotionally available for the yeses you do give to others,
after due consideration. After all, you can't emotionally give out

the attention, love, or support that you don't have yourself, so take time out to look after yourself, to rest and recharge. It is a necessary skill to learn for sleeping goddesses. Setting boundaries can be challenging, but the reward can be so beneficial for people in your life and, most importantly, for you.

———

A DURGA CONTEMPLATION FOR YOU

I ASK: In what situations, or with what
    people, are my boundaries weak?
I RECOGNIZE: Boundaries keep me safe, healthy, and free!
I CONNECT: Eyes closed, hands on belly, breathe,
    and feel the energy of boundaries.
I DECIDE: I will set boundaries and maintain them with integrity.
I ACT: Where my boundaries are weak, I clarify
    them, follow through, and stay firm.
I REMEMBER: Like Goddess Parvati, I fiercely defend my boundaries!

CHAPTER 6

DEFY STEREOTYPES TO LIVE LIKE A GODDESS

We bow to Her who is extra gentle and extra fierce at the same time.
APARAJITA STUTI, VERSE 5

Have you noticed how Durga embodies independence, freedom, and polarities with such ease? Durga's many manifestations as herself—the fearless yet compassionate Durga, angry but true Kali, nurturing yet fierce Parvati—show that the goddess is not stuck in any rigid stereotypical role, such as goddess of the home, goddess of war, or goddess of sex. She is all of these at the same time. She takes new forms as she chooses or finds necessary, and Durga displays the full range of how a woman can embody self-respect in society.

TO MOVE FORWARD, REINVENT YOURSELF

When Durga was battling asuras as Kali, identical asuras kept coming in waves. This is just like dealing with negative thoughts: no sooner do we get rid of one than more flood in, trapping us in a never-ending spiral. Durga had to recreate herself again and again to outwit and annihilate these self-perpetuating demons, which symbolize egos, representing ignorance at the deepest level. It was a holy battle that every sincere seeker of greater consciousness will face one day: a quest to purify and rid the mind of all self-limiting, self-betraying, self-sabotaging thoughts.

Durga did not give up until she triumphed. Undaunted and unstoppable, she gained more motivation and power every time she was attacked. By facing our abusers and fighting our inner asuras of voluntary subjugation, we can finally awaken from our unconscious agreements to accept any kind of abuse that we have internalized or become okay with over the passage of time. We forget that whether we have male or female bodies or mixed-gender bodies, we are divine goddesses inside, and we deserve much more than what has been our lot.

Similarly, Durga is not limited to stereotypes: mean or nice, logical or emotional, selfish or accommodating, virginal or erotic, married or single. She can be who she wants, as it suits her, as is needed in the moment, and always in service to a greater consciousness. This is a potent teaching about connecting to our feminine power. Goddess dares us to be who we are, even if it means we are different from the norm.

But, without such liberating archetypes to refer to, and with centuries of brainwashing by patriarchic values, women worldwide constantly limit their choices, putting themselves in narrower and narrower boxes to fit the molds of patriachal ideals. And out of our feminine guilt, we allow ourselves to be stuck in society-defined pigeonholes.

If you ask me, Eve worked too darn hard to be nice, to be approved, to be liked, and to be allowed to share this planet with Adam! Women have falsely concluded that they must hold themselves back for the sake of others or that they can only express themselves in certain ways at certain times. We do not dare to display all the colors that secretly bloom in our inner goddess garden. But Shakti symbolizes out-of-the-box womanhood. The goddesses teach us how to live unapologetically—royally!—like the divine beings that we are.

Sadly, many women have internalized patriarchy to such an extent that we feel incomplete without men—another stereotype. Deviance can result in being unsupported and un-embraced, even by womenkind.

Fortunately, society is evolving, but often, if women are still single and childless by a certain age, they feel something is wrong with them. Shame comes up. It is as if they need the security of a partner, the age-old archetype of happy domesticity photos on their Instagram, to validate them and help them feel good about themselves.

At one of my spiritual retreats in California, I met a woman who was beautiful, confident, and successful in her career, with a taste for all things sensual and spiritual. She had achieved so much and seemed to be in touch with her inner goddess, but it was not the case. When she spoke the words, "I am single," her eyes filled with terror of loneliness and self-shaming. She spoke about her pain and her emptiness, as if nothing else mattered. It was as if she was not a person but purposeless powder that had scattered everywhere in the universe, without a male partner to hold her together in a container.

When she unburdened her heart, I realized that she was not acknowledging what she had created for herself, by herself, without a partner, or in fact any constructive male influence in her life. She was penniless when she ran away from her home at age seventeen. She had run for her emotional survival; she needed to escape the total denial mindset of the women in her family. Every night, her dad would drink himself into a resentful place, and he would shame her mom and two sisters subtly—on their looks, on their lack of intelligence, and how he was stuck with them. Yet in the morning, everything was back to usual. Dad would be sober, off to work, and her mom would cook and look after the house. "Am I the only one who feels this is not right?" she wondered. She was told she was overreacting; her dad was stressed. The only way to reclaim emotional congruence was to leave.

On her own, she built a whole life, putting herself through college at night while waiting tables during the day. When we met, she had a condo of her own in an up-and-coming neighborhood, she took vacations and gifted herself spiritual retreats, and she enjoyed above all an intimate circle of friends who believed in her and looked up to her. But still, once she hit forty, nothing she had achieved seemed to matter anymore. She had become depressed at her failed relationships with men and her inability to find true love. She withdrew from an active social life. With her drop in self-confidence, her business began to suffer, and she had to take antidepressants. She had come to my retreat at the cajoling of a concerned friend.

She was grieving what she lacked and not celebrating what she had, which had success written all over it. She was like this not because she was intellectually challenged, but because she was emotionally deluded (like we all are at some level). She had grown up valuing having a man as a husband. She was breathing in the beliefs of patriarchy from birth onward. And sometimes even if a woman knows her own mind and chooses to remain single as her preferred lifestyle, her women friends tell her that this will change when she meets the right man! The same is true with having children.

Worldwide, if a man remains unmarried beyond a certain age, he retains his dignity. He is considered "too independent" to be hitched. He can get away with feeling superior to or smarter than his married buddies and can make jokes at their expense. But women have no such option. They may be okay about their marital status as single, but other women often continue to remind them of what they are missing. Sure, there are plenty of people who do support single, gay, trans, and gender-diverse people who don't choose conventional marriage, but more universally, thanks to internalized prejudice, most women are shamed for remaining single after a certain age. A woman is assumed to be unwanted if she does not try, or desperate if she is trying, at once a figure of pity and scorn. We all know about the list of eligible bachelors that includes men of all ages on it, but have you ever heard of such a list for women? I think not. In fact, single women of a certain age used to be referred to as spinsters—talk about judgment!

Durga is a goddess with seeming contradictions. Durga is the most beautiful woman in the universe. She is powerful, and she shines with her inner light. She likes to remain independent. Her stance is not against marriage or for marriage. Her life, which is a blessing to the whole universe, is simply a gesture of self-fulfillment (*I am enough*).

Durga teaches us through her myth to neither minimize the need for a male partner nor overrate the need for one by constantly focusing upon it. Being a goddess means recognizing your divine, true nature of wholeness and self-fulfillment. Your Self is enough. You complete yourself.

Durga's spiritual feminism is a beautiful and befitting answer to patriarchy. She represents a lifestyle that is not traditionally bound by gender roles and expectations. In fact, she shows us how to confront life's ups and downs, losses, disappointments, danger, disease, death—*like a heroine*, in a heroine-centric movie!

Rather than focusing on partnership, let us begin exercising power over our own selves and false disempowering beliefs, shall we? For starters, we can recognize whether we're unconsciously influenced by the patriarchal narrative that a woman becomes fulfilled only if she is married and has given birth, or by those who ascribe to it.

At the retreat, I sat down with the participants in a sacred circle, with the explicit intention of connecting with our inner goddess. I reminded the women around me that the goddess dimension of our being is really our own higher Self, which is by cosmic design ever fulfilled, never needy, and overflowing with love and joy. Those who are self-fulfilled don't necessarily need the companionship or security of a partner, least of all so desperately that it begins hurting them and making them lose self-value.

The woman who had achieved so much yet felt shame about being single looked up for once, and spoke up, a bit overcome: "Well, Shunya, if I listen to you, I'll just remain lonely all my life because I won't go out to meet people. I think being a goddess is lonely!"

I responded: "What you are searching in the world is already within you."

Imagine two women going to a party. One is cognizant that deep down she is a goddess. This one will show up fulfilled from within with greater awareness, self-worth, and standards, not neediness. Her consciousness will be as vast as an ocean. Another, who only thinks she is a body (one that is aging fast) will walk in feeling like a vulnerable drop of water that can evaporate at any time for any reason. She may think, "I am only a drop of water, I am so small, I am unimportant, I am invisible, I should slip away." But if you are an ocean, then you will show up to the party full from within, enjoy yourself from inner fullness, and come back full—without needing to bring someone home or to walk down the aisle with you. That's what goddess wisdom and acting from this knowledge is all about:

you decide if you want to lead your life as a woman like an ocean or a drop of water.

The woman smiled. She was getting the idea that being Durga is about embodying new self-valuing attitudes. Becoming aware of this choice in the realm of the mind is a step inward to reclaiming our inner Durga.

Some years later I received an email from her.

> *I have wondered many times, "Can I be the person I am meant to be, to let the goddess shine though me, as I am, and as my life is flowing right now?" "Yes," I have finally told myself, "I can." One day when I took a walk, I realized that all daisies look the same from afar, yet if you look closely, no two daisies, no leaves, nothing in this world is an exact replica of each other, even the faces of twins. It is all vividly original. Then why should I allow my mind to bend out of shape in copying other women (my sister who is married and friends who have babies) to like myself more? You will be happy to know, I have befriended myself as I am, at last. I still date, but I am not frustrated nor in a hurry. I have found a genuine friend along the way (who wants to marry me, but I am happy to have him as a friend). I am not sure if I have touched my inner Durga yet, but I think she is touching me, more and more on many days. Thank you.*

Our existential crisis is not because we are single, but because we are goddesses inside, and we've forgotten our right to be different and original! We need reminders and guidance, and we must do this lovingly, without scolding ourselves.

TO BE DIFFERENT, RE-OWN YOUR POWER

One reason we don't dare to be different—or rather, be who we are as we are—is because we are afraid of our power. We're led to believe power is bad, that we should not talk about power or want power in relationships.

We need to change our relationship with power so we are neither afraid of it nor are we cocky or arrogant because of it. The power that we want must be pure, raw, goddess power so we can become successful in all our efforts and relationships.

Since Self is inherently connected to the most powerful mistress of this universe, the power of the whole universe lives inside you. When we start connecting with our goddess power, we start surprising ourselves. What is this power? It is a "just" power, it is a "benevolent" power, it's a "creative" power, and it's your power, given to you by your divine Self. This power is a win-win power. It's a good power, it's a healthy power, and it's a noble power. And above all, it is a stable, non-fluctuating power.

Shakti as Durga teaches us critical lessons on sheer courage, strength, and the ability to rise above our challenges and challengers. Shakti as Lakshmi tells us how to do this with a higher consciousness, or by embodying ethical values known as dharma. And finally, Shakti as Saraswati gives us the knowledge to discern what is our true identity—a mere limited woman, or Shakti incarnate as a woman? That is why in my life, all three goddesses are my teachers of *true power*. We really cannot embody true power without three dimensions to our human power: strength (Durga), ethics (Lakshmi), and knowledge (Saraswati).

Here is a story shared with me by another modern-day goddess who used my teachings to approach the profession of a yoga teacher from a different perspective. And when she did that, she felt a greater connection with true power.

> *I was creating an enormous amount of internal stress*
> *for myself as I tried to start a new business in the yoga*
> *world. My mind was a jumble of expectations about*
> *what a "successful" yoga teacher looks like and what I*
> *must do to grow my business. Though I was teaching*
> *yoga and teaching people how to destress, inside me, I*
> *was a ball of stress.*
>
> *But now, I'm asking myself some big questions: What*
> *is my definition of success? How can I truly serve?*

How can I create my business and live my life based on dharma, which will ultimately lead to freedom? How can I live with goddess grace and ease in the ebb and flow of opposites that this world consists of? How do I live joyfully and enjoy the journey?

I'm finding that when I reflect on these questions and live out the answers as best I can, I feel more grounded. I also feel more joyful, more peaceful, and more connected to the divine being within me and less disturbed by the external world of desires, opinions, and, quite frankly, madness. I flow more soul power now. It does not matter what other yoga teachers are doing to build their practices. What matters to me is what I am doing.

I am glad I dared to be different rather than follow herd behavior because it led me to something deep and wholesome. I'm finally starting to experience the inner peace that I have always sought through yoga.

Through the goddess teachings, we can realize that to embody goddess power is a very big responsibility as well as an opportunity. The more you survey the battlefield of your mind as the goddess you are, the more your increasing awareness will allow you to overthrow inner enemies. You will regain your freedom to think like a sovereign goddess and always dare to be different. You will triumph over the asuras of guilt, fear, anger, and any kind of self-betraying or conditioned thoughts.

It may feel like a big scary leap to start acting like Durga. Perhaps a more manageable first step is to begin "thinking" like Durga. And this is what you have been learning to do thus far in this book.

To battle the darkness in your subconscious mind by simply thinking positive thoughts or repeating affirmations is not enough. That's like pouring a single cup of clean water into a swamp. Instead, we must have the courage to drain the swamp first. It is important to know that when you seem to be overrun by unhealthy thoughts and dark self-sabotaging feelings of "not enoughness," your goddess Self still quietly radiates amazing power and wholeness from within. Remember your inner goddess or be overrun by the inner demons.

To embody your inner Durga, you don't need to be holy—simply aspire to be whole, and from this inwardly sourced wholeness, enjoy radical self-acceptance. Then *you shall rise*, first and foremost, in your own eyes. And in the final analysis, that is all that matters. Imagine, like Durga, you are holding a bow and arrow. Get ready to take aim. But instead of targeting outer approval and permission to love yourself and rejoice in who you are, as Divine Mother made you, what if you changed the direction of this arrow and targeted your own Self?

Once you connect with your own inner woman and become at ease with who she is, as she is—how she looks, talks, and acts—you automatically will connect with something profoundly wonderful, your own self-approval and inner permission to reclaim your inner Durga!

With the conclusion of this chapter, we have arrived at the last of our contemplations on Durga. I hope the goddess mythology with my insights and meditations will help you progress toward reclaiming your own inner Durga. As you connect with her more and more, you can expect unprecedented inner courage toward leading a bold, fearless, guilt-free, and truly blessed life as a goddess-woman of this world!

A DURGA CONTEMPLATION FOR YOU

I ASK: Am I constrained or shamed about how
   I live or express myself? Why?
I RECOGNIZE: I am enough unto myself.
I CONNECT: Standing or sitting erect, eyes closed, I quietly repeat,
   Om Tat Sat ("Truth always is") and know the Truth of Self.
I DECIDE: I will live authentically. I will drop the masks.
I ACT: I live in alignment with my values
   and eliminate that which is not.
I REMEMBER: Like Durga, I radiate wholeness!

PART II

LAKSHMI

CHAPTER 7

GODDESS LAKSHMI AND HER BEAUTIFUL SYMBOLISM

You are Lakshmi; you are beauty; you are prosperity.
VISHNU SMRITI 99.4

Sometimes the goddess roars for sheer pleasure. This is not a roar to announce war on asuras or punish boundary violators; this is a roar of happiness that emerges from living the life of a goddess, embodying the divine light of dharma, and ultimately, enjoying what beauty and comforts life has to offer the one who knows she is a royal, queenly goddess!

Yes, the one who roars from a deeply pleased and self-congratulatory disposition is Goddess Lakshmi, a beautiful and generous expression of Shakti. In fact, if we internalize Durga's lessons on true power and slay our inner demons, such as low self-worth, Durga herself transforms into Lakshmi and leads us forward to enjoy the gifts of purified power, in the form of material wealth, noble fame, supportive relationships, physical comforts, and soulful beauty. Durga herself, as Lakshmi, gives us every possible happiness that can be enjoyed on earth.

Goddess Lakshmi's skin color is all shades—black, brown, white, yellow, saffron—but her radiance is golden, shimmering with an inner light that lights up the whole universe. Her being is said to shine with the *radiance of a thousand suns*. This light is the light of conviction in Self. Lakshmi represents a blossomed and balanced consciousness, established in truth and dharma. Her archetype is bedecked in gold and all the pearls, rubies, and diamonds of the world—representing infinite material resources—reposing on a lotus, which represents Awakened Consciousness.

Lakshmi is said to bestow upon us grace that makes our worldly life so much easier. Indeed, Lakshmi's emergence in our heart spells auspicious tidings, with a wealth of cheerfulness, a radiant disposition, an inner contentment, and a sense of peace with our relationships and with what we possess. Lakshmi drives away anxiety, worry, and gloom and puts us in a perpetually festive mood.

If not for Lakshmi's unsurpassed and infinite generosity, you and I would not be enjoying any pleasures in life, whether small or great. Everything we have, every petal of every flower we have ever smelled, every bead of every necklace we have ever worn, every tickle of spice we have enjoyed in food, every delicious sweet fruit we have bitten into, even every drop of rain we have playfully splashed in, belongs to Mother Lakshmi. She gifts us this whole enchanted world as well as our bodies, minds, and senses with which to enjoy it. In fact, she is the five elements—space, air, fire, water, and earth—shining as our visible universe with its shade-giving trees, breathtaking mountains, and thirst-relieving rivers.

Lakshmi continues to shower us with gifts, giving unconditionally. This is what a mother does. No matter how her children behave or even misbehave, most mothers love unconditionally.

LAKSHMI'S LOTUS: SIGNALING HOPE

Lakshmi is often shown seated on a lotus, surrounded by lotuses, holding lotuses in her hands, and possessing beauty as fragile and as beautiful as a lotus. My Baba used to chant to her from a hymn called the Sri Suktam:

> *Having face pure like lotus, outlook spacious like lotus,*
> *affectionate temperament like lotus, eyes comparable to*

*the lotus leaves, universally loved, attuned to the Greatest
Lotus like blossomed Consciousness, let me repose at your
feet O Goddess Lakshmi.*

There is an interesting fact about this flower. It blossoms in muddy water. It symbolizes purity regardless of the difficult circumstances (mud) in which it grows. Celebrated Vietnamese monk Thich Nhat Hanh even titled his book on how to transform the experience of suffering *No Mud, No Lotus.*

The lotus is a reminder that goodness and prosperity can bloom regardless of any darkness or obstacles we face in our life. The lotus symbolizes inner purity, beauty, spiritual power, life, fertility, growth—even the entire manifest universe. It is a recurring motif in Hinduism as well as in Buddhist and Jain literature.

EXPAND YOUR DEFINITION OF PROSPERITY

Lakshmi's prosperity means different things to different people, but usually it indicates an inner state of fullness or abundance. *To understand Lakshmi's blessings, you must expand your definition of wealth.*

Wealth comes in many forms. Lakshmi is the source and provider of the following well-known sixteen types of wealth:

1 fame
2 knowledge
3 emotional courage
4 victory
5 children
6 valor
7 gold, diamonds, and gems
8 grains in abundance
9 happiness
10 bliss
11 intelligence
12 beauty

13 higher aim, higher thinking, and higher meditation
14 morality and ethics
15 good health
16 long, well-lived life

Wealth is not only financial assets; rather, Lakshmi's definition of wealth includes the things that contribute to a life of meaning, connection, abundance, and generosity. This is true prosperity.

Nature's bounty, true love, fulfilling relationships, inner peace, dharmic prosperity, luck and good fortune, virtues and inner values, a satisfying family life, ample food, land and property, water to drink, air to breathe, willpower, intellect, and character are also gifts of Lakshmi. With the grace of Lakshmi, we receive all these in plenty, along with inner abundance.

Let's look at a modern-day goddess Sandra's connection to abundance and Lakshmi.

Sandra was deeply unhappy with her job as an insurance agent. She felt she was made for something "more," but she neither had specialized skills, nor was she clear about other aptitudes; it was rather a case of her always identifying with something "lacking" in her life. I suggested that before considering what she might otherwise be doing, she first find comfort in where she was so she could make her choices from a place of inner comfort, rather than desperation. She agreed to try that approach.

To start, I asked her to make a list of things she feels grateful about, beginning with the maple tree that she could see from the tiny window in her office cubicle. From this, she was inspired to take plants to her office to care for at her desk while she called people to give insurance quotes. Slowly, she started appreciating the tiniest of things, like a genuine smile from a colleague, a cheery good morning from her boss, or the new coffee maker in the office kitchen. The list of things that gave her pleasure grew, and despite her old habit of looking at a glass half empty, she began to feel more abundant. Her morning commute felt like less of a chore when she thanked the smooth roads, the sun shining in the sky, and the chance to wear her favorite perfume to work. Her pleasure in life began to return.

Eighteen months later, for the first time in twelve years, she was named agent of the year, with a cash reward. When I saw her again eight years later, she was still in the same job, but instead of being depressed, she was roaring with pleasure. By accepting her life and cultivating gratitude and inner enoughness, she had learned to like herself, and she attracted people who liked her more. A few years later, she got married and moved on to cultivating all-new joys with her husband and daughter, while still appreciating the maple tree outside the same office cubicle.

On many days, when she visited me at my wisdom school, Sandra would sit by the goddess altar in my school, clean out the oil lamps, and lay fresh flowers. Sitting so serenely content in her inner lotus, she looked radiant, like Lakshmi herself. I noticed a strange peace had descended into her, though she was as animated and active as before. She was dealing with life's ups and downs proactively, but with a new Lakshmi-like equanimity.

She seldom had complaints about life anymore, even when her new marriage ended after just a few years. She explained that it was for the best, as she and her partner are better off as divine friends. She felt grateful that she now had the inner wisdom to not push square pegs into round holes—the wisdom to discern what was what, because her inner fullness was not making her desperate.

This is an example of someone gently being supported in re-accepting her inner Lakshmi, rather than jumping about chasing the outer Lakshmi.

TO CONNECT WITH LAKSHMI, EMBODY GRATITUDE

To tap into our Lakshmi lucky dimension, we must consciously think abundant thoughts with an expanded definition of abundance. Rather than focusing on the one or two or few areas of lack, we need to "find our maple tree." Be grateful for whatever little abundance is flowing in our life.

Look around you. Many people have "nice stuff"; not everyone is happy. Without Lakshmi's blessings in your deep psyche, which make you feel abundant and fulfilled from within, even with the greatest riches and luxuries surrounding you, you will feel empty, alone, and joyless, despite crowds cheering you and friends praising you.

Those who are genuinely happy are channeling Lakshmi through the practice of gratitude. They avoid a complaining mindset focused upon what is missing. I have met people living in poverty in India who are filled with Mother's grace. They laugh, sing, and bless everyone with a smile. I have met people living with privilege—some unhappy inside their bedecked and bejeweled bodies, because Lakshmi has abandoned them.

Don't get hung up on things you don't have yet. Try to feel joy for even the smallest things that give you even a moment of blessedness. This is a potent way to connect with Lakshmi.

A Harvard Medical School study found that "gratitude helps people feel more positive emotions, relish good experiences, improve their health, deal with adversity, and build strong relationships."[1] And in *Psychology Today*, Dr. Lisa Firestone identified gratitude as "perhaps the most important key to finding success and happiness." Studies have shown practicing gratitude leads to:

- Greater happiness
- More optimism and positive emotions
- New and lasting relationships
- Better health
- More progress toward personal goals
- Fewer aches and pains

- More alertness and determination
- Increased generosity and empathy
- Better sleep
- Improved self-esteem[2]

When our mind is connected to our inner Lakshmi, we instantly experience gratitude for everything. Even in difficult situations, say an accident, you will see a silver lining. As Oprah Winfrey put it, "Be thankful for what you have; you'll end up having more. If you concentrate on what you don't have, you will never, ever have enough."[3]

That is why not only cash, jewels, and real estate but also the ability to appreciate what you have are all associated with Lakshmi. Nothing is too small to be grateful for, nothing too big. Constantly ask yourself: *What mindset do I want to prevail in my life—a grateful mindset or a scarcity-based, complaining mindset?* And deliberately focus your energy there.

EMBODY DHARMA FOR LASTING ABUNDANCE

Lakshmi is a goddess who grants us our heart's desires. But I have met people who have been ritualistically worshipping Lakshmi all their lives, chanting away to her, and lighting incense to her deity without fail, who don't experience any essential change in their material lot. What is missing?

The missing ingredient is *dharma, the conscious way of thinking and living.* When we embrace dharma, we become capable of flowing Lakshmi's grace and help ourselves. Only with dharma can we enjoy lasting abundance.

While Lakshmi is willing to endow us with material riches and worldly comforts, she wants us first to embody dharma, through upholding values like honesty, integrity, and uprightness in our engagement with wealth, relationships, and everything that gives us pleasure.

In fact, dharma is so vital that it is said that Lakshmi resides in hearts that are sincere and essentially dharmic, but leaves, sooner or later, whenever dharma is no longer apparent. While Lakshmi awards her hardworking children and can make a beggar a king overnight, she can also do the reverse.

What attitude will help you cultivate dharma? If you change your perception of where the goddess lives, dharma will bloom spontaneously in your bosom. If you think of Shakti and her manifestations—Durga, Lakshmi, Saraswati, Parvati, and Kali—merely as super conscious entities that live in some faraway land, inaccessible by human senses and mind, then she can impose in you awe as well as fear. Because you can't "see" her, this perception can encourage you to cheat or self-deceive. What's not in front of you can be forgotten! Or you can make her gross symbols, such as money or jewels, into *the goddess*!

Unfortunately, most religions advocate and support this sort of divinity worship, placing the divine's residence beyond the clouds. The Vedas say it's okay to begin this way, especially when we are starting out, but it's naïve to continue thinking of goddess as a supernatural being, located in some unreachable destination. Instead, they instruct us to merge goddess and world into one singular entity.

Goddess is not invisible but visible, in front of you all the time as this world: the good, the bad, the ugly, and the lovely, and all facets of this world become divine from this perspective. From this paradigm, you will find that the goddess dwells in everything, living and nonliving, as the fundamental divine essence of pure consciousness. Lakshmi can manifest for you in the form of a life-changing experience, a direction-giving vision, or a prophetic dream. At this stage of devotion, the world itself is a manifestation of Lakshmi. In every character, circumstance, and experience, joyful or sorrowful, Shakti is hidden, teaching you important lessons to elevate your soul's consciousness. This is the birth of dharma—a higher perception, goodness for the sake of goodness. Each pebble, each particle of sand will become sacrosanct for you—a reminder of Shakti. Even recycling will become an act of goddess worship.

There are psychological benefits as well, when we integrate the goddess with the phenomenal world.

OPEN YOUR HEART TO THE
GODDESS EVERYWHERE

When you look at the world merely through material eyes, you can indulge your ego-based likes and dislikes and behave in an entitled manner, contrary to the spirit of conscious life, or dharma. You may think, *The world is a buffet, delighting my senses. I'll be picky, complain about what I want but don't see in front of me, and I'll even get bored with the things I like.*

But if instead we allow ourselves to call upon and view our world through the lens of Shakti, then our ego gradually becomes motivated beyond quick attachments and aversions to perceive a transcendental goddess principle at work, shining everywhere. Now, whatever I get is sacred, and whatever I lose is equally sacred. Birth is sacred and death is sacred. Health is sacred, and even ill health is an invitation to explore the sacred. The people I know and like are sacred, and the people I don't know or possibly dislike today, upon investigation, will reveal the sacred hidden inside them too.

In the face of a higher paradigm, the petty arithmetic of our ego can dissolve, and then all our experiences lead to uncovering goddess and goddess alone. Following this principle in my life, I tend to view both pleasure and pain reverentially. I am now convinced that all my painful experiences are given to me by Divine Mother, so I can go beyond my ego-attachments and cultivate inner equanimity. All pleasurable experiences are given so I can utilize them to experience gratefulness and unconditional love, and ultimately, recognize what lives beyond impermanent joys and sorrows.

In this way, we can experience our life as a divine experiment, rubbing our egos with goddess, who is clothed in all beings (good and bad) and all experiences (light and dark). What seemed distinct— "world" and "goddess"—are shown to in fact be one, and this is how you access an ongoing, direct relationship with goddess. *Dharma is born in the bosom of each being, simply by recognizing goddess everywhere in everyone.*

When you are able to recognize the goddess in everything, you will feel organically inspired to be more generous, kind, and helpful, and you will practice compassion and embody the values of altruism and service. Unhealthy traits like insecurity, jealousy, competitiveness, striving, enmity, mistrust, and envy will spontaneously dissolve. Purer, more noble attitudes—dharma—will reign, and you will find Lakshmi everywhere you look.

It is the true embodiment of dharma that gives us great happiness because acting from dharma brings us closer to our inner goddess in daily life. If we are exhausted and depleted from an out-of-balance, non-dharmic life, Goddess Lakshmi's gifts of good fortune do us little good. But with wisdom, we can plan our life goals, neglecting none, and live our life as a human goddess in a truly dharmic manner.

WHY DO NON-DHARMIC PEOPLE SOMETIMES APPEAR LUCKY?

If Lakshmi loves dharma, why does she seemingly favor the dishonest and even evil ones at times? The Law of Karma, which is wielded by Lakshmi, explains discrepancies in fortune.

According to this spiritual law of cause and effect, our deeds make a cosmic impression, and just like planting a seed, these later bear fruit in some balancing consequence. Some situation or circumstance, whether painful or joyful, will come along and right the scales sooner or later, either in this current life or in future lifetimes.

Future lifetimes? you may wonder. That is right. I believe that you and I and all of us are transmigrating spiritual entities, and our story does not end when the body made of matter that we inhabit ends or dies. In this case, after death, we simply assume another body in another womb, and the story continues with uncountable subplots. Therefore, often the happiness or sorrow, wealth or lack, fortune or misfortune that we are experiencing in this lifetime (our current story) may well be the consequences of actions taken in a previous lifetime's story.[4]

Goddess Lakshmi is said to be the controller or housekeeper of our karmas, not just related to wealth, but pertaining to all our worldly dimensions—our relationships, health, and jobs.

Mother's impartiality can be seen from the Law of Karma. No one can deceive this law or hide from it. If you have done a dharmic deed privately, unwitnessed, be assured that Lakshmi has witnessed it.

Now, no one can prevent you from getting some good luck in this or another lifetime. Lakshmi will see to it.

Similarly, if you cross the boundaries of dharma and hurt or violate other living creatures, negative karma will also catch up with you. The law is impeccable.

And this is why we see fluctuations in fortune. Sometimes we become wealthy overnight, and sometimes, despite hard work and earnestness, we remain where we are, still struggling, in debt, or have trouble paying our bills. In symbolic terms, Lakshmi comes unexpectedly and leaves equally unexpectedly. No one is permanently wealthy nor deprived in a material sense. This is the way Lakshmi guides the evolution of our consciousness.

Mythology describes Lakshmi as "fickle" because she is seen moving from partner to partner. The word "fickle" points to the restless and ever-changing nature of (karmic) fortune and not to the capricious temperament of Lakshmi's attentions. Lakshmi may come to you because your past noble karmas have come to fruition, causing a sudden windfall in fortune such as a lottery win or an unexpected raise, but for the same reason, she may not stay with you permanently.

We can use the Law of Karma to our advantage. The central premise of the Law of Karma is that the universe is essentially dharmic. So, positive actions are those that are performed in accordance with dharma, but selfish actions almost always overlook dharma and others' needs and feelings.

The pundits tell us to appeal to Lakshmi for wealth and relief from sorrow in relationships. They suggest we ask for money, love, and romance like beggars. I find this amusing. Will Lakshmi come fill our wallets while we sleep in a stupor of unconscious karmas?

What if you instead asked her for all-new inner wisdom and mental strength to deal with any rain of negative karmas you had created in past lives? And all-new blessings to act wisely and sow all-new seeds of positive karma in this lifetime?

Many of us seek wealth that does not snatch others' wealth, as doing so would be dark karma, the opposite of dharma. While such ill-begotten wealth may bring some short-lived pleasures, ultimately it is not lasting. Lakshmi will take it away. And sooner or later, you will uncover the dark side of this desperately collected wealth, which is a wealth of fears, from a fear of being caught to a fear of abject loneliness. Those who are envious of you—thieves, back-stabbers, or cheaters—will surround you, calling themselves friends or lovers. Your well-being will be eroded, even if you wear nice clothes or drive expensive cars!

Dharmic wealth, born of positive actions, does not come with such side effects. It makes you blossom like a lotus, and it comes along with well-being, auspiciousness and luck, happiness, fame, true friends, and opportunities to enjoy the highest worldly pleasures, like royalty. Rather than abruptly departing, this wealth stays and grows. This blessed wealth comes to those devotees of Lakshmi who dare to make another living creature's pain their own pain, those who try to uplift others and offer a helping hand where they can with their wealth and power. They don't feel uncomfortable with wealth they have earned or inherited through karma operating in their favor, nor are they apologetic for being rich. As long as their prosperity has been generated through dharma, they happily enjoy their wealth, enjoy every luxury and comfort of life openly, and share it where and when opportunities to do so arise.

When dharma becomes a way of life, all your current and future karmas become lit up, conscious, and aligned with how Lakshmi would like you to act and behave in life and matters of wealth: with golden self-awareness, truth, and light. If we are sincere in our heart, Lakshmi gives even more than we ask because she is infinitely generous and soft with a mother's heart. She is not a hard taskmaster or a punisher. Therefore, it is never too late to begin walking her golden path, taking conscious karma steps, and embodying dharma with a cheerful can-do attitude.

EXPERIENCE LAKSHMI EVERYWHERE: A GUIDED MEDITATION

Right now, pause and begin appreciating everything Mother Lakshmi has provided you—even this book! Look around you. Do you see the sun or moon shining? Become aware of their constancy. They are present for you, without ever giving you a bill.

Have you breathed the air recently? I mean have you taken conscious breaths where you felt the blessings of life-giving air? "I will take care of you," says the air.

Do you find the stars twinkling? They are shining for you, reminding you to become a star in your own life and not just play a bit part. They hold nothing back from you.

Do you have a warm cup of fragrant tea near you?

Has a new blossom emerged in your garden that says smilingly, "Look at me; I emerged for you"?

Do flirtatious butterflies and talkative bees visit your backyard to keep you company on lazy summer afternoons?

Look into the eyes of dogs, cats, birds, and reptiles in your home . . . oh how they gift you their sweet unconditional love. Appreciate today your kitchen full of food and the appreciative eaters who have come in the past and will come tomorrow, filling your home with laughter, conversation, and blessings; sincere friends who show up when you need them; love, affection, and hugs from beloved life companions; health guidance from genuinely caring healers; and life guidance from genuine teachers who show you the path in all sincerity . . . all these resources will become a source of joy and pleasure in your life. You will feel lucky, blessed, and supported by Lakshmi from within.

A LAKSHMI CONTEMPLATION FOR YOU

I ASK: In what ways do I feel I'm lacking?

I RECOGNIZE: Like Lakshmi, happiness lives within me.

I CONNECT: Looking in the mirror, Lakshmi radiates from my heart to my face, through my eyes, lips, and hands.

I DECIDE: I will nurture my inner light, Divine Mother within, seated on a lotus, blooming.

I ACT: Reviewing the sixteen forms of wealth, I list my blessings and enjoy feeling grateful.

I REMEMBER: Consciousness—dharma—connects me to my inherent beauty and prosperity.

CHAPTER 8

THE GREATEST WEALTH COMES FROM VALUING YOUR SELF

I invoke that Lakshmi with a beautiful smile
who is enclosed by a soft golden glow;
who is eternally herself and makes content all
those to whom she reveals herself.

SRI SUKTAM 4.1–2

Once upon a time, Lakshmi dwelled with the noble-hearted devas and their king, Indra.[1] One day Indra was gifted a garland of fresh flowers by a human sage. Perhaps because Indra was a king and so not overly impressed with a mere garland, or perhaps he was distracted, or maybe he had become a bit arrogant, he took the garland and casually tossed it toward his elephant to wear.

But elephants tend to have a mind of their own, so the elephant tossed the garland too. It went flying into the air and fell with a thud to the ground. It lay there soiled and sorry looking, the petals crushed and its aromatic flowers mixed with elephant waste. The sage was angered. He cursed Indra that, since he did not value a heartfelt gift, he would soon lose his biggest gift. What greater gift could Indra lose than the support of Lakshmi, the goddess of every possible enchantment in this universe?

Lakshmi was visibly upset. You see, she lives in each petal of the garland that was tossed away with disdain. She took the disrespect personally. She had no intention to continue supporting someone who claimed to be a king but lacked basic courtesy. His behavior showed that he did not know how to value Lakshmi; he did not deserve her graciousness.

Lakshmi got up and left. She returned to her original home, the ocean of consciousness. Lakshmi was no longer available as a manifest goddess. She returned to her original non-manifest nature of formlessness. No sooner did Lakshmi leave in a huff than everything in the mythical land of the devas began to wither.

Because Lakshmi represents vitality and health, everyone became weak and listless, especially the devas, who felt the impact the most. With achy bodies and heavy heads, they sat and stared vacantly into space, all joy gone from them. The flowers lost their colors, and buds rotted. Trees became barren. Butterflies lost their wings. Birds stopped singing. An eerie silence was everywhere, and though no one said it, everyone knew deep inside them that Lakshmi had left them. They had bodies, but no health; hearts, but no love; food, but no taste. They were the living dead.

And then the unimaginable happened. Seeing them weakened, Bali, king of the evil asuras, gathered his forces and attacked the devas. It was sheer chaos.

Ousted from their heavenly home, the devas, with their leader Indra, ran to God Vishnu for help, showing that when we value dharma, we always turn or surrender to the higher power for help. Vishnu is the *preserver* of the universe—both inner and outer, which are essentially the same. Vishnu is said to manifest on earth each time there is a disruption of natural order or abuse of dharma.

Vishnu directed the devas to churn the ocean and look for Lakshmi. "Maybe as you churn, she'll come up on her own," he said. The devas were shocked. "How can we possibly churn an entire ocean?" they asked. Vishnu said, "Why don't you ask the asuras for help? This will busy them in a constructive task and stop them from attacking more of your people. Tell them there is a nectar at the bottom of the ocean that makes one immortal, and when it comes up, they can have some of it."

The devas, hopeful with this plan, approached the asuras and invited them to collaborate to churn the ocean together. The asuras, excited to become immortal like Vishnu, Shiva, and Brahma, agreed to collaborate this one time with the devas, whom they otherwise despised.

Vishnu reassured the devas not to worry—the evil ones would surely do something stupid and never get the nectar! He would see to it that they would lose, symbolizing the fact that Ultimate Truth never favors the non-dharmic ones.

The churning of the ocean proceeded. A mountain was used as the churning rod, and a colossal snake who abides on Shiva's neck became the churning rope. The asuras demanded to hold the head of the snake, while the Devas agreed to hold its tail. When the mountain was placed in the ocean, it began to sink. Again, God Vishnu helped, taking the form of a giant tortoise and supporting the sinking mountain on his hard shell. The devas and asuras took turns pulling on the snake's body alternately, causing the mountain to rotate, which in turn churned the ocean.

Symbolically, the ocean is the vast field of our own consciousness. Incidentally, this is the same milk-white ocean that gave gifts to Durga in the story I have previously told. The tortoise that supports the churning indicates that the "nectar of Self-knowledge" only can be obtained when we can control the senses, to pull in our limbs like the tortoise does. And the nectar for which the ocean is being churned is none other than the inner goddess, the Self, the transcendent truth of immortality that exists in the deepest recesses of our consciousness. The devas and asuras represent the positive and negative, or darkness- and light-filled thoughts, that exist in our duality-ridden mind.

The churning process released several things from the ocean. The first thing to arise with the constant churning was a toxic poison. This was swallowed by Shiva to save the world. My interpretation of this is that Shiva represents the aspect of our consciousness that can transcend poisonous beliefs and deactivate them. The transcendence power lives inside us.

Next, animals with supernatural powers emerged. A wish-fulfilling cow was given to Vedic seers because they alone knew how not to be greedy! A royal seven-headed horse who could run faster than any horse emerged and was quickly claimed by the evil asuras' leader, King Bali. A beautiful white elephant emerged, shining with inner light. He was claimed by Indra, the king of the devas. Divine damsels of amazing beauty emerged from the churning and preferred to make their home in the heavens. Varuni, the goddess of wine and intoxication, emerged and was greedily claimed by the asuras.

Then at last, from out of the water emerged a gigantic pink lotus, as big as the moon, upon which sat a radiant goddess. It was Lakshmi, dressed in silks and gold, shining like a thousand suns, jewels gleaming at her neck, waist, wrists, and feet. She held a garland of divinely fragrant flowers in her hands. Her anklets tinkled as she moved. Her dark tresses swayed in the wind. Lotuses, which don't typically grow in salt water, magically popped up wherever her glance fell. Sea animals who rarely come to the shore—mighty whales, sharks, and countless turtles—lined up to gaze at Lakshmi, as if mesmerized.

Indra was both relieved and overcome to see her. Because he was a deva, he experienced genuine remorse, rather than shoving blame onto the sage who had cursed him. He had been seriously repentant since Lakshmi left. His complacency gone, Indra could see with eyes of dharma that indeed he had taken all his gifts, represented by Goddess Lakshmi, for granted. He now knew Lakshmi was not someone he or anyone could "possess," least of all unconsciously. He saw her for who she was, the Ultimate Goddess. This was Shakti herself, the Divine Mother.

Overcome, Indra hurried to fetch a beautiful flower-decked throne for her to sit upon. Bali, the king of evil asuras, was also moved. How could he not be? He ran and brought a colorful silk parasol to shield her from the elements.

Upon seeing Divine Mother as Lakshmi, the sun god, who had been burning everyone up with his intensity, hid himself in deference behind a cloud. The wind that had previously been barely moving began to blow pleasantly with the sound of a heavenly flute. The sweet aroma of every flower growing around the world began to spread everywhere, and the scents excited the butterflies, who had emerged from the ocean along with Goddess Lakshmi. They fluttered and danced in adoration of Divine Goddess, forming a halo around her. Rivers swelled in their banks and made their way eagerly toward the ocean, so they, too, could see their Divine Source.

With a smile hovering on her lips, Lakshmi observed the churning scene with serene amusement. She saw devas and asuras watching her with the desire to make her choose them, not for who she is but for the wealth and joy she could impart to them. She didn't want to be claimed solely for her gifts, because she knew how this would go.

And then she saw God Vishnu. At the same moment, Vishnu looked at her, and their eyes locked. Lakshmi saw in his eyes not just a desire to claim her to fulfill some lack in himself, but pure love, bliss, and consciousness, as that is the nature of God (in Hinduism). Lakshmi found her equal in Vishnu. He didn't want to possess her, but just love her. In that ocean of needy stares, only Vishnu's gaze was like a lotus in the muck. His eyes reflected pure, unconditional, no-strings-attached love.

Overcome by his loving presence, Lakshmi made her way delicately toward Vishnu and adorned him with a garland she'd emerged from the ocean with. In this way, Lakshmi chose a befitting partner for herself, one representing the highest consciousness. Vishnu recognized Shakti as his divine completion because Ultimate Reality is One, not two. At that very moment, aromatic flowers began raining from the sky.

When Lakshmi emerged, spring came back in the land of devas, asuras, and us humans, and all was beautiful and hopeful again! All the devas, including their king Indra, rejoiced. She who is the lifeline of this entire universe was back, and that was all that mattered.

Lakshmi's emergence represents what happens inside our own mind when we persist and ceaselessly churn our own mind's dark (asura) and light (deva) contents to ultimately find our inner goddess Self, smiling, emerging, and blessing us from within. She releases from within our inner wealth, beauty, joy, happiness, and inner fullness.

In the story, the devas and asuras returned to their task of churning the ocean for the last time. Lakshmi's emergence meant they were now very close to the nectar of immortality.

Vishnu, with Lakshmi by his side, saw to it that the devas won, becoming immortal through the nectar, and the asuras were, yet again, defeated. Strengthened thus and made lucky by Lakshmi's blessings, the good guys (devas) were finally able to defeat the bad guys (asuras).

SELF-VALUE IS THE ULTIMATE FORM OF WEALTH

This myth, known as Samudra Manthan, is immortal in its own way, with numerous different iterations. I have a feeling you will find it a valuable reminder to churn the ocean of your own mind and let your inner Lakshmi emerge through the process. I remember this story most vividly from the way my mother shared it with me, with beautiful imagery that sparked my child's imagination.

Several Puranas and the Hindu epic the Mahabharata carry the legend of Samudra Manthan, but what always amazes me when I encounter a modern retelling is that most authors seem to focus on what gifts emerged from the ocean, who got what, and how the devas and asuras tussled for the nectar, with Lakshmi being no more than another item on this list. It strikes me that this minimizing of Lakshmi's role and what that means for women worldwide can be attributed to the patriarchal lens of the contemporary writers, both Indian and Western.

But now, looking again with my fresh eyes, I can see the potential of Lakshmi's mythology to remind women (and all beings) today of the importance of self-value as the ultimate wealth. Lakshmi's example shows us: Don't put up with disrespect. Don't stick around with people and partnerships—personal or professional—in which you are devalued. Sure, Indra was a "king"—rich, commanding, and esteemed in his community of devas—but did he give Lakshmi the same esteem? Most of the time he did, but not this time. That is why she left. Once is enough.

Sometimes women choose partners merely because of their financial worth and social stature. And for the very same reason, often such partners may become so full of themselves, that women who marry them may feel like a tossed garland. But still they stay on.

We're all familiar with studies that report that virtually any marriage is better for health and happiness than no marriage, particularly for men. And conservative groups have long argued that "putting a ring on it" contributes to better economic, health, and general personal welfare. But at the same time, one woman in four will suffer some form of abuse from her partner during her lifetime, and in England and Wales, two women are killed each week by a current or former partner. Those promoting marriage at whatever cost rarely offer any realistic strategy for keeping a long-term relationship going—let alone how to ensure mutual respect between partners.[2]

Ultimately, whether we are entering a relationship or preparing to leave one, can we make self-value an ongoing dharma to cultivate and uphold? We must do so not only in our romantic relationships, but also in job situations and friendships, too, and not put anything or anyone above that value.

Our being is infinity emerging, yet due to self-betraying beliefs, we can hoodwink ourselves into thinking that we are helpless, power- less, small, stupid, undeserving, or beyond repair. At times, we can ramp ourselves up into an ongoing underlying anxious state or even a panic attack, needing no one else to disempower us. Self-pitying thoughts create self-degradation and a low self-image. It's up to us to see through these self-defeating thoughts as they arise and "pop" them, like we would pop a balloon, with the needle of Self-knowledge.

When we find ourselves in a relationship or situation where we are being disrespected, we likely feel some degree of emotional pain. From a spiritual perspective, this pain is your best friend, earnestly wanting to make you healthy at every level—physical, emotional, intellectual, social, existential, and ultimately, spiritual. It wants you to take respon- sibility. It won't go away until you do the work you need to do. It tells you where you have become too attached or become unconscious or willing to be tossed aside. Pain wants you to find the highest version of yourself—your goddess version—and not be content with uncon- sciously performing the script of being helpless, powerless, small, stupid, undeserving, beyond repair, or whatever it is for you.

Perhaps the best medicine for this kind of pain is to remember that we belong to Lakshmi, who dwells within us. She would never want us to degrade ourselves. Your inner goddess may be asleep right now, but with self-value, she will awaken and roar from within with the power of this universe.

Always remind yourself that you have at least this one qualification: you are a goddess deep inside you, one that can roar at any moment and reclaim her lost territory at any time. Never forget that!

When Lakshmi left, she was merely Indra's wealth-manifesting resource in the background. But when she reemerged from the ocean, after reassessing and reasserting her worth, she was roaring with self-pleasure, as a *world goddess, no less, the ultimate source of everything that is beautiful, worthy, and joyful.*

ACT LIKE A GODDESS: SPEAK UP

In the summer of 2020, Ted Yoho, the US Representative from Florida, muttered an insult to Alexandria Ocasio-Cortez (AOC), the youngest woman ever to serve in the United States Congress—in clear earshot of a reporter. The comment arose from the fact that AOC dared to make remarks on increasing crime and its connection with poverty, remarks Yoho found threatening enough to want to rein in the woman who made them by calling her, without a second thought, a "fucking bitch."

The word "bitch" is a derogatory term used by men all the time, to put women down, especially powerful women or women who have opinions. Of course, when spoken along with the *F* word, it compares women who possess opinions and simply won't shrink in the face of misogyny to four-legged she-dogs in heat, mating distastefully in the open. Women so referred to, no matter what their achievements, position, ideas, valid concerns, or sensitivities, are reduced to caricatures of vulgarity and debauchery, and their authority and esteem dismissed as no more than a lewd display of misplaced and unwarranted passion.

The insult *bitch* "taps into and reinforces misogyny: its contempt for and anger at women simply for being women. Simply for being," says Georgetown University professor Deborah Tannen.[3] Women who dare go against or stand up to male bosses and colleagues are "fucking bitches." Wives who demand their due attention or share are "fucking bitches." Daughters who determine their own sexual orientation are "fucking bitches," and any women who say no to unwarranted and unwelcome sexual attention are also, you guessed it, "fucking bitches." Finally, a woman who dares to run for the highest political office of our nation is apparently no more than a "fucking bitch." T-shirts sold at then-candidate Trump's rallies hooted "Trump that Bitch," and "Trump versus Tramp," "She's a Cunt," "Hillary couldn't satisfy her husband, she can't satisfy us!" And you can order a T-shirt on online that asks the president to "Ditch the Bitch" and impeach Speaker of the House Nancy Pelosi. According to Kory Stamper, lexicographer and author of *Word by Word: The Secret Life of Dictionaries,* "Calling a woman a bitch tells her that she's too loud, too forward, too obnoxious, too independent, too-too; calling her a bitch reminds her that she should, like a hunting dog, be controllable."[4]

You may wonder why I am discussing the phenomenon of *fucking bitch* in a book about reclaiming the inner goddesses. It is because if we truly want to have the last roaring laugh, we cannot bury our head in the sand and pretend all is well and divine when it is not. Which human goddess has not come dangerously close to being called a "fucking bitch" at least once in her life? We've also seen the goddess wings of our mothers, sisters, daughters, and woman friends torn off, with this insult thrown in their face, sometimes even by the very men, lovers, husbands, fathers, brothers, and sons who claim to love them.

Is it even possible to be divinely content like Goddess Lakshmi in a world where our feminine light threatens an entire gender to go dark? Women's sheer existence is an affront to some men, as explained by the term *misogyny*, which is derived from the ancient Greek word *misogunia* and means "hatred toward women." In his book *A Brief History of Misogyny: The World's Oldest Prejudice,* author Jack Holland explores the roots of misogyny, which he says can be traced back to ancient Greek mythology, specifically to two poems written by farmer-turned-poet Hesiod in the eighth century BCE. In the world imagined by this poet, a time did exist in the history of the universe when men alone existed. Indeed, before women came into existence, men were coexisting peacefully as companions to the gods until Prometheus decided to steal the secret of fire from the gods, which angered Zeus, the father of gods. Zeus punished mankind for tricking the gods by gifting them Pandora, the first woman ever, who carried a box that was never meant to be opened (per the instructions of the gods). But Pandora, being a woman, could not contain her curiosity, and by opening the box, she unleashed all the evils being faced by mankind up through today, such as pain, sickness, old age, chronic suffering, and death.[5]

I doubt men today believe in the Pandora's box explanation, but misogyny nevertheless clearly exists. That is a fact. But by actively choosing to be discontent with her situation, AOC acted in a way truly worthy of her inner Lakshmi. She did not take misogyny lying down! Instead, she stood up and made a memorable speech in the House of Representatives, one that clearly channeled her (timely) goddess-like discontent. An article in HuffPost details her response, as well as commenting on her admirable behavior:

> This morning, Ocasio-Cortez, along with a group of her colleagues, including fellow women of color Rep. Pramila Jayapal (D-Wash.) and Rep. Nydia Velasquez (D-N.Y.), eviscerated Yoho and his casual misogyny . . . Ocasio-Cortez made it clear that Yoho's own speech had prompted hers.
>
> "I could not allow my nieces, I could not allow the little girls I go home to, I could not allow victims of verbal abuse and worse to see that, to see that excuse [from Representative Yoho] and to see our Congress accept it as legitimate. And to accept it as an apology. And to accept silence as a form of acceptance. I could not allow that to stand."
>
> She also made clear that having a wife and daughters—something that is often used by men who are trying to deflect from their own gender-based abusive behavior—does not tender men automatic entry into the club of Truly Decent Men.

*"I am someone's daughter, too," she said. "My father,
thankfully, is not alive to see how Mr. Yoho treated his
daughter. My mother got to see Mr. Yoho's disrespect on the
floor of this House toward me on television, and I am here
because I have to show my parents that I am their daughter
and that they did not raise me to accept abuse from men."*[6]

The word "bitch" being tossed about so often these days as a
demeaning slur on women reminds me of my grandfather, my Baba,
who really knew never to toss away Lakshmi, in any form, ever! He
told me once of an incident from the life of his father, the Vedic sage
Acharya Shanti Prakash, whom I call "Elder Baba."

THE GODDESS VISITS US IN
ANY FORM SHE WISHES

One day, when Elder Baba sat down to his lunch after his morning
prayers, meditation, and teachings, his disciples served him hot
fluffed chapattis (Indian bread, made of non-fermented wheat dough).
When Elder Baba's eyes were closed as he was chanting a mantra and
offering his respect to the food, a sweet-looking female dog appeared
in our open courtyard out of nowhere and slyly slicked the chapatti off
the plate and ran for her life!

Elder Baba opened his eyes just in the nick of time and realized in
an instant what was happening. He saw the escaping dog's back, her
short and stiff tail wagging happily in the air at her triumph. Elder
Baba lost his poise. He picked up his entire plate and ran after her,
and it looked like he was going to throw it on the dog with rage! People
said only a yogi like him could run like an athlete at his age. And yes,
he caught up with the canine all right, since she was cornered in a
narrow alley that came to a dead end!

Elder Baba's disciples caught up with him and were surprised at
what they saw! Elder Baba had flung himself on the ground, next to
where the dog was now cowering. Elder Baba was talking to her . . .

"O Devi, you are hungry, you ran with the bread alone, but you did
not take any ghee (clarified butter), so here, have this . . . eat this . . .
You must not eat chapatti alone without adding ghee to it."

Elder Baba chatted with love overflowing from his speech, eyes, and heart at the flea-infested dog, gradually winning her trust and then feeding her with his own hands every morsel on his plate. Tears were flowing down both of their eyes. The goddess-dog then remained around our home for many more years and gave birth many times, and her descendants still live in and about my home in Ayodhya.

Elder Baba of course was convinced that that day, he had fed Divine Mother herself, through this blessed momma-dog body. He showed her not only love, but profound respect, as he did with all animals, birds, and fishes, as well as the suffering and hungry men, women, and poor children who came to our door. Everyone was welcomed, fed, loved, or at the minimum, blessed with true kind words, prayers, and presence. Divine Mother, the Great Goddess Shakti, dwells in every particle of this universe, and when she is pleased with us, she gives us divine vision.

The devi dog had open access to our home's temple. She would come and go as she pleased. From that day forward, she often accompanied Elder Baba in his prayers and meditation. This story left an indelible impression on my heart. In a wisdom culture, where even the actual bitch is respected, how can we not respect the woman?

In the end, I hope you've never found yourself tossed away like a garland. And if it ever happens in the future, I hope you will find ways to value yourself, even more than before. And you, too, will become a blessed and abundant Lakshmi version of yourself when you refuse to be a tossed garland. The one who listens to the self-valuing and self-respecting voice of the goddess within becomes beloved to Lakshmi and receives her grace!

A LAKSHMI CONTEMPLATION FOR YOU

I ASK: What would life look like if I regarded
   self-value as my greatest wealth?

I RECOGNIZE: Patriarchy undermines women's worth and must be
   checked with Divine Feminine power in service of self-value.

I CONNECT: Standing erect, legs apart, firmly grounded, shoulders
   back, I radiate power. I radiate self-value. I radiate self-worth.

I DECIDE: When I am devalued, disrespected, or
   disregarded, I will respond powerfully to restore
   self-value, self-respect, and self-regard.

I ACT: I make a plan to reclaim self-value. I
   take the first step and keep going.

I REMEMBER: My inner Lakshmi, who teaches me self-
   value, is the ultimate source of abundance.

CHAPTER 9

THE FOUR GOALS OF LIFE AND GODDESS LAKSHMI

*O Goddess, you bestow worldly enjoyment
and spiritual liberation to all beings.*

DEVI MAHATMYA 11.7

oddess Lakshmi is said to possess four hands. They signify her power to grant the fulfillment of four universal goals of life, collectively called *purushartha.*

1. *Artha* represents seeking material security through pursuit of job, family life, relationships, and other material intentions.
2. *Kama* entails enjoying the age-appropriate sensorial and sexual pleasures of life.
3. *Dharma* represents the pursuit of higher consciousness in everything we do.
4. *Moksha* means pursuing spiritual knowledge to connect with the inner divinity.

A long time ago, everyone understood why Lakshmi was associated with the four goals. But now, these are just words to most.

Let me bring these words back into a living teaching so you can adapt them into your own life. Then you will make goddess-manifesting, smart choices, and you, too, will feel blessed with Lakshmi's absolute prosperity and abundance from within. For a true goddess-like life, the Vedas suggest that we aim to achieve all four goals in life.

MATERIAL SECURITY (ARTHA) IS FUNDAMENTAL

It is easy to see why the quest for material security, or artha, is a universally prescribed goal. The Vedas are a mature spiritual tradition. They do not promote a spiritual life that overlooks or bypasses a materially stable, even abundant lifestyle. The quest for food, clothing, shelter, and health, as well as the money and power related to procuring these, is programmed within us universally. Birds make nests and find mates, and humans open bank accounts and try to start families! There is no one single person on earth who is not "driven" to not only survive but thrive. Though efforts and intensity may vary, no one chooses to be materially insecure. Even a wandering monk needs food and water, a fresh pair of clothes, and a place to rest for the night.

PLEASURE-SEEKING (KAMA) IS IMPORTANT TOO

However, if you work all the time to become materially secure (artha) but forget to play and relax (which is the goal of kama), you will burn out. Pleasure and play are also important. Without gratifying and fun activities, life will feel like a burden. Kama relates to our physiological and psychological quest for pleasure, be it sexual, or aesthetic, or via recreation and leisure. Kama is your birthright. You are built for pleasure!

At the same time, if you are simply leading your life in quest of pleasure, you may never save for the rainy day. Therefore, both material security and inner permission to enjoy life's pleasureful moments are important goals to pursue, according to the Vedas.

A HIGHER PURPOSE (DHARMA)
IS THE MISSING PIECE

Despite a life that is materially stable (artha) with ample opportunity to enjoy the varied pleasures life has to offer (kama), your heart can still feel empty without a higher purpose to your existence. Unless you can selflessly become a source of happiness for another living creature (human or otherwise) or act from higher consciousness no matter what challenge you face externally, you won't really feel fulfilled with your life deep down. This is where the goal of cultivating higher consciousness, or dharma, gains importance.

The pursuit of dharma makes humans want to raise their game and become dependable, responsible, worthy, and valuable beings on our planet. It is an impulse from within to ascend in our own esteem, walk our talk, stand for truth and justice. But unlike artha and kama, which are our intuitive goals, pursuit of dharma has to be a conscious choice. It comes from an inner decision to walk a greater path. Hypothetically speaking, if all humans were choosing to be dharmic, exploitative beliefs like patriarchy could not have lasted so long, nor would humanity have become divided between oppressors and oppressed! Alas, that is not the case. Therefore, let us try to embody dharma, shall we?

Dharma, when activated, makes us want to be proud of ourselves— who we are and how we choose to act—and allows us to begin exploring our greater potential, beyond the need to oppress another or remain a victim ourselves. Then, we live our lives not just from our gut fears or conditioning (which often drive us in the sphere of jobs, relationships, and search of pleasure), but for the sake of higher ideals like self-respect, self-value, and commitment to authenticity. The greater the dharma, the greater the sense of responsibility toward self and others who depend upon us. Ultimately, dharma asks you to embody greater self-worth and stay away from self-diminishing and self-trashing attitudes.

Imagine if women were universally taught to seek a higher consciousness along with seeking wealth and fun. Their self-esteem would not be based upon what they own or don't, or how thrilling their life is or isn't, but instead based upon what kind of awareness they cultivate deep down, what they believe in, how they show up in their own life and stand up to oppression, seduction, greed, and manipulation with dignity, and a resolute discernment between what is worthy of pursuing and what is not. The goal of dharma can make women immune to the pulls of quick wealth or desperate pleasure.

In fact, with dharma, one begins approaching all activities—be it a job, paying rent, raising kids, seeking a life partner, seeking sexual fulfillment and recreation—intelligently, mindfully, ethically, and resolutely—and without compromising personal standards.

This is why the Vedas promote dharma, asking us to look beyond quick gains and setting us up for long-term, deeply satisfying success. Dharma quiets anxiety and turns our senses inward and upward toward the goddess, where we find our inner Lakshmi, our hidden talent, creativity, abundance, generosity, gratefulness, and spiritual okay-ness despite adversity.

FREEDOM (MOKSHA) IS MOST IMPORTANT

Once dharma is in place, you must take up and accomplish the fourth and final goal called moksha, which literally means "freedom." Moksha means freedom from your own spiritual ignorance that makes you settle for less. The Vedas say, why not make the acquaintance with your true goddess Self an official goal? Once you do that, you will no longer be afraid of challenges and challengers. You will operate from greater soul-power, an inner permission to lead a more abundant life and experience constant connection with Divine Mother, Shakti, and your own true Self. You'll become free from the obstacles and doubts posed by your own ignorant ego.

If you decide to value moksha, then reading spiritual books, like this one, makes complete sense. Taking workshops or retreats with teachers who help you connect with your hidden, divine abilities also makes sense.

Upon achieving moksha, you will remember who you were all along, before the world told you its version of who you are and who you are not. Once you realize your true goddess-like Self, then money, sex, relationships, joys, and sorrow may come and go in your life, but nothing and no one will have the power to capsize the boat of your well-being. Recognition of who we really are deep down—a roaring goddess, no less—is the ultimate freedom. This is moksha, a state of complete sovereignty.

The goddess rewards those brave ones who don't remain satisfied with transient toys alone, who continue to journey through dharma within, until they come face to face with their inner divinity (moksha). From being dismissed, invisible, and broken, you can become a proud, roaring woman. You will stop apologizing for being awesome.

When you remember who you truly are, the game changes.

GODDESSES LEAD BALANCED LIVES

With her four hands, Lakshmi is saying embrace all four goals, not just one or two. Work hard to be reasonably well off and start a family if that helps you feel more stable (artha); don't forget romance and play—have fun whether you are a single or in a relationship (kama); make sure you don't hurt yourself or anyone else on the planet in the process by remaining conscious and principled (dharma); and finally, don't forget to ask the bigger non-worldly questions like *Who are you deep inside you?* and *What is the relationship of your Self with the goddess?* (moksha).

Cultivating a balance between stability-imparting activities, like a job and family (artha), pleasure-seeking ones (kama), value-expressing ones (dharma), and spiritual seeking (moksha) will ensure greater luck in everything you do. In fact, the word "Lakshmi" means "luck." But this luck is activated by choosing to lead a balanced life. Don't look down upon money, material comforts, cultivating relationships, and enjoying sex just because you are a spiritual person. Don't neglect spirituality and dharma either, just because you like shopping and worldly comforts. Be a balanced person and make time for all four goals.

Only a balanced personality can hope to be lucky in any real sense. Otherwise, even if Lakshmi comes knocking at your door, your addictions to pleasure, your workaholism due to never having enough money—a state of mind more than the reality of your bank account—or even your false beliefs that somehow you must give it all away to be pious or be downright poor and self-denying to prove a spiritual point will block you from manifesting abundance.

Lakshmi's divine animal is the owl. The owl signifies the patient striving to observe, deeply see, and discover the right path of dharma, particularly when surrounded by the darkness of hedonism and self-ishness. It remains awake during nights but sleeps during the day. As a bird reputedly blinded by daylight, the owl serves as a symbolic reminder to refrain from blindly performing scripts handed down by a sleepwalking society.

Lakshmi's owl shares an important quality with awakening souls. As the Bhagavad Gita affirms, the enlightened ones are awake metaphorically when others sleep, and they are asleep to the illusory enchantments of the world. When others are busy chasing illusions in broad daylight, the owl happily sleeps.

Like the ascetics, the owl prefers living in relative seclusion, as if purposefully detached, to listen to its inner voice rather than be caught up in mass mentality. Therefore, rather than mindlessly mimicking worldly activities and worldly roles, modern Lakshmis cultivate an authentic relationship with their inner Self. They lead an ultra-balanced way of life, by always pursuing the spiritual goals (dharma and moksha) along with the pursuit of wealth and plea-sures (artha and kama) like everyone else. While Lakshmi represents wealth, abundance, relationships, and plenty, her divine animal the owl represents discernment and detachment.

When we are not balanced, we get in our own way. Then, no amount of lucky charms, mantras, or rituals will work because our inner god-desses will be buried under our own self-ignorance. Therefore, to be truly abundant like Lakshmi, going forward, try to be balanced in your material and spiritual quests and endeavors.

GODDESSES SAY YES TO UNAPOLOGETIC PLEASURE (KAMA)

If you are one of those women who feel ashamed at seeking out pleasureful activities or sexual joys, stop that! While all over the world religious pundits have decried sexual pleasure as sinful or only meant for procreation in shameful privacy, and others prescribe celibacy as a path to awakening, in India, another goddess manifestation of Shakti is celebrated, called Goddess Rati, who supports sexual passion and enhances our joy of lovemaking!

Goddess Rati is the goddess of love and passion. She represents the pleasure for pleasure's sake aspect of sexuality, carnal desire, lust, and passion—not pleasure "justified" by childbearing and mother-hood. In fact, several sexual techniques and positions derive their Sanskrit names from hers. Her other names describe this enchant-ing form of Shakti:

- *Kama-daayani,* she who awakens sexual desire
- *Kama-kala,* art of kama
- *Kama-priya,* beloved of kama
- *Raga-lata,* wine of love
- *Priti-kama,* naturally sensual
- *Rati-priti;* naturally aroused
- *Shubhangi,* one with auspicious limbs

Goddess Rati is also symbolic of the female seed. She is the "Aphrodite" of the Hindus. Not surprisingly, because sexual passion frees us from our body and unites us with our lover in a nondual union, Goddess Rati's shape is not fixed. She is said to shape shift at will, and each shape she takes on is ultra-sensuous, alluring, and enchanting. In fact, when you are truly aroused and experiencing your sexuality with abandonment, it is *she*, Goddess Rati, who is said to become awakened from inside you. It is she along with you who enjoys your orgasm. It is she along with you who surrenders in the sweet embrace of your lover, only to become the dominant one, seek-ing indulgence and fulfillment of her desire.

In her every form, Lakshmi is playful and present in every plea-sure possible—be it through food, the arts, or sex. Lakshmi herself is adorned with the finest gems and rubies. No wonder the Vedas gave the pursuit of "pleasures for pleasure's sake" an official sta-tus in our life. The *Kama Sutra* is a two-thousand-year-old ancient Hindu text that summarizes sexuality, eroticism, and emotional fulfillment in life. The text paints a fascinating portrait of an India that existed once upon a time (before the Islamic cultural invasion), whose openness to sexuality gave rise to a highly developed expression of the erotic. The first translator of the *Kama Sutra* treatise to English was Richard Francis Burton in 1883. But his Victorian puritanical sensibilities were overwhelmed by the *Kama Sutra*'s sexually explicit language and the Hindus' ability to imagine sexual play and pleasure and give themselves the inner permission to enjoy sexuality with soulful abandonment. In this text, premarital and extramarital sex are not frowned upon, as long as no one gets hurt and dharma is upheld.

Contrary to popular perceptions, the *Kama Sutra* is not just a manual of sixty-four sex positions; it is a complete guide to living a life with fulfilled kama. It teaches the art of living, the art of happiness, the nature of love, finding a life partner, maintaining one's love life, and other aspects pertaining to pleasure-oriented faculties of human life.

Religions fear kama universally and issue various prohibitions against it. Some even suggest celibacy as an ideal way of life. Christianity considers most sex sinful. Islam prohibits indulgence in even wine, music, and dance for the sake of austerity. Modern Hinduism is prudish and holds that sex is only for procreation, not pleasure. But the Vedic tradition of original Hinduism, which came before all sex-fearing traditions, is clear: sex is divine and an all-natural requirement of a healthy body. In fact, if sexual pleasure and sensory gratification are suppressed—even in the name of spirituality—our inner Self won't be pleased! Ill health, rage, and sorrow will fill our heart! Providing a context of wisdom (dharma) is more important than a mass prescription shaming the desire for kama in the form of sex, music, or dance. You don't need to explain or justify why you must have pleasure; simply enjoy it with dharma by your side. Become full of pleasure, but never self-indulgent; discern what is enough.

A pleasurable life feels prosperous. Of course, dharma ensures the pleasure is ethical, and moksha ensures you will never become addicted to it. Compare this realistic and pragmatic Vedic advice to philosophies and religions that "guilt" you just because you enjoyed sex, found a new partner who supported your soul's kama-quest, enjoyed a glass of wine, or even gifted yourself a well-deserved new pair of shoes!

Open up to the ways you can cultivate pleasure in your life. This will please your inner Lakshmi immensely! Besides enjoying (dharmic) sex without shame or obligation, can you do the following few things daily to enjoy goddess-like kama?

- Can you clean and beautify your home regularly and keep it lovely and serene enough for Lakshmi to come pay a visit? More than buying expensive items to decorate your home, your intention to keep it vibrationally pure, clean, and organized is what matters.

- Can you adorn your home with flowers—store bought or wild picked—burn incense, light candles, especially at dawn and dusk, or decorate with natural objects, like rocks and crystals, when possible?

- Can you pick up after yourself and share the delight of a spacious, uncluttered home with family members? If they don't cooperate right away, can you start with your personal space at least? Even if you live in a cramped space, you can still pick up after yourself, mindfully.

- Can you love your body by feeding it fresh-cooked foods whenever possible, set the table nicely, and eat with pleasure and good company when possible? If you can invest in whole organic foods, or better yet, grow them yourself or barter for them, they will give your body extra Lakshmi energy to shine with!

- Can you take up a daily self-care ritual like gazing at the rising sun, meditating under the full moon, self-massaging your body with warm oil, starting an exercise routine, or practicing yoga? Taxing your budget or your time is not pleasure producing, so simple choices lead the way to sublime self-care.

- Can you wear clean clothes, made of natural fibers
  when possible? Even if you have few clothes, regularly
  wash, iron, and wear them with a goddess smile.

- Can you adorn your body with beads,
  ornaments, essential oils, and perfumes more
  often, suitable to your taste and budget?

- Can you try to grow flowers, vegetables, or herbs? Take
  care of them, like you would take care of your own children.
  When you are visited by birds, butterflies, hummingbirds,
  and bees, kama energy will exponentialize in your home.

- Can you enjoy or patronize music, painting, singing, or some
  other form of pleasure-giving artistic activity? Anything
  that makes you feel relaxed and uplifted will work.

- Can you spend time walking or meditating outdoors,
  listening to bird calls, and watching trees dance to the
  tune of the breeze? Spending time with Mother Nature
  is akin to spending time with Mother Lakshmi herself!

- Can you invite a friend or two who are respectful
  to your inner being and fun to be with for
  cozy meals and chitchat? Can you plan picnics,
  camping, or movie marathons together?

- Can you open your heart and home to pets—cats, frogs,
  bunnies, hamsters, and reptiles—because these creatures,
  representative of Lakshmi, fill our hearts with delight?

All in all, don't neglect having fun in your life. Surround yourself
with pleasure-imparting people, hobbies, and activities, and make
time to just be, sweetly indulgent of yourself, from sheer pleasure.
This is one true way to worship your inner Lakshmi.

GODDESSES SAY A POWERFUL YES
TO MATERIAL WEALTH (ARTHA)

To live like goddesses, women worldwide must square their equation, not only with kama, but with artha, too, which can be obtained two ways. One is by marrying into wealth. The other is by earning, investing, and saving wealth yourself.

Many women view being a homemaker as a duty to their family and part of a greater good. All is well with this sentiment, as long as this is a healthy choice and not imposed (but many times it is) and stay-at-home spouses are treated with respect, as equals (yet many times they are not).

Unfortunately, unless we raise the awareness around the sacrifices and contributions stay-at-home women make, this setup gives their men a chance to say, "You wouldn't be enjoying this life if it weren't for me." Financially dependent women must compromise their wishes and desires at every step and rarely exercise autonomy in any area of their life.

That is why, given the slippery slope of outsourcing your artha to others, I recommend that most women stand on their own feet, even if that means working only part time. It's true that women in some cultures are still discouraged, and sometimes prohibited, from working. So this is a catch-22 situation. But financial freedom does not simply happen; it is a choice. And I encourage women to take baby steps where possible toward the goal of financial independence. Besides, if a marriage does not work out, women who financially rely on their spouse become not only emotionally insecure, but materially too.

Outsourcing artha to the man in their life is the number one reason women have become victims of institutionalized patriarchy. For too many years, even in America, men were the sole breadwinners; women's reliance on their fathers, husbands, and sons for security ensured men had the upper hand. That is why in the cultures where women are the head of the household, or at least bringing home the bread as much as the men do (if not more), they enjoy maximum freedom in determining their own life.

Yet, even in the more liberal societies where women have equal if not greater opportunity, the fantasy of *being taken care of financially* still persists even today. And equally saddening is the quickness with which some women forfeit their career goals to become full-time homemakers to make things easier for their spouse. What I am trying to say is, dare to be a goddess and plan your moves carefully. Follow your goddess calling and, when possible, fend for yourself. Don't forfeit your right to hunt (for artha), if that is what you feel called to do and have the opportunity to do so.

Yes, great men exist—they always have, and they always will. They provide, they nurture without strings attached, and they respect their moms, wives, and daughters as equals. I have been lucky to have received nurturance from such a father, grandfather, and husband. And I also contribute artha to my family in my own dharmic way.

Why take a risk? Why not prepare yourself for life by taking your material goals into your own hands? Men do. Why should we not as well? Why not become the Lakshmi version of yourself—truly abundant, not only in wealth, but in attitude, too—by taking on responsibility for yourself?

Far too often, operating under false beliefs, we women become disenfranchised when it comes to commanding wealth. We block our inner Lakshmi from manifesting abundance. We don't speak up. We don't ask. We don't demand. It's no wonder, then, that despite opportunities to live with financial independence, many women worldwide continue to choose emotional subservience over self-reliance, and dependence over independence in every imaginable way.

Many women who do make money report feeling embarrassed at how much money they make or feel it's not proper to talk about money—not polite, or not womanly. Still others exclaim with pride, "I don't know what I have or how much I make. I let my husband handle our finances." Some say a complete "no" to money-making opportunities knocking at their door because the man in their life will feel threatened by their success. Others feel unworthy of an increase in wages when colleagues don't get the increase too (collaborative to a fault). No wonder women worldwide earn less than their male counterparts in the same job and become passive when asking for a pay raise, meekly going along with the universal disparity in pay scale. They may even give away their hard-earned money to unworthy partners, relatives, or causes owned by patriarchal influencers and feminine-guilt inducers who don't take no for an answer.

True artha does not include vicarious pride in sacrifice, dependence, poverty, shunning wealth, or even abandoning the material reality of our existence to create some image of a pious money-shunning, impoverished holy goddess. Get this: self-endorsed and self-enforced destitution, fiscal dependence, and emotional enslavement do not make you a better woman, nor do they rubber stamp your goodness. In fact, it disgraces your inner Lakshmi. Your goddess commands independence and complete abundance. And activating that abundance requires you taking responsibility for your own artha. Period.

On the other side of the coin, here's an artha tip for those of you who are partnered: If you are a homemaker or stay-at-home parent and your partner berates and shames you for not contributing fiscally, don't feel bad any longer, O goddess. Stand your ground. Nothing short of queenly behavior is expected of married women. Nothing short of the status of a queen is what the Vedas prescribe. They go even further and bless a new bride by saying *murdhaanam patyuraroha*: "May your husband [wife] keep you on his [their] head," meaning, "Let him [them] respect you."

Dollars alone don't make you fiscally secure. Nor can a ring on your finger make you feel emotionally secure. It is your recognition of your inherent value from within that brings you security in this case. If you don't work outside of the home, you are contributing day and night to make your home a safe space for you and your partner and children (if you have any) to live in; it is clean, comfortable, and restful, and above all, a safe haven from the slights and attacks of the world.

This sense of being held in a sheltered space, too, is securing artha. You may be procuring and cooking foods and nurturing the well-being of everyone in your home. Without comforting food, without the health that comes from it, without inner nurturance that comes from predictable family life, who can be truly secure? And you are creating all the above. In fact, as a stay-at-home parent, you work day and night and hold various jobs and skills such as personal chef, tutor, nurse, chauffeur, and house cleaner, so your annual salary should be around $178,201.[1]

The sense of satisfaction and the sense of comfort that comes from a home that is a sanctuary of the soul, thanks to the homemaker, cannot be matched by hotel rooms and restaurant food, no matter how fancy they may be. Sooner or later, everyone craves the refuge of the familiar household, the heartening voice of the homemaker, the bark or meow of animals, the laughter of children or chitchat of familiar neighbors and invited guests to dinner. All of this is artha—activities and engagements that spell physical protection, emotional safety, and social well-being. And you enable all this, dear goddess. You truly are the queen of the den—act like it. Roar with pride and satisfaction!

Whether you are earning money yourself or you are supporting your partner in earning it, here are a few ways you can bring higher consciousness (dharma) specifically into your wealth-related attitudes and engagements.

Understand that wealth is of three types: Any wealth legitimately earned or enjoyed by upholding dharma is called artha. Wealth gained by bypassing dharma is called *anartha*, meaning "disaster" in Sanskrit. And finally, when you simply horde wealth, and let it rot, it is called *vyartha*, which literally means "useless." What you want to do is maximize the first kind of wealth!

- Prioritize earning money. Don't ever dismiss money. Appreciate what you have. Work toward earning or saving enough for your needs in the future. Thinking about money in a responsible way does not make you less womanly or less spiritual in any way.

- Never undervalue yourself or your services, least of all because you are a woman.

- Try to step outside your comfort zone—and your culture's description of what is appropriate for women—and think of creative ways to manifest material stability. Try to look beyond the status quo to what is *possible, even if it has not been done before.* You can do this because you are a woman!

- Attending seminars, reading books, and listening to wealth-enhancing podcasts are all good ideas. Knowledge is power. You can also consider working with financial planners.

- Keep money flowing; don't unnecessarily hoard money, nor throw it away. Lakshmi likes responsibility, attention, and care in handling money.

- Share when you can, with appropriate people and organizations. This includes being transparent about your earnings to your government and significant others (not hiding money).

- Avoid swinging between total distaste for money and total greed for money by bringing Lakshmi into the consideration. Then you will be willing to treat money more holistically, as a source of sacred power and force of goodness, for yourself and for your community.

- If you are feeling unworthy of receiving and enjoying money, remember you are a beloved child of Goddess Lakshmi and in every way as deserving as another being in this universe.

- To say no to what gifts are coming your way is to disrespect Lakshmi.

AND BEFORE YOU BECOME HOOKED . . .

Sometimes our search for artha can become exhausting as well as obsessive. Similarly, in the beginning, we think we are enjoying kama—*only one sip of whisky, one pat of butter on our toast, one more game of dice, or one more one-night stand*—and then soon, kama begins to enjoy us instead. Before we know it, we are hooked. Kama, or the desire for pleasure, is never satisfied by satisfaction of the desire. It grows each time it is quenched. And this addiction makes us totally powerless!

Therefore, restoring connection with dharma is important. It is all too easy for women to see themselves as objects of pleasure (kama) and view men as sources of security (artha). Alternately men become predators of women for "pleasure" and champion themselves for the "material security" they (supposedly) provide . . . but at what cost? These are non-empowering positions. We all need to stop selling ourselves so cheap and take dharma and moksha into consideration!

Only with dharma can women say no to the casting couch model of sexual favors for some supposed advantage. And men with dharma will not invite you to the casting couch either; instead they will distribute whatever opportunities they offer based only on merit. Once again, let me remind you: The battle is not between men and women. It is between the grabbing and greedy "asuras" of all genders, who put aside considerations of dharma and live and manipulate for wealth and pleasure at any cost; and "devas," who may sacrifice money and comforts if necessary to uphold their values (dharma).

A seeker who had a chance to glean a new way had this to share:

> If only I had known about the four goals, then I would
> not have undergone as much suffering as I did. I was
> dissatisfied in my marriage. I married right after high
> school. We fought about everything. My marriage
> suddenly ended when I slept with a guy I met when I was
> out drinking on a girls' night out. My lover moved into
> my home, promptly after my husband walked out on me
> because I cheated on him!
>
> Life was idyllic for a while, until I realized I was bored
> again. He felt like a burden. So, I asked him to leave. I
> thought I was doing the right thing, except my children
> went into a tizzy. They missed him even more than they
> missed their dad. They wouldn't talk to me for days.
>
> Unknowingly, I kept hunting for security from the
> men in my life (artha) while seeking pleasure like a wild
> animal every night I could find someone to watch my
> children (kama). Then one day, my mother forwarded a
> video of a teaching about the four goals. At first, I balked.
> But something in me continued listening. I learned that

money and sex are worthy and to be fulfilled, provided I
do not hurt or abuse myself or another and do not impede
my own journey of feeling good deep inside me (dharma).
Despite my immediate resistances to what the speaker was
saying, it made sense. Slowly, I started making changes.

Instead of dreaming to be "provided for" and
"pleasured" 100 percent by my lovers just because I have
something they want, I am now trying to stand on my
own two feet. I still date. But I don't bring the men home
no matter how nice or rich or smart they are. I started
laying my cards on the table even before the first date,
letting the men I met know clearly that I was looking for a
life partner, not a lover, and I had children. I have yet to
meet the man who will meet my children. I have started
spending more time with my children, reading stories
or taking walks together. When their dad visits, I feel
appreciative in my heart.

I am finally liking myself more, and though this feeling
is new, I really like that feeling of self-respect, called
dharma. Maybe this is the beginning of moksha. I will
find out.

When dharma informs our quest for pleasure and wealth, it feels good to be honest and say no to seduction or manipulation. It feels good to speak the truth even if it leads to some unpleasant consequences, like losing a prospective lover. It feels good to restrain our own impulsive nature before pointing fingers at others! Therefore, dharma will restore your goddess well-being and protect you from your own plotting, scheming, greedy mind when it comes to any artha or kama overdose while teaching you how to respond with fairness and power to asura-like minds who may want to take advantage of you.

Dharma, in the ultimate sense, restores power back to you and puts you in charge because you are responding not reacting, are discerning not impulsive, and are willing to earn your worth and not feel worthless in any capacity. With dharma, you will feel like roaring with inner satisfaction!

A LAKSHMI CONTEMPLATION FOR YOU

I ASK: Of the four goals of life, where am I
abundant? What needs work?

I RECOGNIZE: Prosperity is uniquely within me and up
to me, not outside of me and not up to others.

I CONNECT: Resting attention on my heart (the fourth chakra), I sense
potential for expression of my loving, powerful, abundant nature.

I DECIDE: Pursuing the four goals, I will practice
discernment and detachment.

I ACT: Where I am unbalanced, I make a plan,
take the first step, and keep going.

I REMEMBER: I am Lakshmi. My four hands create every
kind of abundance, material and spiritual!

CHAPTER 10

THE VALUE OF DISCONTENTMENT IN A GODDESS'S LIFE

The body shines, the character shines, the conduct shines, when Lakshmi shines her blessings on you.

VIJAYALAKSHMI STOTRAM, VERSE 13

I n the last chapter we explored the value of pursuing four integrated goals. As an embodied goddess, you must enjoy wealth (artha) and pleasures (kama) unapologetically, while acting from a higher consciousness (dharma) and seeking spiritual goals (moksha). Once we grasp the wisdom of the four goals that aid us in reconciling materialism with spirituality in our lives, we still need to work not to forget them. If we get caught up in chasing material wealth and crumbs of ephemeral pleasures, we can lose our peace of mind, and sometimes our health too—not a very goddess-like state to be in! But the foresighted Vedas promote cultivating a special dharmic attitude called *santosha*. Santosha means proactively choosing to cultivate contentment and being satisfied with a life free of material greed and acquisitiveness.

Contentment arises from a divine source—the goddess Self within—which money and material possessions cannot purchase. Goddess is the giver of wealth, but she is said to impart a greater wealth when she imparts us with contentment because this gift alone makes us feel fulfilled and whole. It gifts us peace, well-being, and inner pleasure. It's no wonder another name for Goddess Lakshmi is *Santoshi*, the one who is ever content.

CULTIVATE THE DHARMA OF CONTENTMENT

Santosha is a deliberately cultivated attitude connected with neither being wealthy nor poor. Rather, it is about trusting a higher power— trusting that Lakshmi has a plan for your life, whether you are going through a period of material scarcity or abundance.

Santosha is always an inside job. It involves your thoughts, values, beliefs, and attitudes, and not what is going on outside you. Santosha has only one source; that source is found in a soul-satisfying relationship with the Feminine Divine, who cares for you, through and beyond life circumstances.

The spiritually content truly appreciate life, regardless of circumstances, because they have connected with the goddess within. This contentment is a choice, an inner attitude that gives rise to a sense of "enoughness," divine protection, and personal power. Truly, the desire for wealth never ends. One never arrives at a point when one says, *I think I have enough!* Bottomless wanting is pure powerlessness; contentment is power.

Lacking the bigger picture—estranged from inner Lakshmi, who is smiling with contentment—and ignorant of our inner nature, many of us become trapped into believing our restless mind and its scenarios of "missing the bus" or being "doomed for life." An attached, desire-filled mind builds up its ignorant forces, attends workshops and bootcamps to get rich overnight, grinds in a toxic job situation just because the pay is good, or cheats and manipulates others for money, marriage, or sex. It lies; it withholds, schemes, and abuses; it hurts others, and gets hurt itself—all for crumbs of artha (money) and kama (pleasures). Estranged from its inner goddess abundance, the unexamined mind never really arrives upon true abundance. The solution is to cultivate contentment.

To do that, we must change our core beliefs about our neediness and be willing to see through our own lust for ever more wealth and ever more material pleasures. You will know you have lust for money—versus a legitimate need for it—if you find yourself stressing about money despite having money, possessions, and property to your name. You may also be lying and manipulating others for monetary gain when under the influence of money-lust.

Be aware of any such sorrow-causing attachment to wealth. Inculcate in yourself the qualities of contentment, which include detachment, generosity, sharing, caring, and selflessness, which free you of any survival consciousness that fuels insatiable fears, greed, envy, and malice. When you awaken the goddess inside you, your mind becomes enriched with contentment and you feel inwardly rich too. When envy arises because others have more than you, deliberately think spiritual thoughts. For example, if you are feeling jealous of someone's wealth, think one thought about them that is generous, such as, "Lakshmi knows why they are more successful and wealthier than me in this moment in time, and since goddess wills it so, I am happy for them." Then try your best to sincerely feel glad for them.

Discontentment traps us in a stressful life by adopting purely material goals: more, bigger, and best. The dissatisfied mind fills with greed. In our material discontent, we can become like the mythic asuras—principle-less, power-lusty, and insatiably greedy, shadowy versions of ourselves. Therefore, discontentment must be seen through and set aside, and contentment nurtured, mindfully. This is Lakshmi's wisdom. Without contentment, even if you have savings, you will remain stressed about losing what you have by future unforeseen events. Such anxieties are unrelated to an actual lack, but rather an *imagined* loss. It is a virtual suffering created by our own mind. Instead of settling down and enjoying what we have, we remain hypervigilant against losses, often sleepless with worry.

You may wonder, *How can I cultivate contentment when I am dealing with adversity or lack? Is Lakshmi still with me, or has she forgotten me?*

Let me reassure you that even in poverty, Lakshmi is still with you, in her twin incarnation as Goddess Alakshmi, who is the ruling divinity of poverty. Yes, Goddess Alakshmi is the goddess of poverty and deprivation. So, if you practice a degree of contentment in poverty, too, while trying to change your lot through enterprise and hard work, material lack and even difficult circumstances can become rich fodder for the growth of characteristics like perseverance, patience, surrender, and fortitude. For example, when material wealth goes away suddenly, through unexpected losses in the stock market or by losing your wallet full of cash, it means Goddess Lakshmi is saying to you, "You got this . . . you can walk on your own feet of devotion and trust in your inner goddess, and reach my infinite locker, where you will never ever be needy again—in this and future lifetimes."

If you are currently struggling financially, instead of repeatedly thinking thoughts like *I am cursed, I can't afford it, I am always struggling, I never have enough, goddess has abandoned me*, ask yourself:

> *What is Lakshmi trying to teach me as Goddess Alakshmi?*
> *Does she want me to see through my attachments?*
> *Does she want me to embody dharma?*
> *Does she want me to work harder?*
> *Am I being asked to rethink my attitudes?*
>   *Change my life strategy?*
> *Persevere despite challenges?*
> *Move toward selflessness?*
> *Be more selfconcerned?*
> *Forbear?*
> *Let go?*
> *Awaken the inner entrepreneur?*
> *Become fearless? Invent? Explore? Resolve?*
> *Learn determination when my resolve*
>   *is tested through adversity?*
> *Cultivate contentment in what little I possess?*
> *Cultivate a rich and ethical spiritual life anyway?*
> *Understand the value of less?*
> *Discover my inner esteem unrelated to outer circumstances?*
> *Empathize with other beings in similar circumstances?*
> *Learn to experience compassion?*

Discover my inherent spiritual fullness?
Tap into my hidden spirit gifts (such as an ability
    to serve, co-create, and share generously in
    community, cheerfully accepting life as it comes)?
Understand that true poverty stems from estrangement
    from our higher truth (Self and Goddess) and not
    from merely a lack of material resources?
Discover that dignity, contentment, hope, kindness,
    ease, grace, and love are spiritual currency?

Ultimately, the goddess is neither about material richness nor material lack. She is divine contentment herself, and her expression, supported by cosmic wisdom, can be in the form of inner fullness and inner richness, despite an impoverished material life. She can also bless us with unexpected material wealth. Understand and rejoice in this fact that everything in the universe—including poverty, scarcity, and material lack—is a manifestation of goddess, and her blessings of abundance are hidden in darkness as much as in light.

CONTENTMENT HAS NOTHING TO DO WITH FATALISM

Santosha never means flat resignation or giving up. It simply means being okay with your situation in the "now" while working peacefully—without frenzy or desperation—toward a more optimal "future." Contentment isn't denying one's feelings about wanting and desiring what you don't have; it's a freedom from being controlled by those desires.

For example, two decades ago when I was just starting out as a teacher on the world stage, emerging from my self-imposed spiritual hibernation, my husband Sanjai lost his job, and our house foreclosed. Due to our faith in Lakshmi's plan for us and our practice of santosha, we did not lose heart nor peace of mind. We both accepted this material loss and material inconvenience over a two-year period as Lakshmi's will. It gave us great inner solace to know she has our back. We rode the materially hard times out. We did not go into a self-pity mode. Our trust in Lakshmi's housekeeping was undeterred, and that kept us feeling positive, creative, hopeful, and even happy in the hard times. I did not once deviate from my goal of bringing Vedic wisdom to the world. And thanks to my practice of cultivating moment-to-moment santosha, I planted so many beautiful seeds in that time of scarcity that my life has become an aromatic, abundant garden today. In time, Sanjai got better and better paying jobs. We bought a new, much more beautiful home atop a hill. And my spiritual and humanitarian work has now spread to all continents.

Remember this: Whenever you actively choose to practice santosha, you activate Lakshmi within. And soon enough, Lakshmi from inside your heart will begin shining as Lakshmi outside you—in the form of wealth, health, pleasures, friends, and fame.

BEWARE WHEN CONTENTMENT BECOMES CONTAINMENT!

There is a vast difference between when santosha is taken up voluntarily as a spiritual practice against acquisitiveness, covetousness, materialism, and greed, and when premature contentment becomes our delusory go-to emotional mechanism, engendering a false sense of satisfaction. When this happens, we begin telling ourselves all is well when clearly all is not well. If we are not careful, an unconscious practice of contentment can give a false sense of "okayness," leading us to bypass real-life issues that need addressing.

In my own life experiments, I have come to know that we must practice contentment when it comes to acquiring wealth and pleasures. But we must remain *dis*content when it comes to pursuing dharma (values) and moksha (freedom). There are no limits to how evolved you can become ethically and spiritually, and this includes forever pushing yourself toward inner evolution, expanding your self-awareness, self-definition, self-respect, and self-value!

Never settle for crumbs in these matters. Always attempt to show up in the world as the best, most dharmic version of yourself, and always insist upon being treated with dharma too: with respect, consideration, and equality. As the goddess that you are, you must not fall asleep at the wheel, prematurely becoming "content" with less than fair and equitable treatment. Expect more from yourself and expect the same from others.

Cultivating the value of contentment is universally supported by religions, but often to the point of dogma and mute acceptance of unfair treatment. This over-the-top contentment, preached almost exclusively to women, asks them to turn a blind eye to real-life issues, even of domestic abuse, inequality, and discrimination in the name of cultivating contentment! Instead of freeing women from their inner bondage, contentment has historically been the most effective tool to "contain" the (dharmic) feminine angst.

Therefore, women who want to truly roar like a goddess must keep their eyes open to any religious, cultural, societal, or simply habitual conditioning when practicing contentment. Before you take pride in how content you are, or how *stoic* (frankly this word makes me nervous due to its historically masculine construct and adoption), you must examine the politics of mandatory contentment before you know you truly are exercising your heart's free will. Getting caught up in the same old feminine guilt can allow us to sleepwalk our way through life and relationships, professing satisfaction in our less than satisfactory life circumstances.

Throughout history, male religious and societal leaders have prescribed contentment as a "godly ornament" to be worn especially by women. This ornament gives women courage to "suffer through" and ultimately be there as a support to their "unpredictable man." After all, organized religions tend to be *androcentric*, which is the practice, conscious or otherwise, of placing a masculine point of view at the center of one's worldview, culture, and history, thereby culturally marginalizing femininity and the feminine divine—and requiring a stoic, content woman to play along. Religions are products of a certain era; they often have outdated rules, many of them sexist.

Women belonging to every major religion are coerced into contentment of some sort, which demeans them and makes them easy targets of institutionalized containment—and these rules are unfortunately encoded in their religious texts. For example, eight rules known as *Garudhammas* relegate the women nuns to a status inferior to the male monks. These rules were purely based upon gender due to traditional Buddhist attitudes toward women associating the feminine with the sensual realm as opposed to the dharma realm. Women are depicted either as lustful temptresses who threaten the spiritual welfare of monks or as the maternal source of man's anguish and pain. As an example, here are four of the eight rules, each one reflective of the fear of women:[1]

1. A nun, even if she has been ordained for one hundred years, must respect, greet, and bow in reverence to the feet of a monk, even if he has just been ordained that day. (Monks pay respect to each other according to their seniority, or the number of years they have been ordained.)

2. A nun is not to stay in a residence where there is no monk. (A monk may take an independent residence.)

3. A nun may not reprimand a monk. (A monk may reprimand a monk, and any monk may reprimand a nun.)

4. From today onwards, no nun shall ever teach a monk. However, monks may teach nuns. (There are no restrictions on whom a monk may teach.)

Lama Rod Owens, a modern-day Buddhist teacher, observes, "At the heart of patriarchy is a duality between power and weakness. The female body becomes a symbol of any-body that is designated as weak, including queer bodies, transgender and gender expansive bodies, disabled bodies, bodies holding different beliefs, and even young bodies. In orthodox Buddhist culture, patriarchy often renders the female body as an impediment to enlightenment, a tool manipulated by the male imagination to achieve enlightenment, or an object for pleasure."[2]

A woman's status is relegated as inferior to a man's status in Islam. It decrees that men are a degree above women in authority and responsibility.[3] It suggests that women who disobey their husbands must be first admonished, then forsaken in bed, and finally, as a last resort, they may be beaten.[4] And then, in dividing the inheritance, even today, a female gets half of a male's share,[5] *and* a woman's testimony counts half of a man's testimony.[6]

In Christianity, women are told, "In pain you shall bring forth children, yet your desire shall be for your husband, and he shall rule over you."[7] And a woman must exercise silence in church,[8] as well as practice submission to her husband, without the right to question it.[9] And here is the ultimate advice on cultivating contentment without having a say in the outcome of a rape: *An unmarried woman could be compelled to marry her rapist, as long as the rapist could pay the standard bride price and the woman's father was comfortable with the marriage.*[10]

In the essay "Discontented Women" by Amelia E. Barr, we find the author, a prominent voice of her time, scolding American women in the nineteenth century: "Every human being has a complaining side, but discontent is bound up in the heart of a woman; it is her original sin. For if the first women [Eve] had been satisfied with her condition, if she had not aspired to be 'as gods,' and hankered after unlawful knowledge, Satan would hardly have thought it worth his while to discuss her rights and wrongs with her."[11]

With Hinduism, we see the opposite forces at work. While its core scriptures, like the Vedas, Upanishads, and Bhagavad Gita, embody positive ideals toward women and incorporate the Divine Feminine along with Divine Masculine and are even gender-neutral at times, the Hindu society today is mostly a man's world, where women are conditioned to be submissive. *A good woman is an obedient woman.* So, in Hindu society, patriarchy has a social and historical genesis more than a religious one.

This happened because over time Sanskrit (the language of the scriptures) was forgotten by the masses, and gradually a culture of male pundits (known as *purohits*) emerged as translators and keepers of the religion and prohibited women from studying the Vedas (despite the fact that women sages contributed to the Vedas). They also prescribed restrictive customs and conditions for women and curtailed their freedom, which was previously guaranteed by the Vedas. For instance, female widows were prohibited from remarriage, and a widow remarrying is still frowned upon by most members of Hindu society today, whereas the Vedas encouraged widows to remarry.

Hinduism is more a way of life than a religion and encourages eclectic worship that's open to personal interpretation. It does not have a centralized churchlike institution, only one god, only one holy book, or only one set of religious practices or ideals. So gradually, newer but less progressive ideas, far removed from the original Vedic ethos and often influenced by colonizing powers that ruled India for more than a thousand years, began entering the Hindu way of life. Over time, a society that was once equal became tainted with gender inequality. The implicit or clandestine patriarchal customs endeavor to make sure most Hindu women today—who are largely unaware of the Vedic invitation to be bold like a goddess—stay "disturbingly content" despite the patriarchally oppressive society that emerged with the passing of time.

Of course, conditions for women and the religious attitudes toward them are changing in Hindu, Buddhist, Christian, and Islamic societies worldwide, slowly and surely. Many modern theologians in every religion known to humankind acknowledge that their scripture was written during a different time and age and that a new interpretation is warranted in some sections, while holding to what is beautiful and worthwhile in the remaining scripture. And for this, we must not only thank progressive religious scholars but also the women in those societies who became discontent with things as they were and began roaring for a change!

The degree to which women became discontent corresponds to the degree in which we find reform and restitution in the religious domains and adjunct society.

THE REAL REASON LAKSHMI IS CONTENT

In my mind, the secret behind Lakshmi's contentment is her ability to become *discontent* for the right reasons. She does not turn a blind eye to things as they are. Instead, she addresses them. She can do that because she is emotionally sovereign, resting in her own inner fullness, freedom, and autonomy.

Let's not forget that Lakshmi is no other than Durga. Only after she has won her righteous battles and defeated the enemies of dharma does Goddess Lakshmi roar with delight from punishing boundary violators! She is content because she is never complacent about abuse, nor does she compromise her self-respect or dharma of self-value. No wonder Lakshmi can afford to be serene, because she has dealt with the darkness that came her way—not made a hasty peace with it, nor looked the other way, in the name of societal or religiously mandated "contentment."

Lakshmi is the goddess who *moves about a lot* of her own independent will. Devdutt Pattanaik, author of *Myth=Mithya: Decoding Hindu Mythology,* observed in an essay on Lakshmi that though nowadays Hindus accept Lakshmi as the eternal consort of Vishnu, the preserver of the world, in her long history the *roaming* goddess has been associated with many other deities, including asuras like Virochana, devas like Indra, and even the Hindu God Shiva. "With Vishnu, she was domesticated. No longer fleet footed, she sat demurely by his side, on his lap or at his feet."[12] Thereafter, Lakshmi became the paragon of domestic contentment, and generations of women from my country were told to keep quiet and simply "be content like Lakshmi."

But here is what I know from the mythology shared by my mother: Lakshmi does not simply sit content by the side of her partner Vishnu, either. And if she does that, she does it from sheer love and not from conditioned, sleepwalking behavior. As his equal, she questions the choices and actions of Vishnu and she is happy to answer his questions to her as well. They work as a team in the accurate versions of the stories. She actively chooses to remain his partner because he gives her reason to trust him, not from a subscription to blind contentment. No matter what the pundits would have women believe, I want to tell you that Goddess Lakshmi is ever watchful, unwilling to hypnotically settle for crumbs of satisfaction, love, affection, or equality. She wants the real deal because *she* is the real deal—and she knows it. In fact, mythological tales tell of Lakshmi getting up from her lotus, straddling a lion, and going to battle herself.

Remember, myths are allegorical. They remind us of our forgotten business, locked away in the dark recesses of our mind. Just because she is Lakshmi, the goddess of contentment, does not mean that she sits back, sipping the pina colada of patriarchy and enjoying her celestial life like a trophy goddess! She stays on her divine toes at all times, and if she finds any darkness lurking about her—such as false contentment, or even a little bit of residual codependence—suddenly her arms become bedecked with weapons, the lotus she is sitting on transforms into a roaring *I am hungry for blood* kind of lion, and her gentle demeanor transforms into a fierce one. Then the discontented Lakshmi gets to work piercing the heart of darkness, until she can restore the light that had become concealed in her own heart, first and foremost. Lakshmi uses her own discontentment to restore what is true and worthy for all beings in all worlds.

WHEN LAKSHMI MUST WASH
HER HAIR IN BLOOD

Once upon a time, King Draupad prayed to the Divine Mother asking that she emerge in embodied form as his daughter. From the sacrificial fire where he was chanting Vedic mantras, she materialized as a beautiful human-child-princess. He named her Draupadi. It was clear from the beginning that she was no ordinary child, but an embodiment of Shakti.

When Draupadi came of marriageable age, her father arranged for her to meet several suitors. Each was more handsome than the previous, with valorous resumes, wealth, and illustrious family backgrounds. Draupadi, too, was a breathtaking beauty, with ebony-colored skin, eyes like lotus petals, and dark, wavy hair. Her body's scent was like that of a blue lotus; it perfumed the air for miles around her. None was her equal in majestic beauty and purity of heart.

And this beautiful goddess's heart was won over by a quiet but intense-looking prince, Arjuna, whose mischievous cousins had managed to exile him, his four brothers, and their widowed mother from their own kingdom. They all lived in the forest in a makeshift humble home of thatched bamboo. Arjuna dressed simply and had no pompous airs about him. Yet, his eyes shone with princely light, and Draupadi was enchanted by him and his skill in archery, which he had demonstrated to win her over.

When Draupadi reached Arjuna's humble abode as his new bride, Draupadi consented to become the wife of all five brothers. This was a consensual situation and not entirely untraditional at the time.

Draupadi enjoyed her marital life—and yes, her sexual life, too, unapologetically—with her five husbands, and bore five healthy children, one from each partner. All was well, until the mischievous cousins invited Draupadi and her husbands to their home, supposedly for a conciliatory family reunion.

Everything was fine until the cousins cornered Arjuna's elder brother in an unfair game of dice. The man lost everything, and finally, in a moment of desperation, he even lost himself, his brothers, and by extension, their common wife, Draupadi! In that one unfortunate instant, they all became slaves to the wicked cousins, who became their heartless masters!

Draupadi, who was resting in the private women's chamber, was horrified to learn that she had been staked in the game and now she was a slave of those wicked cousins (asuras)! This was a gross injustice to Draupadi—betrayal by her own husband, the father of her child, who had gambled her away like a mere object! She was livid. But that was not the end. The mischievous cousins, technically now her masters, dragged Draupadi by her hair from the bedroom out into the main court where sat all the noble men and dignitaries of the kingdom. One of the cousins attempted to unrobe their new "slave-woman" publicly, making lewd remarks about her polyandrous sex drive at the same time—suddenly she was no longer a queen of her husbands, but a royal whore!

After her enslaved and powerless husbands failed to assist her, the helpless Draupadi prayed to Lord Krishna (who is none other than God Vishnu) to protect her from this public humiliation. Then, a miracle occurred. No matter how many layers of the fabric covering her body were forcibly unwrapped, the layers of Draupadi's garment (sari) kept growing. Eventually the cousins, exhausted, stopped the disrobing, and Draupadi's modesty was preserved.

Draupadi, being the "wife," was expected to keep the peace and cultivate contentment with whatever fate came her way through her marriage and her husbands. But this Lakshmi was raging like Kali. Rightfully, she was spewing venom. From that day onward, she left her hair loose and refused to wash it. She declared to her husbands, "Unless you destroy your wicked cousins and bring me back the blood of your cousin who forcibly dragged me by my hair and then tried to disrobe me, I won't wash my hair or tie it either (as was the custom for respectable married women of that time). I will wash it only with the blood of your vile cousins who publicly tried to disrobe me . . . who you must slay in this war! Period."

The family then returned to their home, once a place where everyone was happy, but which had now lost its peace and joy. The men were ashamed and humiliated. Draupadi was cold as ice but furious like Durga. The husbands wanted to forget this trauma and move on, but an indignant Draupadi saw to it that her five husbands became real men for a change and went to war against the wicked cousins to avenge her insult and to get back their lost kingdom, too, that belonged to them, not the cousins. And, she thundered, "Do not return without the blood of my molesters!"

The war, which lasted eighteen days, came to be known as the War of Kurukshetra, and is chronicled in 100,000 verses in the Hindu epic Mahabharata. This war was devastating like none before. Each and every one of the one hundred wicked cousins died, and their supporters, too, in the millions. But Draupadi was unrelenting in her discontentment until she had drenched her hair with the blood of her molester. Then, and only then, did she tie up her hair, and finally become content again inside herself. Draupadi the Empress of India was not only the queen of the lost empire now regained through righteous war, but also the sovereign of her personal dignity, now regained through righteous retribution.

Draupadi gave up her affection for her partners, but she refused to give up her burning fire of discontentment. Draupadi gave a healthy outlet to her outrage and effective resistance to her oppressors through defiance, anger, and contempt when she suffered outrageous attacks on her body and spirit (just because she was a woman), was treated as an object, and was let down by her husbands and sexually abused by her accosters. If she had somehow found a way to live with this abuse—as many women do, swallowing their pain, blocking their memories, suppressing their anguish, and pretending all is well—no women would ever be safe again. Draupadi was Shakti incarnate as a woman after all, modeling to the rest of us future goddesses how to behave with discontentment instead of contentment when asuras come for us, and when the devas in our life—like her good-hearted but slave-minded husbands—fail to protect us. They may even, as in Draupadi's case, jeopardize our safety. Then we have to take a stand for ourselves.

In one sense, Queen Draupadi is our planet's first-ever feminist because she spoke up. She was able to subvert the objectification and commodification of women in society through her resistance. Instead of staying silent when ill-treated, like a "good wife," Draupadi was vocal, lamenting the despicable treatment she received from all the males in her life.

In Hindu mythology, Draupadi is considered Goddess Lakshmi and Goddess Kali, both. She is worshipped in villages throughout Southern India under the name "Draupadi Ammal," and women turn to her for inspiration when they are dealing with domestic abuse and can't find their inner strength!

Naturally, the patriarchs in Hindu society do not endorse Draupadi for the fact that her bold image does not encourage Hindu women to conform. But the open-minded ones adore her! She remains a heroine to most women (and to many fair-minded Hindu men too). She cannot be forgotten. Notwithstanding all the shame and humiliation meted out to her, Draupadi stood her ground and survived abuse and trauma—and in fact, turned the tables upon her shamers and made them pay, with their own blood! Despite her humiliation, Draupadi emerges a victor, roaring like a goddess, because she has her own will, her own determination, her own capacity to be content and discontent for the right reasons, and most of all, she owns her own sexuality and her ever-confident, self-valuing, self-celebrating existence!

Goddess lessons on contentment are never about unexamined and unconditional acceptance, but rather how to utilize spiritual discernment, and when appropriate, utilize discontentment for *waking up, growing up, and showing up* in the world to do what we must do! Our willingness to be content with whatever is meted out to us by the asuras in our life advances their tyrannical deeds. Our silence feeds their lust. However, one courageous woman, Draupadi, stood her ground thousands of years ago and voiced her dissatisfaction when she felt wronged. I consider her the epitome of gender resistance, and also applaud the Vedic sage Vyasa, creator of the epic tale of Mahabharata, for such a memorable character and for raising the plight of all women through her!

Only when we have done the work we need to do, like Goddess Draupadi, can we really enjoy goddess-like contentment. And like Goddess Draupadi, we must move beyond cultural versions of "mandated contentment" into the open fields of truly liberal spirituality . . . to true goddess contentment, even when it requires expressing our discontent for a change.

BUT I ONLY WANTED TO STUDY: MALALA'S STORY

Malala Yousafzai is a beautiful example of someone who became discontent for all the right reasons. Malala, growing up in a far-flung mountain district of Pakistan, was like any other teenager in any part of the world—enjoying music, television, and attending school, where she connected with her girlfriends and learned about the world. Unfortunately, everything changed when Malala was eleven years old. The Taliban, an Islamic extremist group, moved into her village and banned everything Malala and her friends enjoyed, including school! Any rule breakers would be punished, even killed.

This situation was unacceptable to Malala. With the support of her father, who was a teacher at her school, she started expressing her discontent by blogging about it for the BBC's Urdu website. Gradually Malala's words caught the Western media's eye, and she rose in prominence, giving interviews in print and on television. One day, in 2012, while on a bus, she was shot by a Pakistani Taliban member in an assassination attempt to retaliate for her activism; the gunman fled the scene. She woke up ten days later in a hospital in Birmingham, England. After regaining her health and obtaining the opportunity to study in Oxford, Malala was more determined than ever to continue her fight until every girl could go to school. In 2014, she became the youngest co-recipient of the Nobel Peace Prize. Malala is often quoted saying, "I tell my story, not because it is unique, but because it is not. It is the story of many girls."[13]

A GODDESS MEDITATION ON
CONTENTMENT AND DISCONTENTMENT

In truth, any progressive changes that have transpired for women on this planet have emerged from the dharmic discontentment of women who said *no!* That is why to roar like a goddess, I would like you to adopt both dharmas—of contentment and of discontentment—and judiciously activate only that which serves higher values (dharma) and your inner freedom (moksha) as an embodied goddess.

The Vedas say that the breath is inherently connected to thoughts. In fact, they are gross and subtle versions of each other. To cultivate awareness that connects you to inner freedom, simply begin breathing slowly, fully, deeply, mindfully as you read each statement below:

I am content with who I am.
I am content with what I have.
I am content with what I don't have.
I am content with those who are with me
and with those who are not with me.
I am an ancient being; I am an immortal goddess.
I can experience inner contentment without reason.
The houses come and go.
Lovers come and go.
Relationships come and go.
Aspirations come and go.
Wealth and jewels come and go.
I experience pure contentment.
Because my inner nature is of pure contentment,
there is no future aspiration to this contentment,
there is no time requirement for this contentment,
this contentment is emerging right now in me.

I am an ancient being, a true Goddess.
I can separate from situations and people at any time,
to discern when they are not conducive to my or this
planet's best interests.
If I suspect or see malevolent intent,

then I shall allow myself to stop being content.
A raging tempest of divine discontentment arises within me.
Then, I shall become
the blade of the goddess's sword,
the blaze of the goddess's fury,
the might of the goddess's will,
and rest not,
until I burn through the darkness facing me,
and thereby become
truly content again,
truly content again,
truly content again.

A LAKSHMI CONTEMPLATION FOR YOU

I ASK: How does contentment and discontentment
appear in my life? Is it dharmic?

I RECOGNIZE: I'm only truly content when I
deal with dharmic discontent.

I CONNECT: What does contentment feel like in my body?
What's it telling me about discontentment?

I DECIDE: No system, culture, or individual determines
my worth or holds me to false contentment.

I ACT: I choose one situation in which I am discontented
and take steps to resolve it with dharma.

I REMEMBER: Lakshmi's contentment hinges
on discontent for the right reasons.

CHAPTER 11

LAKSHMI SHOWS THE PATH TO GENEROSITY

O Kind and Generous Lakshmi, You are the banisher of poverty, sorrow and fear for all beings.

SHAKRADYA STUTI, VERSE 16

When you, too, adopt and cultivate a generous temperament by becoming a relaxed and joyful giver, sharer, and helper, you are in sync with Lakshmi energy.

Once again, this is not superstition; this is a divine science. The Vedas say, *Yad Bhaavam Tad Bahwati.* This means that you become what you believe. If you believe you are the mistress of infinite resources and it won't hurt you to share bigheartedly, then you will become an infinite mistress of this universe. No goddess is ever pensive, coiled up in worry and fear of scarcity; she is always giving away gifts and sharing from a trust in a spiritual plan. The more you exercise generosity, the more fulfilled you will become.

Since time immemorial, the Vedas have been reminding human beings that we are not merely consumers but benefactors, and that our thoughts and actions influence and shift not only our consciousness, but the entire cosmos.

The Vedas say to recognize and be grateful for the peach tree because the peach tree grows peaches not for itself but for you. The rivers carry water not for themselves but to quench your thirst. The flowers bloom not for themselves but for your senses to feast upon. The cows produce milk not for themselves but for you.

See how the cosmos co-creates an amazing life experience for you, making existence a gift from generous givers. Notice how everything in the universe is a natural "giver," while a human is mostly being a "receiver" or "enjoyer."

Thank everything you notice with your eyes, smell with your nose, hear with your ears, touch with your hands, and taste with your mouth. Perhaps this grateful contemplation will lead you to wonder: *How can I, too, become a giver in the universe? How can I give back in my own unique way? How can I shift from being a mere receiver and enjoyer, to becoming a contributor, giver, helper, and sharer in the cosmos?*

We may be dealing with very real cycles of poverty, but once we start giving back, even something as simple as a smile, and continue expressing cosmic gratitude, our daily choices become naturally aligned with Mother Lakshmi's own temperament of radical generosity.

A WORD OF CAUTION FOR TRUE GODDESSES!

Is your inner Lakshmi going to be happy with your practice of radical generosity if you forget to value yourself? I think not. She lives in you, and she wants you to be happy, comfortable, and valued, too, so she can roar with delight—without exception.

Responsible self-value, self-respect, and self-care is Lakshmi worship of the highest order. Becoming a martyr, giving to a fault, and not valuing your own presence, knowledge, skills, or talents is akin to disrespecting your inner goddess. If you are whimpering and not yet roaring, then it is time to make some changes to your agreements, be they with loved ones, friends, colleagues, or even students.

Sometimes, over-giving can be a sign of codependency. When we are codependent, we lack self-esteem deep down. And we make up for it by giving (to a fault) to receive praise and attention (at any cost) to make up for our missing esteem. But this is ungrounded esteem that does not come from within but from without.

Women worldwide give to a fault. We take subconscious pride in being scapegoats or saints at home and at work because that is what we are indoctrinated to do. Disenfranchised by a millennium of patriarchy, women unconsciously tend to over-explain themselves, over-do, over-care, and over-prove themselves at every step, far more than their male counterparts (and for a lesser wage too).

That same feminine guilt strikes again and again, until our goddess roar becomes drowned out by an avalanche of soothing and reassuring words like: *Of course I can help you (even if it hurts me to do that). You can count on me at any time of the day or night (even if you have not been there for me). I take pride in my duty. This is my job, leave it to me. Trust me, I'm there for you (but am I there for myself?).*

Remember, the opposite of generosity is not grotesque selfishness. I am simply asking that you remain generous, as that is the nature of Lakshmi, but you include yourself in that circle of generosity. Do not leave yourself out. Continue evaluating what is the right amount of giving before resentment takes over or you become a codependent version of yourself, overcompensating and denying your real feelings. Ultimately there is no point to gathering crumbs of outer esteem while your inner esteem plunges.

The Bhagavad Gita teaches ancient lessons on the dharma of giving and describes three types of generosity in action—unconditional, reciprocal, and addictive, which is the worst kind of generosity.[1]

WHAT IS UNCONDITIONAL GENEROSITY?

The Bhagavad Gita answers this question pointedly: "The enlightened or best kind of charity is given from a sense of purpose, responsibility, or duty [toward the cosmos], without expectation of return [unconditional], at the proper time and place, and to a worthy person or cause alone."[2]

While generosity is upheld as a great dharma, there is no recommendation for being generous unconsciously or indiscriminately. This means that true acts of goodness are not borne from guilt, conditioning, or fear, but from a cognition of soul-ability to act generously. Mindfully examining *worthiness, time, and place* curbs impulsiveness and acting out of mere habit, which results in objective discernment.

True charity arises from our thoughtfulness and spiritual consideration of our role in the cosmic scheme of things. We can aspire to act from compassion and greater consciousness and give our time and energy to help another human being in a large-hearted way. But we only do so after checking the worthiness of the person we plan to give to and evaluating the cause we are contributing to. True generosity has the following features:

- Emerges from spiritual insights and thankfulness to goddess (or god, supreme power, universal intelligence)
- Readiness to give freely, without strings attached
- Giver feels fulfilled in the act of giving
- Involves more than just outward behavior—the underlying thoughts, feelings, and motives are generous too
- A genuine giver remains humble before and after the act of giving

Genuine generosity is not merely an outer action. It stems from *attitudes* of compassion and kindness. Because goddess power is always feminine, you will not feel empowered through masculine-oriented ways (of needing to feel superior over another or needing to decry your own mistakes and learning curves), but empowerment will come from feminine Vedic wisdom—by acting from kindness and accommodating others when it is reasonable and respecting their choices and reality too.

THE DHARMA OF ACCOMMODATION (KSHANTI)

Goddesses accommodate as much as reasonably possible in relationships. This does not mean being a docile doormat; it means acting from patience, tolerance, and forbearance toward people—their peculiarities, their life goals, and their learning curves through their life. It also means practicing acceptance toward apparent differences in color, race, religions, political beliefs, sexual and gender orientations, and cultural ideologies. This is the dharma of accommodation, or *kshanti*. Accommodation makes us broadminded and bighearted. It means you won't drive yourself crazy with judgments, frustration, blame, or feeling victimized, nor will you try to change others in order to force an outcome. Rather, you will remain truly generous in your outlook toward all sentient beings.

Accommodation is certainly not a passive attitude. It takes goddess-like courage to tolerate the irritations of life and people with whom you have minor differences in opinion. And if you need to bring about a change, you will do so with a generous amount of patience, with care.

While Goddess Durga teaches that we must exercise judgment and sometimes not accommodate boundary trespassers for the sake of dharma. Lakshmi teaches us to generously accommodate our own learning curves and mistakes to continue growing and to stop being nasty to ourselves.

Ultimately, we accommodate from an inherent sence of generosity because *being human* makes us all equally vulnerable; we are all still finding ourselves. Each time you accommodate versus react; practice patience versus push, pull, and force outcomes; or tolerate some discomfort versus denounce and pronounce dire verdicts quickly, you experience goddess tranquility through recognition of your spiritual core, which is unconditionally generous and thereby accommodating.

THE DHARMA OF KINDNESS (DAYA)

Kindness comes from recognizing the goddess-like Self in each other and acknowledging that everyone is suffering because we have forgotten our inner goddess. The least we can do is act kindly toward ourselves and each other, demonstrating sensitivity, empathy, and friendliness.

Kind people exhibit care, concern, and consideration for others' suffering. Therefore, sensitivity of the heart is another generous quality we aim to cultivate.

Durga says we must exhibit kindness to worthy, dharmic beings. Toward the non-dharmic beings, our kindness transforms into teaching—or calls them out. Lakshmi's kindness blossoms as the lotus of self-love and self-care extending outward as generous affection and heartfelt concern for all sentient beings. She asks us to act with extreme kindness toward ourselves, until our every act of genuine kindness is a prayer. Our kindness ripples out to everyone we touch, helping others lead fruitful and positive lives in peace and harmony with all other beings.

It is possible to exist like a peaceful flower that generously spreads her fragrance of kindness and compassion everywhere. With kind thoughts, you become self-healing, self-soothing, and self-uplifting, and through the agency of your own kindness-filled heart, you become a boon for everyone on the planet.

The Vedas not only encourage embodying generous attitudes of accommodation and kindnesss but also suggest five ways you can act generously and put the dharma of accommodation and kindness into action.

1. Act Conscientiously Toward Mother Nature

To connect with your inner goddess deep down, recognize Divine Mother in her manifestation as Mother Nature. Rivers, mountains, trees, and even rocks are worshipped as manifestations of Lakshmi. Deliberately, leave no stone unturned to act generously toward Mother Nature in whatever way you can, like planting tree saplings or picking up the litter of fellow humans.

2. Act Kindly Toward Parents

Your parents gifted you your body. If you have a relationship with your parents, thank them. Act generously toward them; go out of your way to be there for them, especially as they age. And even if they were not perfect parents, let your inner goddess find the inner strength to accommodate their minor faults, forgive them, and act kindly. And if they were veritable monsters, understand that not everyone obtains the knowledge to rise beyond their unconscious asura nature! You need not condone their actions, but by understanding them, you let your inner goddess shine from thoughts of generosity.

3. Act Bigheartedly Toward the Less Privileged

Generosity, kindness, charity, and going out of our way to honor and help distressed human beings are essential aspects of living like a goddess. Can you extend a helping hand to those less privileged than you? Generous and compassionate thoughts are door openers to the portal of conscious goddess existence. Whenever we go beyond our egoic self-absorption and offer a sincere helping hand to those truly in need, our mind becomes filled with the light of our inner Lakshmi!

4. Act Appreciatively Toward Divine Forces

To connect your ego to a greater divine existence, offer gratitude to the all-pervading, omnipresent, supreme Divine Feminine power. Grateful practices, like meditation, mantra chanting, placing a flower on your altar, lighting a lamp or a candle, or even simply acknowledging the fact that goddess dwells everywhere and in your heart are ways to connect with the goddess via grateful thoughts. This keeps the human ego beautifully connected to its divine and deeply generous source, Divine Mother!

5. Act Gratefully Toward the Teachers in Your Life

The Vedas instruct us to experience humbleness and gratefulness toward the teachers of sacred wisdom and to offer selfless service (known as *seva*). After all, these great teachers introduce us to our goddess potential and show us the way to lead lives worthy of a living goddess. We should serve them generously because without their presence in our life and their honest preservation and transmission of timeless wisdom, we would not have the knowledge that introduces us to our divine potential.

WATCH OUT FOR RECIPROCAL GENEROSITY

True generosity is never a business deal. It does not come with strings attached. True generosity is a sacred act, and it emerges from a sacred attitude of true compassion and care. But reciprocal generosity is more like a business deal. And like any business deal, problems occur if the contractual agreements are not spelled out and room is left for ambiguity.

Reciprocal generosity is connected to ego, as explained in the Bhagavad Gita: "Charity performed with the expectation of some return, or with a desire for fruitive results, or in a grudging mood is said to be charity driven by the ego, for egoic satisfaction and gains. This is lower than the charity offered with selfless motives."[3]

Reciprocity-based generosity is typically the guiding principle behind fundraisers, political campaigns, giving to worthy causes, and even agreements between friends. When terms are laid out transparently, then it is neither robbery not manipulation; it is simply a fair exchange, done with an explicitly stated expectation of return, such as:

If I buy you lunch today, you've got to buy me lunch next time.
If you give me a ride today, I'll drive you in future.
If you vote for me today, I'll advance your cause.
If you smile at my jokes, I will laugh at yours.
If you donate to my causes, I will wine and dine you.

In many ways, our world is dominated by a system of reciprocity, or conditioned generosity, more than pure heartfelt generosity without expectation of return. Reciprocal generosity has the following features:

- It is directed to those from whom we expect something in return in the near future, not toward the truly needy.

- There is a secret desire for a return and frustration when our generosity is not matched in some way.

- There is a wanting to be appreciated, in person or in public, and an angry or resentful feeling when generosity is not acknowledged.

The downside of this kind of generosity is that if the terms of reciprocity are not met, then sooner or later, the giver feels misgivings toward the receiver, somehow cheated of what they gave "willingly," or robbed, resentful, or persecuted. Take the example of volunteers who generously offer their skills and time for a cause. The ones who believe in the worthy cause give from their heart and feel fulfilled in the act of giving itself. These people are acting from optimum generosity. But the ones who have a private desire for reciprocity—such as public recognition, maybe a plaque, social benefits, a photo with the president of the organization, or time socializing with the people higher up in the organization—feel miffed. Though they had signed up voluntarily to donate money, time, or skills and were quite enthusiastic in the beginning, they feel "taken advantage of" or "abused" as time passes and their needs for reciprocity are not met. They contribute less and less and complain more and more.

This is why the terms of reciprocal generosity should be spelled out each time, both by the giver and the receiver. If you are on the receiving end of this sort of generosity, watch out. Remember, the expectation of reciprocity may be hidden, even if it is not vocalized. At the least, show your appreciation for the generosity that is directed toward you. Let the person know what their generosity meant to you. Say it out loud. Mean it.

Sometimes, reciprocal generosity can be used for ulterior purposes, especially when it is almost imposed upon you. I have met women who were presented with unrequested acts of generosity by a lover, boss, colleague, or even a good friend and later beleaguered for it. For example, at work, they received unexpected gifts, support, or even an out-of-turn promotion and salary increase, only to discover later that they were now expected to give sex or some other benefit in return. The generosity was not unconditional; it came with invisible strings attached.

In such cases, generosity is not dharmic. It is a coercive generosity exacting returns, even resorting to violence at times. It becomes a tool in the hands of asuras to first oblige and then exploit the unsuspecting devas!

Goddesses go beyond blaming the bad guys who take advantage of women. We must increase our *net wisdom* from which we operate in life so we can see through genuine and non-genuine kindheartedness and make better decisions.

WHAT IS THE WORST KIND OF GENEROSITY?

Real giving is done from a place of true generosity, when we have an excess of something to offer and we feel it is our cosmic responsibility to show gratitude by giving or helping where and how we can. Reciprocal generosity is also passable if the terms and conditions of giving and receiving and the expectations on either side are clearly spelled out. The worst kind of generosity is more like a drug to feel good about ourselves. "The worst kind of charity is one given with contempt, to unworthy person(s), at a wrong place and time," explains the Bhagavad Gita.[4] We become addicted to giving, to seeing ourselves as noble, smart, wise, capable, ultimately generous and selfless people.

This kind of giving is most non-goddess-like. Its impulse arises from societal conditioning, such as, *All good women behave from a charitable disposition. They are always kind and compassionate to a fault. A true woman forgives readily and loves unconditionally. She extends herself beyond capacity. She is a super mother, a dedicated wife, and a wonderful hostess.*

Essentially, the same old *feminine guilt* has done a number on female psyches. It forces women to over-give; they think they "should," "ought to," or "must" give even while they resent (hold in contempt) the very person they are giving to! This giving is compulsive and does not involve any joy or abundance for the giver.

Thanks to the insidious snake of conditioning in patriarchal societies, often women try to outdo each other in demonstrating their generous nature, to redeem themselves and be recognized as better than the rest, or as "rescuers" and "caretakers," even at the cost of going against their own inner voice and crossing their own goddess boundaries. Such compulsive generosity conceals guilt, feelings of inferiority, and the wish to infantilize or control the other with our (unasked for) gifts.

In the twenty-first century, even in most advanced nations, many women overwhelmingly suffer from the disease of compulsive and relentless generosity, persistently giving away themselves—their time, money, sexual attention, care, affection, love, nurturance, and unique feminine talents—and always putting themselves and their needs last. This is the reason why such giving and generous yet self-depleted women get taken advantage of repeatedly, and overwhelmingly suffer from lower self-esteem than the men in their lives. They settle for lesser wages than their male colleagues, put up with inequality in intimate relationships, and internally allow underlying rage to take a toll on their health and well-being. Sadly, this is all learned behavior due to a misinterpretation of what it means to be "generous."

For example, according to the Vedas, while charity toward a teacher who is guiding us toward our greater truth of Self is a worthy enough reason to be generous with our volunteered hours, skills, or donations, continuing to support an abusive teacher (who is no longer worthy of being called a Guru) is not a wise use of our charitable nature. Where is the cognitive discrimination? Similarly, supporting our life partner who is currently without a job is a noble act of generosity, undoubtedly. But to continue to support a fiscally irresponsible partner is anything but noble.

In the same vein, when we ourselves need help or are feeling depleted and fragile, it may not be the right *time* to give. But, it may be the right time to ask for help. After all, even givers need to take care of themselves and be helped. Although giving to others can refill us spiritually, it is important to remember that there is a limit to our emotional and material resources.

We can all learn from Lakshmi's myth and her decision to never be a "tossed garland." This simple story teaches us where to relax a boundary (to give without restraint) and where to enforce a boundary (to withdraw giving without guilty explanations). If we don't employ discernment in matters of generosity, our kindness, niceness, and spirit of accommodation make us pushovers. Not knowing the difference between selfishness and self-love is a prime cause of disrespect, exhaustion, and misery. And self-love should include the goddess-like ability to say *no more*, asserting boundaries and honoring our needs and limits.

Naturally, our goddess generosity and how it plays out cannot be cast in stone. I like being able to at least discuss options and possibilities, versus scripted behavior. Question yourself every single time: Is generosity appropriate in this circumstance or not? How should my inner Lakshmi act?

THE PHENOMENON OF THE TOPPLING GODDESSES

Nowhere is the phenomenon of misplaced generosity more evident than in India itself, the country where Lakshmi's generous archetype first originated. In India, daughters-in-law are ubiquitously called Lakshmi, crowned the reigning goddess of the family. It sounds very charming at first, and newly married women even now beam with pride when they are extolled with honorifics by their in-laws. Except this title is often little more than hogwash, camouflaging an underlying exploitative patriarchal setup.

The "Lakshmi of the house" sobriquet unleashes all kinds of unspoken expectations upon the new bride. It is a decoy to seduce women into an unconditional attitude of round-the-clock giving. And she must give these gifts—be it domestic labor, sex on demand, or birthing grandchildren for the in-laws—with a smile on her face, or else she is no goddess! After all, isn't Lakshmi the ever serene and cheerful giver of gifts?

However, this is not respectful recognition, nor the official position of the Vedas. Recognizing how to be truly generous and being equally self-nurturing was the original Vedic way, not running out of fuel while serving a patriarchic agenda. Here are a few examples of what the ancient Vedic texts had to say about married women:

> When a woman marries, she enters "as a river enters the sea" and "to rule there along with her husband, as an Empress, over the other members of the family."[5]

> No man, even in anger, should ever do anything that is disagreeable to his wife; for happiness, joy, virtue, and everything depend on the wife. Wife is the sacred soil in which the husband is born again, even the sages cannot create men without women.[6]

To my great shock, I found "toppled goddesses" in Western culture too. The authors of a 2021 article titled "23 Ways Women Still Aren't Equal to Men" provide the evidence that women are still shouldering more of the household burden than their male partners; at a greater risk of rape and domestic violence; more likely than men to live below the poverty line; and not being given the same opportunities at work nor equal wages for the same job.[7] Women are also far more likely to be victims of human trafficking. In the arenas of policymaking and government and state institutions (including the armed forces), women and women's issues continue to remain grossly underrepresented. And in the cultural domain, women's sexuality still remains suspect and susceptible to being mocked as either overly sexual (deemed too slutty) or not sexy enough (earning the labels of prude, hag, or killjoy).

Charlotte Higgins, chief cultural writer for the *Guardian*, opined the following in a 2018 article entitled "The Age of Patriarchy: How an Unfashionable Idea Became a Rallying Cry for Feminism Today":

> *In this moment, the concept of "patriarchy" has offered itself as the invisible mechanism that connects a host of seemingly isolated and disparate events, intertwining the experience of women of vastly different backgrounds, race, and culture, and ranging in force from the trivial and personal to the serious and geopolitical. For it allows us to ask, according to the philosopher Amia Srinivasan, "whether there is something in common between the Weinstein affair, the election of Trump, the plight of women garment workers in Asia and women farm workers in North America, and the Indian rape epidemic. It allows people to ask whether some machine is at work that connects all the experiences they're having with all the experiences others are having." The return of "patriarchy" raises the question: Does the naming and understanding of this invisible mechanism offer the key to its destruction?[8]*

Therefore, when we are trying to emulate Goddess Lakshmi's behavior of generosity, a strategic consideration of how much generosity is appropriate—and what kind—is in order within a culture of institutionalized patriarchy. We women must not continue to slumber in any area of life if we truly want to roar like a goddess!

~~~~~

A LAKSHMI CONTEMPLATION FOR YOU

I ASK: Is my giving unconditional, or is it reciprocal or addictive?

I RECOGNIZE: Generosity includes kindness toward myself too.

I CONNECT: With my arms held wide, I receive gifts
from this generous universe and, like Lakshmi, I
radiate generosity back toward this universe.

I DECIDE: I will never act from generosity that is addictive,
depleting, conditioned, compulsive, or mindless.

I ACT: Where I give too much or too little, I take steps to find balance.

I REMEMBER: Patriarchy weakens generosity by fuzzing my
boundaries. Lakshmi roars to remind me of my inherent
capacity to "give" by being willing to "receive" too!

PART III

—

SARASWATI

CHAPTER 12

SARASWATI'S MYTHOLOGY AND AWAKENING INSIGHTS

Those who meditate upon you who O Goddess
who is Supreme Knowledge incarnate,
they attain liberation from worldly sorrow
and spiritual self-ignorance.

SHAKRADYA STUTI, VERSE 9

While Durga represents the raw power of Self and Lakshmi represents fullness of Self, the Saraswati archetype represents sacred wisdom—the knowledge and the realization of the goddess-like Self within.

When Durga accomplishes what she sets out to accomplish, which is to annihilate the forces of darkness in your mind, she becomes Lakshmi and rewards you with expansive prosperity. Now knowledge dawns—and not just ordinary knowledge—in this final stage of inner growth and fulfillment. Knowledge of the Self, *the Inner Goddess*, will dawn along with the realization that there is no manifestation of goddess apart from the Self. As moonlight is not different from the moon, the Self is no different from the Goddess. They are one and the same. To aid you in this final step to reclaim your true Self and the lasting peace that comes with this recognition, Durga who is Lakshmi, becomes Goddess Saraswati.

The literal meaning of Saraswati is "the essence of the Self" as *saara* means "essence" and *swa* means "Self" in Sanskrit. She is the divine muse, and her blessings include spontaneous emergence of freeing knowledge, feminine intuition, artistic inspiration, music, and spiritual insights. She symbolizes Shakti's qualities of knowledge, purity, and virtue. Saraswati is the patroness of the arts, being a celestial poetess, musician, and skillful composer. When we meditate upon Saraswati, she mysteriously transmits divine light toward us.

When the goddess roars from ferocity, she is Durga. When she roars from pleasure, she is Lakshmi. And when she roars serenely, almost melodiously from the sheer sweet recognition of her own, ever-radiant truth of divine creativity within, she is Saraswati. And Saraswati, whose roar is more like a self-celebratory song, dresses in white flowing drapes with white fragrant flowers adorning her hair and her body, which is luminous like the full moon. She is often depicted in art as playing a lute and riding a white swan or a gorgeous white peacock in the vast, expansive blue skies with calm white clouds floating by. Simply gazing at her deity arouses clarity, peace, and joy within our hearts. She's the Goddess of Knowledge or Higher Wisdom, and Bestower of Peace because knowledge of Self is the final gateway to abiding peace.

Goddess Saraswati is hailed as the *Mother of the Vedas*. In association with her divine partner God Brahma, she is believed to have given the four Vedas to humankind; as one of the hymns dedicated to her says: "Salutations to Goddess of knowledge Saraswati, who is known by Vedas and is the light of the Vedas."[1]

Like Durga and Lakshmi, Saraswati is a popular goddess. She is beloved across southeast Asia, where Hinduism and Buddhism, the two religions that both venerate Saraswati, thrived in ancient times.[2] She is everyone's goddess, adults and children alike. She is beloved to householders, scholars, and students (and their teachers and parents alike), and of course spiritual seekers adore her because she bestows that rare wisdom, both secular and spiritual, that leads to happy, fulfilled, and above all, spiritually sovereign lives. She purifies our speech and enhances our perceptive, cognitive, and imaginative faculties. No wonder her image frequently appears in textbooks; adorns walls in libraries, schools, and classrooms; and is even inscribed on writing paraphernalia in India. I remember chanting this mantra to her every morning before commencing with studies for the day:

Salutations to Devi Saraswati, who is
the giver of boons and fulfiller of wishes. Goddess, when
I begin my studies, please bestow on me the capacity
of right understanding, always.

I would chant this mantra at home before starting on my homework. I prayed to her while walking to school when I had not prepared enough for an exam and, miraculously, it seemed she would open up my higher mind to ensure I got a good grade! I felt like Mother Saraswati was my invisible friend through the trials of academic life. I knew my good grades were a result of my hard work plus something extra—the wisdom that emerges from emulating Goddess Saraswati's archetype, which helped me cultivate clarity of mind so I could focus and bring my best self forward.

Awakening Saraswati within your heart is a blessing. Her wisdom shall reveal to you (as she did to me) your real status, worthy of self-reverence and full of life's boundless potential to self-heal, self-actualize, and self-realize. She shall lead you to the Ultimate Truth: you are a goddess inside you, no matter what!

As you connect with her archetype, your limiting beliefs that estrange you from your inner goddess shall become exposed and loosen their grip on you. She drives away anxiety, worry, and gloom as your mind is illumined with her divine light. When Saraswati is present, no possible illusion about who you are can exist. Truth alone is present—bare-bones perfection in imperfection, light in darkness. Saraswati's emergence in our heart spells auspicious tidings: a wealth of cheerfulness, radiant emotional disposition, inner contentment, and a sense of peace with what we possess and even with what we don't possess. We feel joyous as a peacock and serene like a swan floating in water.

SARASWATI'S ICONOGRAPHY AND SYMBOLISM

As you know by now, the Vedas are full of symbolism, and symbols have their own language, communicating ideas in nonverbal ways.

Goddess Durga is often depicted dressed in red and other vivid colors to indicate her valorous mind, raw power, and courage. Lakshmi dresses in green silks, symbolizing nature's fertility, and saffron-gold, symbolizing spiritual fullness and contentment. Saraswati is dressed in all white. In almost every culture, white is regarded as the color of purity, non-attachment, and inner serenity (versus passion). She wears white because she represents a way of life that transcends the cravings of the flesh and rejoices in the sovereignty of Self. She embodies wisdom and all that is pure and sublime.

Saraswati's seat is a giant, white lotus. She also holds a white lotus in her hands. The lotus blooms in muddy, stagnant water, representing the spiritual ability to use one's powers of discernment and detachment to rise above our senses that have become filthy (muddy) with attachment, greed, clinginess, and obsessions. While still being in the world where our senses hold us down, like the lotus we can try to reach the sun (light) and rise far beyond our material bondage. Therefore, her lotus represents the invitation to rise to the final journey to realize our inner Goddess.

Saraswati's deity displays four graceful hands, each representing a unique dimension of the human intelligence: mind, intellect, memory, and ego. In her four hands, Saraswati holds a palm-leaf book, a rosary, a pot of water, and a lute. The palm-leaf manuscript represents the ancient scrolls of the Vedas. The rosary symbolizes mindfulness. The pot of holy water signifies purification. At other times, rather than holding the aforementioned sacred objects, she is shown raising one of her hands in the "giving gesture," while in the other she holds a white lotus flower, representing her power to grant liberation.

You may appreciate another popular hymn to Saraswati that I grew up chanting—and sometimes, even dancing to its tune:

> May Saraswati, whose complexion is fair like the
> jasmine-colored moon,
> who wears a garland of pure white flowers, too, that look
> like frosted dew drops;
> who is adorned in radiant white attire,
> on whose beautiful arm rests the veena [a lute],

and who sits on her throne which is a white lotus;
who is surrounded with and adored by Brahma, Vishnu,
and Shiva,
May she bless me too;
May she help me overcome my physical lethargy, mental
sluggishness, and spiritual ignorance.

SARASWATI AS LORD BRAHMA'S CONSORT

As per Hindu lore narrated in the Puranas, when God Brahma was creating the universe, he started meditating. A beautiful celestial feminine presence emerged from this field of cosmic awareness.

Brahma, the creator, asked, "Who are you, O radiant one?"

"I am Shakti, the power, awareness, and intelligence inherent in your mind. I can help you in your creative manifestations," responded the Divine Feminine presence.

Brahma responded: "May I call you Saraswati then, because you are a continuously flowing, expressing, creating awareness?" Brahma continued, "You will stay on the tip of every sentient being's tongue as speech, through which they will express this awareness. Your second form will be that of a mighty life-giving river. For your third form, I invite you to join me as my ongoing inspired co-creator in the co-creation of this universe."

Saraswati agreed. They gladly divided duties. Brahma would create, and Saraswati would fill this creation with awareness, order, and intelligence. Brahma's creating would populate the creation with all kinds of creatures, and Saraswati would impart these creatures with intelligence and speech—and in the more self-aware ones, wisdom.

Before Saraswati engaged with the creation, a great confusion existed in the universe because everything emerged spontaneously in Brahma's dream. For instance, all the celestial bodies, including the sun, the moon, the stars, and other planetary systems, were chaotically emerging together. But once Saraswati joined Brahma, she brought order along with her wisdom. Thanks to her, the oceans became contained, the seasons started changing rhythmically, and we humans began asking ourselves deeper questions like, *Who am I, and what is my relationship to the divine?* No wonder the Vedas describe Saraswati as "the awakener of our intellect who shines as the embodiment of universal awareness and wisdom."[3]

In the beginning, the entire creation was awe-inspiring. Beautiful and pristine, but soundless. It was Saraswati who enabled the faculty of higher thinking as well as speech in all living creatures. Suddenly the whole world was full of chirping sounds and buzzing sounds and laughing sounds and mating sounds. Ecstatic Brahma now hailed Saraswati as *the goddess of speech*.

Brahma said to Saraswati: "I couldn't have done this without you, O embodiment of Great Shakti. You are my co-creator indeed, the compassionate mother of this universe, and all its creatures big and small are your children. Only due to you, all thinking, feeling, imagining, and desiring hearts enjoy the urge and faculty to express themselves through speech, writing, and artistic impulses, your divine gifts, no less."

Saraswati, the consort of Brahma, is often painted as his wife in mythology.[4] She is very much Brahma's equal and respected associate, representing the highest forms of creative awareness, intelligence, consciousness, and embodiment of the knowledge that supports the creative acts of gods and humans. Saraswati *and* Brahma are essential for co-creation because to create anything requires both a creative will (Brahma) and creative intelligence (Saraswati). That is why they always coexist. This being said, Brahma and Saraswati are not considered a couple in the romantic sense. Theirs is more of an intellectual partnership that can best be described as a conceptual marriage; metaphysically speaking, Brahma represents the cosmic ego, and Saraswati the cosmic consciousness that dwells near the ego and is yet never limited by the ego.

SARASWATI AS A RIVER IN THE VEDAS

In the *Rig Veda*, a "River Saraswati" is revered as the "best of mothers" and the "best of rivers." Historians are fairly confident that at one time, a river called Saraswati flowed in the northwest part of India, and it is here that the early Vedic civilization thrived. As the *Goddess of Water*, her wrath manifested as floods and torrential rains, and her blessing was the fertile land. It was said that the river is Shakti incarnate. Her true abode is heaven—and yet, from sheer compassion for living creatures, she has come to stay amidst us, manifested in physical form as the river of plentitude and protection.

Water, an abstract element connected with Saraswati, can play two roles in your spiritual life. When you are not conscious, it can make you overly emotional and attached (to your detriment). With consciousness, water can act like an inner purifier, generate creative flow, strengthen your ability to endure, and enhance love and care for your own self. You will also gently let go of what is not serving you; it flows away, cleansing you of your attachments and addictions, like pure water would clean up something muddy and dowdy and make it glisten with freshness.

Saraswati's physical form as a great river satisfies physical thirst. But formless Saraswati, as the river of cosmic consciousness, quenches our spiritual thirst! As the goddess of speech, she is entreated for a flow of inspired words by the Vedic sages, like these: "O best Mother, best River, best Goddess, Saraswati, as soon as we are without [the power of] words, O Mother, create for us the right words."⁵ That is why in art, her clothes are always depicted as flowing. When you are ready to venture deeper and beyond form, you will find the Saraswati "flow" of creativity within your own mind.

In humankind, Saraswati represents the *flow of feminine creativity*. She gives us the confidence to accomplish great things in the material world with our creative intellect and inspired imagination. She bestows energy to do all our actions with great heart and beauty. In fact, Saraswati can be considered the cosmic source of all forms of creativity—the root of secular and sacred knowledge, literature, painting, drawing, music, sculpture, and theater. Her blessings include spontaneous emergence of wisdom, intuition, purity, excellence of expression, refinement in communication, artistic expression, higher insights, truth, and inner light. This is how great music, art, science, or philosophical ideals are born. That's why she is a favorite goddess for all artists, musicians, authors, and teachers. (From this perspective, I want to share that I truly feel Goddess Saraswati is writing this book through me for you!)

A SARASWATI CONTEMPLATION FOR YOU

I ASK: What thoughts come up as I read about
Saraswati and all she signifies?

I RECOGNIZE: The goddess and Self are one and the same.

I CONNECT: Sitting in meditation, I contemplate
the mud and the lotus.

I DECIDE: Like the lotus, I rise to the light.

I ACT: I open my mind and heart to Saraswati wisdom:
pure, authentic, discerning, creative.

I REMEMBER: Knowledge of Self is the gateway to lasting peace.

CHAPTER 13

THE GODDESS PATH OF DISCERNMENT AND SOVEREIGNTY

O Saraswati who resides in the whole universe as its Mother,
you who resides within me in the form of Higher knowledge;
Destroy this darkness and ignorance that exists within me.

VISHVAMBHARI STUTI, VERSE 1

Durga rides her lion to victory, and Lakshmi sits in abundant pleasure on her owl of dharma. Goddess Saraswati enjoys two divine animals: the swan and the peacock. The swan, known as *hamsa*, is representative of the true Self. One who realizes the *inner hamsa* shines because veils are lifted and doubts are destroyed, revealing calmness, clarity, and above all, psychological wholeness.

Then there is the peacock, which is a gentle bird, known for its beauty, elegance, poise, and dancing skills. The peacock dances with joy to its inner music. It suggests that you can seek the help of Saraswati if you, too, want to dance to your inner music, and especially if you are pursuing higher education, fine arts, esthetics, dance, music, theater, or craft.

When I examine Saraswati's swan with deeper eyes, I grasp a subtle teaching, that of spiritual discernment. The swan is believed to be able to separate milk from water. In the Vedas, the swan represents the power of *subtle discernment* between good and bad, true and false, real and unreal. This is symbolic of the informed intellect capable of "knowing better" and separating the real from the unreal, or truth from untruth. All women have a powerful discernment ability, despite our intellect being historically suspect or mocked, and we must use it!

We must become swans ourselves and question default beliefs and conditioning. We must look objectively for the underlying truth to give ourselves permission to listen to it, especially when it goes against the status quo.

HOW TO PRACTICE DISCERNMENT

Essentially, discernment is the willingness to step back and evaluate a situation with dispassionate eyes, a conscious act of examining the contents of your own mind. It is not ordinary thinking, like when we casually think about things while listening to music in the background or while we chop vegetables. This is the kind of examination we do by focusing on a single issue and combing through our own beliefs, especially the ones that make us shame, doubt, and under-value ourselves and others of our gender. Discernment can teach you how to hone your thinking, eliminate distracting thoughts, and go deeper to see the real picture (not just see what you have been conditioned to see)! You can ask yourself:

> *What do I understand?*
> *What don't I understand?*
> *What do I need to know?*
> *What do I need to inquire?*
> *What do I see behind what is simply meeting the eye?*
> *What do I hear, really?*
> *What do I feel below and beyond the numbing*
> *   or quick default reactions?*
> *What do I think now that I have sat with*
> *   the situation some more?*

If all women were to become simultaneously discerning, we would see through the institutionalized *dumbing down* of women over centuries. We would listen to our inner whisper, sit with it, and clear away the ignorance and blind-sightedness until knowledge starts to emerge from the deepest recesses of our goddess-like selves. We would dismiss our wrong expectations, our false identifications, and self-diminishing agreements. And what remains would be the gleaming truth of who we women *really* are!

Discernment, known as *viveka* in the Vedas, is a sacred cognitive practice, a powerful self-discipline to not just become women with beautiful or sexy bodies and warm hearts, but women with exemplary, shining intellect.

A modern goddess shares what discernment means to her.

> *Discernment helps me to take a step back, take time to notice my feelings and the situation in its bigger picture, and then it helps me to choose the appropriate response. I can recognize that no matter what others assess about me, that is not who I really am. Lack of respect from others or lack of recognition from others is not something I truly need to address, since I am complete from within and loved unconditionally again from within, always. Thanks to discernment, I can step back into my greater reality, and return into the grace inside me, and remind myself all that I truly am.*

Discernment includes asking yourself if certain feelings, attitudes, and ideas are worthy of your inner goddess's time, energy, and dignity. Your inner goddess may prompt you to leave the room versus confronting the person! Maybe your inner goddess shows you how being healthy is more important than being skinny at any cost. Maybe your inner goddess will guide you along a path to truth that has fewer followers but feels wholesome. Consistently ask yourself: *What is real, and what may be merely the projection of others that I have internalized?* Hold the intention to release everything that is distorting an accurate perception of your own capacities, worth, and truth. Whenever you feel or act defensively or offensively, simply stop. Take the time to discern your real position, in this moment, and act accordingly. The key is to avoid being either reactive or gullible and to be more grounded in reality.

You won't dismiss yourself. You won't scold yourself to "reel it in" just because others are uncomfortable with your power. You'll catch yourself when you feel yourself becoming unnecessarily apologetic. This is especially important for women today because in a climate of patriarchy, where industry, education, media, and most religions (or their mostly male keepers—scholars, pundits, priests, and clergy) are upholding a version of women that is vastly different from our own reality. This incongruence must be examined by us, otherwise our beliefs and our inner knowingness about our own self becomes delegitimized. Saraswati's beautiful peacock eats snakes. This symbolically means you can strive to transcend the snakes of internalized misogyny too. We let others make decisions for us and even allow them to tell us when we are happy and when we are sad—without letting ourselves feel our own emotions.

While Saraswati is celebrated as the ultimate sovereign goddess in the Vedas, patriarchy-stained legends involving Saraswati and her partner emerge in post-Vedic Purana texts, wherein Goddess Saraswati has to face patriarchy herself. Fortunately, she uses her power with discernment before she acts with conviction.

In one such story from the Puranas, Brahma organized a sacred fire ritual. In India, it is traditional for the wife to always be by her husband's side in such rituals. In fact, the wife carries such importance that the husband cannot qualify for the ritual without her.

But Saraswati is no ordinary spouse. She never forgets who she is! While her loyalty, her heart full of divine love and service to all sentient beings, and even her support for her partner's creative projects are never in question, her free spirit and her time are her own. She does not blindly put her partner's needs above hers. So, on the day of the fire ritual, she was off doing her thing, and therefore, was running late. Brahma grew restless waiting for her.

Indra, the king of devas, an invited guest to the grand ritual, offered unsolicited advice to Brahma. He suggested approaching Goddess Gayatri (another invited guest) to stand in for Saraswati in the ritual, since she, too, is the embodiment of Shakti. After all, the goddesses are really all ONE—surely Saraswati wouldn't mind, reasoned Indra.[1]

But Saraswati, who arrived in the nick of time, did mind. She was not at all pleased with the power dynamics going on behind her back and Brahma's enthusiastic acceptance of Indra's ill-considered advice. She was not jealous of Goddess Gayatri, as some patriarchic versions of this myth propagate, happily pitting one goddess against another. But I dismiss those sexist versions that perpetuate the idea that womanhood is an ongoing competition rather than collaboration, where women are also often described as "catty" toward each other, forever vying for male validation. Gayatri, who is a great goddess in her own right, had nothing to do with what transpired. Saraswati, being the ultimate intelligence of this universe, could easily discern the real perpetrator.

Because she was Saraswati, the ever-flowing one, instead of jealousy, she experienced compassion for both Goddess Gayatri and herself. Instead of sadness, she felt rightfully angered. And instead of feeling invisible and fearful that *she was not enough and she didn't matter*, Saraswati felt extra visible and valuable to herself in that moment, full of inner enoughness. It is this radical self-worth, borne of self-knowledge and self-awareness, that guided her next set of actions.

Ultimately, Saraswati was upset with Brahma for making socially dictated expectations more important than her. Brahma had let her down by reducing her to the status of an object, replaceable by any other body with a feminine body. Brahma's role in this mythological tale represents how men can be generally conscious, even honoring the women in their life, and yet behave in inconsistent and disappointing ways due to the entitlement present in a male-centric society. Women, when faced with prejudice, are often socialized to smile it away or look away. But Saraswati discerned it was time to leave this party, but not before setting an example for us. Saraswati, who mostly remains peacefully self-absorbed, spoke up firmly, and chose to publicly censure Brahma.

Saraswati said: "Going forth, no one shall worship you, O Brahma, because you set a poor example for males in how they treat their female partners as objects."

Brahma was the creator—he could have created another reality where Saraswati did show up on time, but he did not. He was a godly being, after all, and this was divine play, an agreement no less between Divine Masculine and Divine Feminine, to teach all human men and women dharma. So, he gracefully accepted his part in this story, but still, the die was cast!

When Saraswati speaks, it becomes so.

From then onward, the legend goes, Saraswati neither played a dutiful wife to her cosmic partner, nor bore him children, nor kept his house! Instead, she roams the universe as a self-possessed goddess, shining the light in each wisdom-seeker's heart, provided it is sincere. Saraswati's unwillingness to live as a "dutiful wife" shows the nature of the dynamic relationship between creator and creation: awareness has no boundaries, nor containers; it never stands still for ego's sake, but forever morphs, changes, and tests, furthering the limits of our imagination. Yes, Saraswati remained married, but because this was an atypical marriage or association to begin with, it was more a relationship emerging from the ties between a creator and creativity. Saraswati became even more detached from Brahma and became her own independent deity, rarely worshipped alongside her partner.

To me, their marriage represents the first *contractual marriage* in mythology—a marriage that is based on agreements, not romantic love. It also represents to me a marriage of convenience where the female partner calls the shots for a change, and chooses to remain in it for a select purpose—in this case, the co-creation of a greater reality that was beyond their roles as husband and wife. Saraswati and Brahma worked together as cosmic partners, while their pairing failed as intimate partners—yet Saraswati chose to hold on to what worked and made insignificant what did not!

In my eyes, Saraswati responded to patriarchal maneuvering in a manner befitting a goddess. She neither became reduced to a weeping, lamenting, spurned wife who felt powerless and hopeless in a male world, nor did she turn into a mean and nasty cosmic vamp, plotting to avenge her humiliation in more and more cruel ways. She really shines like a goddess—because she never forgets who she is—walking away in cool detachment from an unfulfilling personal relationship to lead the life befitting a goddess on the world stage! She had other more important matters to attend to, such as awakening ready souls like you and me. She knows her priorities. Yes, she expressed her annoyance. She said her piece. And then she left the scene. And never again do we hear of *Saraswati the wife*, nagging Brahma while participating in birthdays or anniversary celebrations in mythological heaven—she had emotionally detached, for good.

Here are ten goddess teachings on discernment that I glean from this legend:

1. Saraswati discerned: *It is not me!* Typically, if women become upset, they are told they are being overly emotional, hormonal, hysterical, or crazy. Saraswati did not buckle under self-doubt, self-hatred, guilt, or shame because she trusted her own feelings.

2. Saraswati discerned: Saraswati understood what would enable her flow and what would obstruct it. When you are aware of who you are, you have a much clearer idea of what you need to say yes and no to and what people, situations, actions, and outcomes best support you in being you and what do not. An intimate relationship that opens you to disrespect, even once, must undergo changes, and new understandings must be reached.

3. Saraswati discerned: Saraswati resisted from higher consciousness and dharma, not simply to pick a fight. It's important to recognize when our rebellious self is acting out in a way that's not in our best interest, when it might be harmful to those around us, and when it is imperative to resist the bait of another's unconscious ego.

4. Saraswati discerned: Instead of making herself unforgettable by plucking her eyebrows, pumping

her lips, exaggerating her eye lashes, or tucking her tummy, Saraswati decided to go about her own life, celebrating her essence, which she never once forgot!

5 Saraswati discerned: Saraswati knew repressing her real feelings would have disempowered all womankind and created inner misery, so she spoke up truthfully and expressed her concerns openly. This way she did away with the big three: resentment, anxiety, and frustration!

6 Saraswati discerned: Saraswati would not allow anyone to pit her against Goddess Gayatri. She deemed she will not perpetrate societally reinforced toxic disrespect toward other embodiments of Divine Feminine. Saraswati remained rooted in sisterhood with Goddess Gayatri. Indeed, challenging one's internalized notions against feminine solidarity begins with understanding the power of divine womanhood.

7 Saraswati discerned: Saraswati possesses radical self-awareness—a sense of self that is forever separate from her partner (and everyone else). That is why she chooses wholeness over half-ness and self-compassion over self-censure.

8 Saraswati discerned: Saraswati knew what she must express to others and what she would retain inside her heart, when she needed to act, and when she could let go and focus on her own life. She teaches us when to be silent and when not to be, when to remain a partner with someone and where to draw the line.

9 Saraswati discerned: Saraswati knew there is no point in forcing unity, harmony, and obligatory peace through enforced love. She knows unconditional love begins with self-love. And self-love has no room for self-loathing and self-blame. (*Oh why was I late? I could have arrived*

ten minutes sooner!) Instead of not feeling good enough,
pretty enough, or smart enough, Saraswati thought
enough is enough, and that is why she is a goddess!

10   Saraswati discerned: Saraswati realized it was time to tune
in and honor the pain she was experiencing, and using this
pain to fuel her divine activism and make her voice matter
for the women of this world. Power stems from knowledge of
Self. Clarity returns when we become radically present with
ourselves. To be present with herself, Saraswati gave herself
the permission to feel ALL her feelings, including sorrow and
rage, allowing each feeling to have a moment, to be seen, felt,
experienced viscerally, and let go of. First, underneath all
the frustration, she encountered sadness that Brahma, her
beloved creator, a mighty well-meaning god, would let her
down, even if not on purpose but by association with Indra's
advice. She honored this insight because instead of bypassing
her grief, she could be there for herself. She became radically
present to the uncomfortable sensations of feeling unloved
and unwanted and even experienced the anger that befits
a goddess. And then finally, after she was present with her
rage, too, self-love and unconditional recognition in her own
worth rose in the garden of her divine heart. She could feel
a rock-solid presence inside her that was deeply nurturing,
and that is how she moved on in her life, not from a place of
fear but love. She teaches her human daughters that there is
no greater goddess power than being able to transmute your
rejection into radical self-acceptance through self-knowledge,
until you express the creative, most self-assured, and deeply
peaceful (with your choices) roar possible from deep within!

Thank you for being such a great role model to me, O Saraswati!
Saraswati mythology, or at least the way I have reinterpreted it,
has shaped my own behavior in relationships. I don't hesitate to give
them new shapes and forms or forge new agreements in old affilia-
tions. Sometimes, it is time for me say goodbye—a real goodbye—and

move on without regret. And sometimes, after discernment, I gift myself the opportunity to emotionally distance myself, just enough (but not physically distance myself). There is no failproof formula when it comes to relationships, but emulating Saraswati's quality of discernment can always help you strike the right note too! There is a difference between giving up entirely and knowing what to let go and what to let alone. When you let go of what actually isn't, you will make room for what could be.

Saraswati asks all women to live from radical authenticity. This is the goddess route to cultivating lasting peace in your own heart. Don't cultivate a single fiber of self-deception. I implore you— dig in (discern), and see what treasures lie within you. Stop trying to decorate the body alone by dressing or undressing it to present it "perfectly" to the patriarchal world. No one has the right to judge your intrinsic value. You don't have to spend years keeping up some external standard or trying to prove you are deserving—good enough, smart enough, thin enough, white enough, straight enough, bright enough, wealthy enough, fertile enough, sexy enough, woman enough.

You, too, can develop all-new beliefs through discernment, beliefs that spell greater conviction and trust in your inner voice and a Divine Feminine cosmic order. Become responsible for writing and creating your own life script, O goddess. Like Saraswati, be a straight shooter. You can express yourself with clarity and integrity without callousness or disregard for others' feelings. If we women trust ourselves, our inner light, and each other, ours will be a very different world.

> Don't chase.
> Don't want to be met.
> You have nothing to prove.
> Simply remember you are enough,
> Because you are.

Saraswati shows us that we must not hesitate to walk the uncommon path, if that is what it takes to connect with our true voice, talents, dreams, and desires. And it is never too late to live the life you are meant to lead as a goddess! Let's clear away the patriarchal conditioning that compromises our understanding of feminine intuition and blocks it. Such conditioning—rendered more potent by the gender-shaming, racist, classist, sexist, and guilt-inducing scripts of humanity handed down ad-infinitum—corrupts your innate wisdom. But Saraswati says, "Wake up! Examine your beliefs. Drop what is false. Choose what is true. Keep what is worthy. Let go what is not."

Yes: darkness, when faced and dealt with, ushers in light.

Self-awareness, self-value, self-prioritization, and self-determination rebirthed Saraswati from a "partner" goddess to a "sovereign" goddess. Just as if you've ever sincerely persevered in the face of personal attacks, emotional neglect, or social humiliation, and yet you endured (or even prevailed) and there was a part of you that never let go of your belief in you and your worth. Then that challenge itself, that darkness that shaped you and morphed you, though uncomfortable to begin with, ends up rebirthing you.

While I never suggest being hasty in your censure of others, nor impulsive, cold-hearted, or egocentric, if you want to live by goddess teachings and roar like Saraswati, retain your right to think originally and make major life decisions for yourself. Self-determination, birthed from discernment, represents the sacred emergence of divine knowledge and spiritual will, and not self-centeredness or selfishness. When goddess-like Self-recognition emerges from within, your self-confidence will blossom spontaneously. Your ability to make sound decisions will be enhanced exponentially. Your inner Saraswati is roaring to be heard, expressed, and honored. Do this by leading the life you must lead in service of evoking your inner goddess.

Sadly, successful, talented, strong, and intelligent women are viewed with suspicion in patriarchal societies. Female leaders and politicians tend to be covered by the media less for their ideas and contributions and more for their clothes and hairstyle. Saraswati never shrank in the face of male gods when her own partner reduced her existence to a mere replaceable object! Did she suffer in silence? No; she ensured her voice was heard and went on to lead the life she was meant to lead. Therefore, never suppress your voice, vision, or dreams, just because someone significant does not think much of you or your ideas. Anyone who can't respect and honor you for your light, wisdom, skills, and progress is not worth your time.

Even your female well-wishers may have conscious or subconscious reasons to hold you back or advise you in ways that don't support your inner goddess. Their advice for you may emerge from their own perceptions, experiences, and traumas due to patriarchy and might not have anything to do with you. That is why to think for yourself is paramount to living like Saraswati. The more autonomy you have over the decisions in your life, the more confident you feel in your ability to achieve your true Self.

The very fact that you are reading these words means that, beginning now and onward, Saraswati wishes to awaken you from your sleepwalking stance, in case you are subscribed to the patriarchal gossip that you don't matter and that the goddess lives far away from you. There are no goddess haves and have-nots. Everybody got goddess! Therefore, all of us need to work toward undoing this illusion of smallness. We are infinite beings: goddesses, no less.

NEITHER GIVE NOR ACCEPT ABUSE

An important discernment you can exercise is between being the abuser or the abused. You saw how Saraswati refused to be a victim of her domestic situation. She did not tolerate her partner's insensitivity. Nor did she react abusively. Yes, she censured Brahma openly, but it was for dharma that she did so, and that is all. Saraswati used her wisdom and power of discernment to remain inwardly peaceful, at peace with her life, anchored in her true identity, and focused on her joy as the divine awakener of ready souls instead. Have you played aggressor or are you a victim? Let's find out.

WHO IS A VICTIM?

A victim can be anyone in a state of mind that is largely drenched in self-forgetfulness, blind to the inner Shakti. Victims "believe" they are cosmically disempowered, that the world or even goddess or destiny or the higher principle wants them to remain a victim. These women often shop till they are broke, drink too much, or swallow more medication than needed to confirm their powerlessness. Victims are more prone to being ill-treated or sexually and physically abused because they simply unconsciously expect to be trodden upon. They have poor or no boundaries and no personal power, really.

Metaphorically, their inner goddess is completely asleep. They don't realize there is no victim in a real sense (or at least, not forever) and that there is power and choice, as well as the freedom to wield it, fully. The invitation is to find the power and joy of *simply being who we are: divine!* Just like Saraswati did not walk around perpetually exhausted, emotionally burnt-out, moping, crying, and feeling sorry for herself for eternity, you, too, can say no to victimhood (even if it is justified in the moment) because persistent self-pity has the power to steal your very life from you!

WHO IS AN AGGRESSOR?

Aggressor mentality is simply the other side of the coin. If victim mentality is one way to deal with what is unacceptable on a patriarchal planet, aggressor mentality is an opposite way to cope with it. We try to make things better by using unwarranted force, whether physical, mental, emotional, sexual, or political. The aggressor asserts their dominance or right to win in an unfair world by intimidating, pushing, and even unfairly punishing. Aggression helps numb emotional pain and fear, rather than processing it healthfully. Aggression almost always involves a drive for greater power. Often, aggressors grab power or appropriate what is not theirs.

Aggression does not always involve loud, belligerent yelling. It can be a cold withdrawal of emotions, hugs, or sex; a polite but cutting criticism; unfair revoking of privileges; or passing biased judgments. Aggressors often abuse and victimize others across gender lines, or even right along them; often, women gang up on other women. In the externalized search for power, aggressors lose touch with what they already have—their inner Shakti. They are totally cut off from source (Self and Goddess, which are one).

Here's something interesting about the aggressor: even as the aggressor appears to the world as a powerful tyrant, at heart this unfortunate persecutor is really wounded with the spear of victimhood. If a mouse is transformed into a tiger overnight, the mouse will roar extra loud so no one suspects she's really a mouse. All vulnerability, all tenderness, all fears, and all doubts are hidden under the mantle of anger, which is projected outward as a compensation for the fear felt inward. The aggressor is indeed an unfortunate "spiritual victim," forever snatching power, yet feeling deeply impotent at every level.

At your core, you are pure unlimited Shakti, not powerlessness, because your Self is one with goddess. The fundamental reason we humans are resistant to the flow of our own true goddess power is that we operate from our mind's limited conception of power. We are ignorant of our inner goddess Self. So, we conclude that we don't have power, or enough of it. We are unaware of our connection to Shakti, which is always enough, overflowing, and available even if we have not yet called upon it. Our minds have bought into the false notion that someone outside us or some external situation is more power-ful than we are—and that will define who we are, as long as we keep letting it.

Until we stop swinging between victim and aggressor conscious-ness, we are unable to transcend. We will keep slipping into one or the other mode of consciousness, again and again. Sometimes, our entire life is spent in the clutches of one or the other state of mind, and even at our deathbed we die the angry unrepentant aggressor, or we die of the unredeemed victim's grief.

But the good news is that the door is always open to Saraswati's path of discernment. As soon as you turn your attention inward and remember that Saraswati is your own Self, you transcend all these petty polarities, and the same difficult experiences you face on a planet wounded by patriarchy will turn into divine opportunities to exercise your higher knowledge, will, power, and creativity. Instead of reacting and hyperventilating, pretending nothing has happened, or making excuses for your offenders, you will discern, then respond. You can be as Saraswati was in her story: balanced and bold yet self-affirming, assertive yet peaceful.

Any time you start feeling or thinking some person or some circumstance gets to call the shots in your life, rethink the situation:

change your self-perspective and say to yourself, "I am a Goddess." Then, act as Saraswati would act, with wisdom and knowledge-borne discernment.

Let us resolve to be neither aggressors nor victims. The word I use to define what is neither extreme, but a compassionate yet empowered alternative, is "sovereign." Only a sovereign mind will do for Saraswati, who became the Mother of the Universe and the Giver of the Vedas, despite her own creator and life partner not acting as per her ideals.

O GODDESS: EMBODY SOVEREIGNTY

Estranged from their inner nurturing goddess core, victims and aggressors become blind to their divinely feminine, intuitive abilities to understand themselves and their situation and the opportunities hidden inside obstacles. They lose touch with their inherent power.

But the sovereign mentality is essentially a "script-less" space. It is also the most intuitively Saraswati-like mindset. It is not the end of the journey. In fact, it may be the beginning, a special adventure in authenticity and enlightened vulnerability.

Sovereign minds possess a *soft, respectful, responsible, and ultimately a wisdom-based* relationship with power, like Saraswati does. You, too, can begin to experience a new raw courage to simply be the best version of yourself (despite your rejecters and mockers) and live peacefully inside your own heart fulfilling your life purpose, enjoying your own soul-music! When you would rather play on your own lute—which is symbolic of doing your own thing and doing it well—you shall neither become a powermonger nor victim, but a successful goddess-woman in your own life!

Sovereign women are Saraswati-blessed women. They are empowered in a healthy manner. They are assertive with the ability to communicate clearly, uphold personal boundaries organically, and respect others' boundaries while fulfilling their life purpose. They have integrated the lessons taught by Durga and Lakshmi, too, so they neither suppress rage nor express it without dharma by their side. They become more and more Saraswati-like by employing wisdom amidst stark power struggles. Instead of acting and reacting from mere scripts and impulses, sovereign minds begin to truly discern and act with self-determination after thinking responsibly and deeply and long enough.

Hanging out in victim or aggressor consciousness feels more and more unnecessary as sovereign mentality becomes second nature through exposure to knowledge like I am sharing in this book. You can also read more about the *sovereign state of being* in my book *Sovereign Self*.

Living a sovereign life, versus conditioned living as victims or attackers, is a totally goddess thing to do. My grandfather Baba used to explain how night does not know what light is because the moment light dawns in the sky, darkness takes flight, nowhere to be seen. The dark night symbolizes the obscurity and ignorance that allows us to forget our goddess essence in the first place. Similarly, ignorance does not know what wisdom is because the moment knowledge dawns in the sky of our mind, ignorance ends.

Yet, as Goddess Saraswati promises, we need not fear darkness, material or psychological. Saraswati represents the dawning of greater wisdom and the enlightened sovereign mindset that leads us to liberation from ignorance and imprisonment in our mind's shadows, illusions, and delusions. That is why she is also called *Ahana*, which means "to illumine." She promises to always come to our aid, especially when our life is filled with darkness engendered by patriarchal obstacles. Once the luminous ray of Self-knowledge makes its presence felt in our mind, the forces of darkness have no other choice than to make way for the light!

May you meditate upon Mother Saraswati in your heart and know her as Ultimate Wisdom, Ultimate Knowledge, and Ultimate Reality.

You can also contemplate: *What attitudes and actions will restore my mind to wholeness?* The daily transactions of living in an essentially unfair man's world can deplete you or put you on the edge, and that is why cultivating the wisdom and practices I am sharing in this book, including the practice of pausing to discern before speaking or acting, are crucial for your womanly survival and potential existence as a goddess in this world. You need not bow mechanically to patriarchal conditioning or mindlessly do what was is expected of you, even though resentment is simmering away inside you. Step back and remember who you are first (discern) and only then act.

By casting aside habitual thought patterns, by learning about the nature of the true Self and its strength and potential, and by practicing the tools offered here, you may start seeing the many opportunities that your life is presenting to you, reach within, and express the truth of your Inner Saraswati. Even if others are blocking you, you will go within and find your inner flow. You will choose to remain unobstructed, untainted, undisturbed, and un-judged! You will just *see* it for what it is: patriarchal sludge!

This I know: If you connect with the Saraswati archetype and meditate upon her wisdom, she will ensure you seek your identity beyond simply being a "woman of the world" who is so enmeshed in her worldly relationships (which largely undermine her) that she forgets to claim her inner goddess.

Whenever a woman in any era looks beyond to ask the deeper questions, such as, *Must I play out roles versus be the authentic woman that I already am?* Saraswati ensures that she gets all her answers. With her grace, you may come to know the answers to your big questions: *Where is my real purpose in life? What is my relationship with the goddess? What is the type of respect, love, and standards in relationships I deserve to cultivate, really?*

For this final journey, to come through the darkness and remember your truth, all women require Goddess Saraswati's benevolent grace. She enkindles the fire of self-enquiry and spiritual aspirations and initiates our final journey to Self. Then you shall be a free spirit who roars peacefully with self-recognition and self-acceptance. You shall roar from ultimate enjoyment of your glorious, divine legacy as a human goddess.

You saw how Saraswati's mythological life is a tale of defiance. Her peace was hard earned by choosing authenticity over attachments at any cost. She would rather be labeled a haughty goddess who is not a good wife, than settle for crumbs and become a man-pleaser. Her speech retains the capacity to bless as well as censure because her speech is fearless, celebrating her free spirit. Imagine if Saraswati had not paused to discern who she was and what she wanted her life to be really about. She would still be the victim: sobbing in her mythological bedroom or turned an abuser or perpetrator of harm and planning revenge with her goddess-gal pals.

Instead, she sits peacefully on her white lotus, surrounded by serene swans and dancing peacocks, playing her lute for her own satisfaction, and what emerges is self-laudatory soul-music that cradles the whole universe in radical self-love and radical self-worth—a true picture of sovereign consciousness that transcends the mundane.

Discernment is up to you. You can choose how you wish to act in life, as damaged goods or as a damager—or instead, as a thinking, sovereign, goddess-like woman who can discern her way back to her power, back to her true Self, to who she is, always!

A SARASWATI CONTEMPLATION FOR YOU

I ASK: Where could I most use more discernment right now?

I RECOGNIZE: Discernment requires a willingness to
pause and step back from scripted responses.

I CONNECT: Sitting quietly or taking a meditative stroll, I observe
the goddess in my third eye. She urges me to discern.

I DECIDE: I am sovereign, not the victim or aggressor.

I ACT: I review the ten goddess teachings on
discernment, noting how they apply to me.

I REMEMBER: Saraswati blesses me with radical authenticity,
creativity, flow, joy, wholeness, and Self-determination.

CHAPTER 14

SARASWATI SAYS WAKE UP AND FACE YOUR TRAUMA

*Saraswati, that Great Wave [of Ultimate
Knowledge] is flowing as a River;
She is the awakener of our intellect and shines as
the embodiment of universal wisdom!*

RIG VEDA 1.3.12

I t is my gut feeling that there is a direct relationship between patriarchy and the generalized or universally prevalent trauma among women. Psychologist Valerie Rein's research confirms my suspicions. In her book *Patriarchy Stress Disorder: The Invisible Inner Barrier to Women's Happiness and Fulfillment*, she defines the term Patriarchy Stress Disorder (PSD) as the collective inherited trauma of oppression that forms an invisible inner barrier to women's happiness and fulfillment. Dr. Rein identifies the deep, unknowable weight that so many of us have been feeling for so long and gives it a name. She coined the term PSD when she discovered a missing link between trauma and the effects that patriarchal power structures have had on certain groups of people throughout history up until the present day.[1]

O GODDESS, DON'T PRETEND ALL IS WELL!

We can't simply remain asleep, believing what the pundits of patriarchy tell us about how good we have it. Honestly, of what use is our feminine wisdom if we can't call it like we see it? Even now I occasionally receive a letter or email challenging my right to be a Vedic teacher because I am a woman. Alas, I may have to face consequences even for writing this book, but write I will because the Saraswati archetype has shown me that I should trust my own instinct. How long can I pretend all is well?

Sadly, we pretend all is well even when our DNA is shrieking with terror. Trauma lives on in the collective subconscious of every woman on earth and, per the science of epigenetics, passes from a mother's womb to her daughter's psyche through gender and genetic memory. And yet we say—or are seduced to say—*all is well.*

On a cellular level, every woman still silently recoils in terror from the cries of 100,000 to 500,000 innocent women (and some historians say the number is 1 million) who between 1450 and 1750 were hunted mercilessly and executed or burned at the stake after being labeled a "witch" as a result of the mass hysteria and Christian moral panic that overtook early modern Europe and colonial America.[2] What was these women's fault that terrified the keepers of the male moral code, other than they played with the supernatural, healing, and self-love?

It's easy to dismiss this terrifying historical episode of mass femicide as the irrational actions of medieval mobs. But this was misogyny, fueled by irrational stories of "witches," who were accused of murdering children and riding "wooden implements smeared with a flight-enabling ointment made of the fat of a murdered baby. They traveled by night to secret witch confabs in which they communed with the Devil, gatherings of a vast, coordinated Satanic sect."[3] This brings to mind how American presidential candidate Hillary Clinton was accused of pedophilia and other incredible, child-related conspiracy theories.

Our feminine DNA also recoils from the mass murder of female babies due to the preference for male babies in many societies, such as China and India. Yes, our collective DNA memory includes being murdered in the womb; rape; torture; sexual slavery, including trafficking and prostitution; incestuous and extrafamilial girl-child sexual abuse; physical and emotional battery; sexual harassment (on the phone, in the streets, at the office, and in the classroom);

genital mutilation, unnecessary gynecological procedures; forced heterosexuality; forced sterilization; and forced motherhood due to criminalization of contraception and abortion. According to Diana E. H. Russell, professor emerita of sociology, whenever these forms of terrorism result in death, they become femicides.[4]

It's time for all of us to wake up and smell the torturous brew of misogyny. Alas, women, no matter how successful they are and whether they live in capitalist, communist, or feudal cultures, are suffering from the trauma of being second-class citizens on a hostile planet. And when I use the word "trauma," I am not just talking about the catastrophic harm rendered toward women through domestic, intimate, and street violence, which in itself is deplorable. I am talking about the emotional toll of a pervasive climate of patriarchy that is subtle but insidious. This is especially hard on women who strenuously defy male dominance. The injuries caused by such tussles and power struggles may not be visible to the physical eye, but surely and steadily, they can bleed the essence out of each one of us. Women become either numb or enraged, compliant or rebellious to the point of depression.

Deep inside our being, in the realm of our subconscious, all women are traumatized from what I can only describe as *shock arising from having to inhabit a hostile planet* and the huge amount of energy it takes to constantly appease the assailants and subjugators. There are women, who upon introspection, may say, "No, I am not burdened by traumatic downloads from patriarchy." But still, the patriarchal gaze is silently assaulting women in our subconscious minds every day; it is shaping our deepest beliefs and informing our expectations of how our lives will unfold in a certain way. As Simone de Beauvoir observes in her book *The Second Sex*, "She is defined and differentiated with reference to man and not he with reference to her; she is the incidental, the inessential as opposed to the essential. He is the Subject, he is the Absolute— she is the Other"[5] This is the "dark energy" that holds women back, despite opportunities. This is the "inner critic" that makes women unable to ever be completely satisfied with themselves. This is the "dissatisfaction with who you are" that makes women spend money they may not have on self-improvement classes, books, workshops, and retreats, or on clothes, shoes, handbags, and perfumes and yet still feel "unfinished," "unready," "unprepared," and generally "unwanted" and "unimportant" so much more often than men.

I am not saying that patriarchy explains all trauma or that patriarchy is the only problem women face. That would be an overly simplistic deduction. But certain repercussions of patriarchy are manifest in trauma because as an ideology, patriarchy promotes the oppression of the weak and vulnerable by the strong and powerful. Thus, patriarchy does not only subjugate women; depending on the dictates and expectations of a culture, men, too, can be subjugated if they are deemed unworthy of the title of a "man." And this behavior is accepted as normal because, as Maya Salam observes in the *New York Times*, men and women "internalize patriarchy without realizing it, pushing aside their best judgment and sacrificing their needs in order to fall in line with how they think they're supposed to behave. By not falling in line, they risk sticking out for all the wrong reasons, potentially driving away friends, partners, or professional opportunities, ultimately resulting in isolation."[6] This is why most people look the other way as patriarchy informs homophobia, racism, sexism, colonialism, and misogyny, and why boys learn that crying equals weakness, while girls learn that asserting themselves is too aggressive a behavior to be tolerated.

Therefore, the goal of wisdom should not be to pretend all is well. We must not merely decorate our cage. We must push against the bars, break through, and fly high. Only then can you sit peacefully and play music sitting on your white lotus like Saraswati does, and at last sing your own song—when *all is truly well* . . .

TRAUMA HEALING LESSONS FROM SARASWATI

I could describe what exactly has traumatized me. But it would not be very different from what traumatizes you. Ultimately, no woman— *not one single woman*—not even the most powerful woman on earth today can claim that she has gotten away unscathed and unscorched from the universally raging blaze of patriarchy!

When we are conditioned by trauma, we cannot think originally in the moment; we are forever playing out scripts to be "safe." Estranged from our authentic goddess nature, we cling to our gender stereotype, watchful in case we are "too big for our britches" or "acting too bossy" or "coming across with sharp elbows" or not "dressing up right for the job" or "not dressing down enough." Some may wonder, "Maybe I should opt for that plastic surgery and fix my boobs first," or even "Having sex might ease the way for me in a man's world." We've even subconsciously (or consciously) learned to sit with legs folded with a certain decorum in public, and to control the pitch and tone of our voice—not for any greater reason like being dharmic and true to yourself, but simply because this is how women must sit and talk if they don't want to raise eyebrows or if they wish to impress the influential males.

We've learned to monitor how much we speak or share our opinions because speaking too little and having no opinions at all will make us uninteresting in the eyes of guys and sharing too much will threaten them. And when some women feel tired of all this hustling (pretending all is well) and at last decide to speak up, to protest, a quick voice inside them rises out of nowhere and alas, fills them with self-doubt all over again: *Am I being unfair, inconsiderate, demanding, whiny, selfish, a drama queen?*

We are all pandering to patriarchy—even if subconsciously from internalized trauma—just to survive, and the women who do seem to thrive are lucky, because the outer demons (asuras) are ready to attack at any time and the inner asuric demons (the trauma or memory of when you or your kind were diminished or dismissed, even raped and killed) hide our goddess strengths from us!

Sadly, trauma of any kind, and from any source, whether personal or collective, insidiously destroys the body and most certainly unsettles the mind. No wonder women feel chronically unsafe and emotionally insecure even with professional success—as if they are waiting for the other shoe to drop! We feel frustrated with not being taken seriously, suffer way more than men from generalized stress disorders, resulting in unmanageable aches, pain, and countless stress-borne diseases, including eating disorders, anxiety, depression, insomnia, and heart conditions![7]

For all these reasons and more, we women must support each other, not pull each other down, and subscribe to a goddess sisterhood by being an ally to women, to remind each other of our buried goddess potential.

Not facing your trauma attacks your confidence from inside you. It makes you walk a certain walk and talk a certain talk, aimed at winning and reassuring the asuras in your life. Cornell University's philosophy professor Kate Manne explains in her book *Down Girl: The Logic of Misogyny* that misogyny is *not* about generalized male hostility or hatred toward all women, as popularly understood. Instead, it's directed exclusively toward punishing women who don't appear to toe the line in a patriarchic setup. As the author explained in an interview, "Misogynistic behavior is about hostility toward women who violate patriarchal norms and expectations, who aren't serving male interests in the ways they're expected to. So there's this sense that women are doing something wrong: that they're morally objectionable or have a bad attitude or they're abrasive or shrill or too pushy. But women only appear that way because we expect them to be otherwise, to be passive."[8]

A question we must ask ourselves is, *What can we do about this*? To start, we must stop going along and saying all is well when it isn't.

Cultivating awareness of things as they stand is critical. Wise up, goddess! In an article in the *Guardian*, Meera Atkinson, a Sydney-based poet and author, writes, "We need to snap out of the fantasy that socialized traumas, like rape and other violent crimes, are aberrations in an otherwise fundamentally commendable and fair society. We need to face the fact that abuses and offenses like these are logical and predictable outcomes of a deeply troubled social system built on the [patriarchal] belief that some individuals, by virtue of certain sex organs, skin pigmentation, physical ability/normalcy, are inherently superior and more entitled than others."[9]

MY EMERGENCE FROM DEEP TRAUMA

Trauma prevents us women from being authentic and behaving authentically. To adapt to patriarchal expectations, often women either withdraw from being themselves or overcompensate. These adaptations, of escalating or shrinking our personality at cue, are defense mechanisms, purportedly helping us stay safe in an otherwise hostile environment. But in reality, they only further disconnect us from our true Self.

I, too, lost myself to trauma, until I found my Self again, in order to lead others back as well, as a teacher. Thanks to my progressive Vedic family and my dharmic roots from childhood, I was a free bird, grounded yet unburdened by patriarchal expectations. But I encountered patriarchy when I got married the first time. And for a time, just to survive on unfamiliar terrain and catch my breath, instead of being authentic, my go-to responses became flight, fight, or freeze!

- To avoid disapproval, I would distract or distance myself or meekly go along with what was expected of me—or worse, pretend that I had no problems (flight response).

- I would pick unnecessary battles when I could have benefitted from a different approach. I did not stop disputing even when I knew I was sounding illogical (fight response).

- I would not even know what I was feeling or thinking and forget what I wanted to make happen and what I had valued in the first place (freeze response).

This last response of emotionally freezing was the most dangerous because when that happened, there was no healthy and happy Self inside me. It was as if I had been abandoned by Divine Mother! My previously confident personality became full of morbid misgivings about my own feminine capacities to nurture. Any inclination to roar like a goddess felt as remote as a fairy tale!

My rejecters, operating from scripts, did not see what a genuinely worthy person I was. They only saw someone who would not follow the rules, and that this was a breach of patriarchy. No one hit me. No one cursed me out loud. No one said anything that could be taken to a court of law. They just gazed at me with disenchantment. They talked at me rather than to me. They moved away physically when they could if I approached them. They disdained my sincere gestures and genuine words because to the men in the new family, I was no more than *a rebel*, and to the women, an uncomfortable *reminder* of their own trauma (which they wanted to desperately deny so they could be at peace with their own patriarchal agreements).

From my family of origin, I was used to high-minded ideas of equality and oneness, freedom, spontaneity, and heartfelt relationships between humans. Now I was suddenly lost, paralyzed, not knowing how to respond to such subtle but undeniable emotional rejection. Had I been physically or verbally assaulted, it would've been easy to walk away. How do you make a case against well-bred coldness that freezes your spirit and contracts your emotions into ice?

I collapsed in a pool of self-doubt. *Am I really a bad person? Should I become who they expect of me?* To cope, I became splintered into shadowy parts. Just to survive, I began to display the so-called "functional part"—the *patriarchally approved self*—while hiding the "disapproved and shamed part" in the basement of my awareness.

Sound familiar?

That's right: when we freeze from trauma, the trauma has eaten into our soul, depriving us of our right to even breathe fully and deeply experience our fears, joys, and sorrows as our own. We become so full of the voices of our patriarchic employers, relatives, husbands, and lovers that we have no inner voice to guide us anymore. This is where Saraswati, the goddess of wisdom, found me, right in the middle of emotional trauma and abject self-abandonment.

We cannot let trauma silence our goddess roar. We must find a way back to the lap of mother Saraswati, and sitting safely in her protection, we must tune in to our soul's music and roar with all the notes intact, in our sheer right to self-reclamation. And I did that. I said *enough is enough* and walked away with my head held high. But I could not walk away until I had glimpsed (discerned) once again what my inner voice was whispering to me about who I am, *a goddess-woman*, and who I am not: *a failed wife, a failed daughter-in-law, and a failed mom* (in the eyes of my critics).

The goddess reclamation work, rejecting who we are told we are by the patriarchal asuras in our life, must be an ongoing contemplation until we reclaim our authentic voice and no longer react from flight, fight, or freeze impulses. As goddess women, we must restore dharma in our hearts and in the world.

Remember, we have devas and asuras, forces of light and darkness, in our minds too! All women have shadows—dreadful memories. These shadows emerge from our encounters with patriarchy. We try to forget about our shadows and pretend we live in light, but darkness lurks in our buried memories. How can any woman possibly experience goddess-like wholeness when she must push away disturbing memories of harm done to her, mocking her, diminishing her? No wonder most women, even the most outwardly confident ones, are unexpectedly diffident at times.

Even when I walked away from my first marriage, a deep subconscious self-loathing set into me for failing, for taking my infant son away from his father. This self-hatred is trauma.

Sometimes, we must go back and heal the residue of the trauma.

As years passed, I chose another partner for myself, this time a more evolved soul, and I cut off any memory of that illogically and unnecessarily shamed, vulnerable, and abandoned young woman who was backed up against a wall of patriarchy. By then, the damage had been done. I was split into parts of me that I liked and parts I did not like—those that my subjugators had blamed and shamed. Thank goodness my teacher Baba had told me something special about Saraswati. He had given me wisdom to see and bring light to all my shadows—*when I was ready*.

Baba told me that the Goddess Saraswati not only lives in cosmic realms, but she also manifests as a life-giving river. He pointed out something significant: "To those who possess inner eyes, this river is flowing inside your own awareness . . . a river of light. When you are ready to venture into your hidden heart and beyond the form, you will find Saraswati's 'light' within, flowing like a torrential enlightened current. When you descend into Saraswati's flow, everything will become wet with awareness, love, and light inside you!"

I never forgot those words, even decades later. I kept thinking about how a river flows. There is something immensely okay and wonderful about this forward, ever-onward flow! A grand river that moves forward with goddess momentum will never leave behind even a cup of herself. Despite unwanted things (shadows) entering her waters, she carriers all of herself, every drop of herself, closely held to her heart, eagerly rushing along to meet the ocean. Finding rest at last in the ocean is her spiritual goal. The ocean represents becoming endless and boundless in her own fullness.

One morning, after my meditation, I thought: *If I truly want to "flow" like Saraswati, then I, too, must accept everything about me.* I decided to practice radical self-acceptance toward my so-called failed parts, which I had banished from my awareness. Then began my journey to love, to seriously love and bring to light all my disowned parts, with all the thunder and passion of a goddess river! At long last, I opened the door to the banished parts of me. I welcomed the failed wife, the failed daughter-in-law, the failed mother of her infant son, to come out in the open from the basement of my consciousness and join me in my daily life.

A much younger and inwardly broken woman with dark circles under her eyes came out trembling, squinting in the light. She had not seen light for decades. But now, every day she smiles in my heart, as she lies in the grass with her head on my lap, singing to herself songs about being a roaring goddess that we had heard from our mother! She knows she is loved by ME (the bigger me, the goddess me), no matter what. And when she does come out to be with me, in full transparency, she is joining me, the fifty-five-year-old respected author, teacher, mother. My inner Saraswati flows again with a joyful ferocity and unstoppable goddess force. There is no drop left behind, not even the cloudy and stained ones—all are divine, each single one of them, so listen up patriarchs!

> *Ah Saraswati,*
> *Who is this river? I did not meet her earlier?*
> *Oh, she is eternally new.*
> *In each pulse of time, she rushes forth to become*
> *what she was not a pulse ago.*

Her watery canvas boldly moves
ceaselessly bubbling, gushing forth,
through the will of her own,
because this she knows for sure,
I will never stop.
The river has no fear
she need not capture her immensity
in a standing pool of fear and ferocity,
because the river is all of herself
she has not left even a drop behind,
and in that wholeness
there is courage for the river
to move, be, and become, untold.

Ever since I opened the door to *all* my memories and became misty in the torrential current of my inner Saraswati, I found myself filled with self-worth and self-love of a new kind, as if it were sparked with goddess magic and stardust!

The journey from *shadow to Self* (which incidentally is the name I gave to my podcast) is not just a journey we do occasionally, but a journey we must do ALL the time if we want to flow in our lives like Saraswati does as a goddess river, full throttle. And even when you've overcome your default way of living in the shadow to living more in the light, our human mind (made susceptible by countless millennia of battling patriarchy) is always being seduced to go into the more shadowy (non-goddess-like) aspect of itself—into the lostness, the self-abandonment, the bewilderment. But as you read, you can breathe. You can exhale. You can go sit in the garden of your own life and picnic with all the shadowy parts of yourself that you had once banished from your day-to-day reality. Then, as your dark, light, and grey personas, past and present, merge into one integrated whole, no one can stop you from flowing forward, with Saraswati showing the way.

Don't lose hope.

An epithet for Saraswati is *the Lit One*, one who is lit like a divine flame of self-awareness deep within the cave of our heart. She is the divine light that ignites our imagination, enkindles self-enquiry, and supports us in processing our traumas. She helps us evolve as free, self-determined women of wisdom, who are peaceful inside their hearts yet powerful, wise, and dynamically assertive inside relationships. Her blessings help us discover our steps back to our unfettered goddess Self because Saraswati lights up each step of the path back to our healed self. This is how we deeply know what to will, what to speak, and how to act in such a way that we come closer to realizing our own glorious goddess within.

Indeed, she symbolizes the power of new beginnings and the joy of a fresh start! With her blessings, traumatic wounds heal, and your hidden goddess Self becomes "illumined" or "revealed" to you spontaneously from within. You need no light to "see" and "know" the truth of your goddess Self—it is "self-revealing."

And ultimately, a time will come when Saraswati herself becomes our mentor. Through a special teacher and their teachings, and books that awaken your inner Shakti, Saraswati will convey to you the highest transcendental truth worth knowing about yourself: that your essence is radical wholeness and no amount of trauma can take that destiny away from you.

SARASWATI SHOWS THE WAY
OUT OF EMOTIONAL TRAUMA

When we women are traumatized, we hear all the time: *Don't be so emotional—we will tell you how to think, feel, and act.* But Saraswati does not suppress her intuitive wisdom or original emotions, as women have been trained to do over centuries. She welcomes her own insights. And when it is time to act, Saraswati neither runs away (flight), nor takes aggressive action (fight), nor remains paralyzed with passivity (freeze). Instead, she evaluates possibilities in the light of knowledge and takes powerful, self-affirmative action. Knowing she is a goddess, she acts discerningly, in a balanced way, without fail. This balance is her music, her poise, her beauty! It is the healing balm for trauma!

One of my students shared the following awakening story:

> To survive through certain situations, we women often
> adopt modes of behavior, such as feeling like a victim or

becoming belligerent like a bully. I now understand how
these modes of behavior obscured my recognition of my
true, shining, unscripted, inner goddess. I no longer bow
mechanically to societal conditioning or mindlessly do
what is expected of me even though resentment might
be simmering inside. By casting aside those scripted
thought patterns, being educated about the nature of
the Saraswati-like Self, and learning about my innate
strengths and potential, I can see the many opportunities
that my life is presenting me and can express the truth
of my Inner Saraswati, who is neither a victim nor an
aggressor but truly sovereign. I am more balanced, wise,
and fearless in every situation.

Nowadays, when I sit quietly meditating on my goddess altar in my study, where Saraswati's deity is playing divine music on her lute, I say to her:

O Mother Saraswati, if it were not for you,
I would have settled for my shadow instead!

I now realize why this goddess can afford to sit in her seat, lost in her own music. Saraswati represents ultimate self-acceptance, and her music emerges from our deepest being, when we dare to bring all parts of ourselves—the heroic, the ashamed, the evolved, and the still evolving—together in one hug, and love and honor them all, unconditionally.

If women were always anchored in the wholeness of Self rather than the split selves, then hypothetically speaking, there would be no more suffering of body, mind, or soul. We would all become aligned with the intelligent cosmos and its Divine Feminine laws, roaring all naturally from our hearts, comfortable in who we are, loving our cracks and fissures, and healing our own wounds, with inevitably emerging goddess love, strength, power, radiance, and joy.

This is not a tall claim. I have repeatedly seen what happens when a previously distraught woman begins retrieving parts of her Self that she banished from her awareness. Different traditions call this practice different things; for example, soul retrieval, inner child work, or inner integration work. I call it practicing radical self-acceptance. As the banished parts are discovered, welcomed, and integrated into the big Self, peace, hope, compassion, kindness, and even laughter, playfulness, creativity, and cheerfulness begin to surface, along with a calm mind. From being split to being more whole, the entire being relaxes in deep, unassailable inner peace. Take inspiration from Saraswati's flow and work with a therapist, if need be, who can help you bring home your lost selves.

The stakes are high. If we don't take matters into our own hands and begin to uncover, accept back, and consolidate all parts of ourselves into one whole self, we can continue to play out our old scripts. This will keep us on the hamster wheel of keeping up appearances for the sake of the world, while being split and cracked apart deep inside. And this is where a relationship with the Goddess Saraswati archetype can come in super handy! I wrote this verse to Mother Saraswati, and you can chant it, too, to connect with Saraswati:

O Goddess of liberating knowledge,
burn away my ignorance.
Consume my darkness, enlighten my thoughts.
I want to know You Goddess
by knowing my own Self and all its hidden parts!
Help me know myself more, help me know myself all.

As you remove the veils that conceal your parts from you and begin thinking and acting like the goddess—courageous like Durga, self-fulfilled like Lakshmi, and seeing through falsehoods to claim the concealed reality like Saraswati—your authentic Self will not remain hidden for long. Your body, family life, and external life situations may remain the same, but your private knowing about yourself will become totally different. Your self-conception or identity will shift from a fearful, split, and fissured "i" to the whole, inwardly integrated, self-assured goddess "I" that you are!

A SARASWATI CONTEMPLATION FOR YOU

I ASK: What trauma or shame do I carry? Is patriarchy involved?

I RECOGNIZE: There are unloved parts of me
I've denied, dismissed, or berated.

I CONNECT: Sit with an uncomfortable memory. Feel the
feelings. Softly let go. Give it to Divine Mother.

I DECIDE: I'm done with being split by trauma and
shame. I am choosing to be whole again.

I ACT: One by one, I bring my banished parts to
light until my inner goddess flows with self-
acceptance, self-love, and self-empowerment.

I REMEMBER: Saraswati, "the Lit One," the divine flame
of self-awareness, resides in the cave of my heart.

CHAPTER 15

GODDESSES DON'T HARBOR IRRATIONAL FEMININE GUILT

O learned woman, the way a river breaks away mightiest of hills and rocks, the learned woman destroys myths and hype through her knowledge and intellect alone. May we all bow to such dharmic women through our respectful words and noble actions.

RIG VEDA 6.61.2

We women are somehow filled with a universal guilt, as if apologetic for our existence, talents, and innate power. But it is time to be done with this guilt that causes women worldwide to constantly explain themselves and subscribe to self-diminishing beliefs and roles.

The emotion of guilt is a feeling of having done something wrong or somehow causing hurt to another sentient creature. It arises to inform you that, knowingly or unknowingly, you may have transgressed another's humanity, goddess-given rights, or earned privileges.

This means that the voice of your conscience is active and expressive, which is a good thing. Our conscience is the part of our ego that remembers that it shares a common Self with all living beings. It indicates that you are human, that you naturally don't like being on the receiving end of pain, and are sensitive to causing others pain. When feeling healthy guilt, you must make conscious amends or you will feel emotionally restless. Healthy guilt leads to making outer restitutions and inner growth.

DON'T FALL FOR THE FALSE GUILT

Yes, guilt serves a purpose in life. But unfortunately, too many of us fall for a guilt that is unnecessary, unhealthy, and unreal! Too frequently women, the other-gendered, and people who belong to minority groups operate from guilt that does not originate in their individual acts or conscience. It comes from guilt in our collective consciousness: from failing to meet the expectations of our cultures, our religion, our family. This in turn fuels our inner critic, who is forever making us feel guilty for not meeting the demands placed upon us. And I suspect this phenomenon is connected to anti-feminine and homophobic religious precepts (which are found in all religions universally, to a greater or lesser degree), patriarchy, and other demeaning myths that are rampant in our society and around the world.

When we don't stop and question the validity of such guilt, our guilt button can be activated for no reason, sometimes disproportionately, which can make us feel responsible, apologetic, contrite, remorseful, and ashamed of our existence. We hesitate to communicate our genuine needs or to own our talents.

This guilt is not easy to self-diagnose or undo because it is not prompting you at a rational level. It is subconscious. I call this guilt that has no basis in reality—which I diagnosed in myself using Vedic insights—"the feminine guilt syndrome." But this syndrome and its aftermath of emotional powerlessness is not limited to the feminine gender exclusively. I am referring to a whole worldview, *patriarchy*, that divides the world into two camps: higher and lower, more preferred or less, with anything "feminine" in the latter.

Therefore, though I refer to generalized "feminine guilt" and "women," I am also talking to you, if for any reason—race, color, or sexual orientation—you have been shoved to the back seat by an unconscious humanity steeped in patriarchy. Because of a generalized feminine guilt syndrome, women worldwide hide their aspirations, often stay in the background, keep their opinions to themselves, don't say what they mean, say yes when they should say no, say no when they should say yes, and in countless ways devalue themselves.

From birth onward through my childhood, I was guiltless, bold with Shakti energy. I was an oddity in my society (which is mostly estranged from its gender-inclusive Vedic ideals). But, as I shared previously, I became vulnerable when my first marriage ended because I would not toe the line of patriarchal expectations. I was fine when I walked away, but very soon, almost as we catch a virus, the guilt got me!

We must be wary of disempowering beliefs catching up with us. No one is immune to such beliefs. They imprison us and take over our thinking. The antidote is to embrace and emulate the goddess of wisdom with your heart. The goddess will teach you how to use the knowledge of your true Self like a sword to annihilate the self-incriminating guilt.

When I moved to the US, I found to my amazement that Western women are buried under the same guilt I saw at home. It was clear that feminine guilt syndrome is ubiquitous. It has no boundaries. The feminine guilt looks different in different cultures, but it damages women's self-worth in the same way.

Some of my guilt was valid and was urging correctional behavior. But most of my guilt was imagined and irrational. Tragically, I stopped celebrating myself, delighting in who I was—the Shakti whose parents had believed in me 100 percent, to whom my Guru had bequeathed his ancient lineage. Yet here I was, filled with abject self-doubts.

Ever since Adam and Eve were banished from God's paradise, out of sheer guilt, every Eve on the planet has been making it up to the sulking Adam in her life, hoping to make him a little more comfortable on earth, at her expense! This disempowering myth is not from my part of the world; I have different memories, and different, deeply empowering feminine myths that tell me that no "God" has any business banishing me from anywhere. Because *I am the Goddess myself. I, as Shakti, pervade everywhere. Period. I power everything—including the people who disbelieve me and shame me.*

It was time I remembered those uplifting goddess myths and roared like a goddess! And I did. It was refreshing to remember how Saraswati in her myths never demonstrated unhealthy guilt for leading the life she leads as a free-spirited goddess, deliberately and consciously choosing to NOT carry the burdens of matrimony. Yes, she has a partner in Brahma, but in every other way, Saraswati and Brahma retain their independence and enjoy separate lives, performing separate cosmic duties, and enjoying the freedom to express their unique divine powers differently.

In all Hindu legends, the goddess not only grants desires, but when she is angered, she can also thwart them. She represents "the disruption of disruption." That is, she restores harmony. The next time I was told I lacked wifely attributes, that I was a poor housekeeper, that I was not a good mom, I said, *enough is enough!*

One day, my ten-year-old son told me I was not a good enough mom. He was upset because I had walked out of my marriage with his father when he was a baby, rather than stay and work on it. Deep down, I knew I had done the right thing to leave an emotionally disparaging relationship in order to find my own Self. And still, I was filled with uncalled-for, yet societally reinforced guilt. Even Western society upholds the right to pass judgment on women who leave their partners.

I remember having this insight: *Yes, people will reject me and criticize me until I accept myself on my own terms. Others will get to define me only until I define who I am. No matter if the world believes in me or not, I must believe in myself. The goddess will guide my little broken self, even though it has become overwhelmed or confused, attacked, mauled, disliked, and defiled. I will love myself unconditionally because I am a goddess, worthy and deserving of that love. Period.*

The world can only diminish the woman who knows her inner goddess for so long. She can only forget herself for so long. Her goddess can only stay asleep for so long.

The conditioned, self-betraying mind can get hung up on past mistakes and will never lose an opportunity to belittle you or generate guilt and shame. Healthy guilt and shame remind us to make amends where appropriate and to learn from our mistakes, but when the self-criticism never stops, your inner goddess must at some point play her lute and tune in to her inner music by thinking self-valuing thoughts. Remember, your thoughts are the mold and life is the clay.

Whichever thoughts take up the most room in your mind, so your life shall become. Hence, first and foremost, you must choose thoughts that are self-valuing in nature.

Silence and soothe the asuras of self-reproach and self-criticism and give your learning, faltering self a huge goddess hug by surrounding yourself with musical notes of self-love and self-compassion. It's all okay. Often, life takes us where we're meant to be, through falling and making stupid mistakes. Each clumsy situation and every perceived slipup are opportunities to learn and grow. When the old tapes of self-blame start playing, sing out loud, *OM Saraswati Namaha* (O Saraswati, I am remembering you fondly). This will stop the out-of-tune tapes and free up a tremendous amount of mental and vocal energy, activating the inner wisdom to finally serenade yourself and celebrate who you are and what you do. *Self-value is an act of Saraswati worship*. With devotion in our heart for outer Saraswati, and the memory that "I AM a Saraswati myself," we shall overcome tossing ourselves away and re-emerge in the infinite garden of our life, as a blossom that never fades. Either way, when you connect with the Saraswati archetype through deliberately exercising self-value and practicing detachment from what and who does not value you, an inner goddess who dwells in the depths of your being will be activated. Yes, Saraswati is that inner power that becomes unleashed by the firm decision to live your life from a self-caring, self-respecting, self-valuing outlook. No wonder it is said that Saraswati's grace is the enhancement of self-love and self-worth. Our inner goddess Self shines when her light falls upon us!

When I had the insight that "I am no different from Saraswati," through my continued vigilance, it became clear that none of my negative self-judgments were true. Slowly and steadily, during my meditations, I realized that I am sincere and authentic to who I am, and that is what matters in the end. The guilt I was buying into was a false construct. My inability to be or become something I am not—remain married at any cost, wear a moral straightjacket, be a super-scripted, suffering wife and sacrificing mom—is not my thing.

This spiritual nonconformity, ultimately in service of a greater dharma of authenticity, is an ode to who I am deep inside me: a goddess-woman. And the spiritual teacher inside me, who has lit count-less hearts with wisdom, and has been making a difference in countless lives for the last two decades worldwide, has arisen from the ashes of the so-called failed wife and mom. My former husband is a friend now, and my son is coming around too.

I am a nonconforming Guru, just like Saraswati is a non-conforming Guru goddess. I am not bound by any mold, domestic or spiritual, Eastern or Western, masculine or feminine, except to be authentic to my own goddess-like Self, in each moment. That is the highest dharma.

I am grateful for goddess mythology and my unique privilege to interpret it from my own original lens, knowing there is no human-set standard that we women need to aspire to and judge ourselves against as adequate or not. If any ideal must be sought, then it is in Saraswati's archetype.

RECLAIM YOUR POWER BY SAYING NO TO IRRATIONAL GUILT

Guilt in useful proportion makes us take ownership and opens the way to make any possible amends, at least in our heart or at our altar. We may have caused the original difficulty—for example, in ignoring an alcohol addiction, which led to losing our job; or staying in an abusive relationship that is now causing trauma. But when guilt is out of control, as well as irrational or spiritually unfounded, it turns poisonous and begins to disturb our psyche. Our reality becomes skewed, and we walk around feeling like a culprit. Self-loathing can set in—disproportionate to the offensive behavior—and we emotionally abandon our own self. We might become paralyzed, not knowing what our next steps should be.

Internalized feminine guilt can make us overcompensate for being born a woman. Stop being so apologetic and overexplaining yourself.

Perhaps you feel your guilt is rational. Then let me ask you: How many times do you want to hang yourself in the courtroom of your own mind? Few things are more painful than excessive guilt that makes us punish and forsake ourselves repeatedly.

All of us have done some wrong in the past. We must atone and, if possible, make restitution. We must seek knowledge and inner strength not to repeat the wrong. Then let it go. To be human is to err. And to learn from those errors and move on is a goddess thing to do.

HOW TO COGNITIVELY
BECOME GUILT-FREE

Through knowledge-based contemplations and attitude corrections, you can start to see through the darkness of your guilt-inducing false beliefs that conceal your goddess essence and disempower you. I was able to finally completely set aside feminine guilt—which all women embody universally—when I created this contemplation:

> Saraswati carries no guilt for being the Ultimate Wisdom bearer embodied in a feminine body with a womb, vagina, and pair of breasts. I, too, will not buy into any guilt that patriarchy-fed pundits have been forcing women spiritual teachers to internalize since time immemorial.
>
> Are women born only to give pleasure, procreate, or feed another? Saraswati neither played submissive wife to her cosmic partner, nor bore him kids, nor kept his house. Instead, she roams the universe shining the light in each sincere wisdom-seeker's heart. Therefore, to give pleasure, procreate, or feed another is a woman's choice, not her moral imperative.
>
> Women do not become less of a woman if they have not given birth, suckled a baby to their breast, or received a (male only) lover inside their bodies. She who comes from wholeness remains radically whole through her womanly incarnation. She remains a gorgeous embodiment of Shakti whether she is married or divorced, straight or lesbian, queer or fluid, sexual or celibate.
>
> Just as men don't have to justify why they are male, women must not justify why one who is a formless divine consciousness took on a female body. Nor should mixed genders and transgenders justify why they are who they are, since they are perfect as they are. We all are always designed by goddess as divine

embodiments of her being. Saraswati (Self) can take on
any type of body, and any guilt arising from this is the
vile legacy of patriarchy.

I must scrutinize my unconscious beliefs and
internalized misogyny under my emerging inner light! I
am Saraswati deep inside me, and I will live each day
from this higher plane of awareness, rather than speaking
and acting according to a script handed down to me by
countless sleepwalking generations.

For me, the overall contemplation theme remained the same, while the exact chain of thoughts would differ every day. But I would not let go of contemplating until I arrived at inner clarity and owned it fully. A guilt-free state of mind became my emotional reality, slowly and steadily.

FORGIVING YOURSELF IS ESSENTIAL

Forgiveness does not mean sidestepping the importance of dharma (morality, ethics, and justice). It means that we accept that we are a work in progress, and we're overcoming our self-ignorance. There is no reason to be unforgiving and punitive with ourselves. Poisonous guilt makes us forget we have the goddess dwelling inside us, which we are still in the process of uncovering. For goddess self-acceptance, forgive any past ignorance that led to actions you regret. This is essential; otherwise, you will drown in guilt.

In this cosmic setup, often our mistakes alone wake us up to where we can find the goddess treasure: inside us. Our mistakes turn us toward spirituality and guide us beyond the one-night stand, the alcohol fix, or the abusive partner who we go back to again and again. Maybe your mistakes are what will finally lead you to your inner goddess awakening.

Right now, stop punishing yourself. Each of us will meet a unique set of circumstances that will challenge us, and in meeting the challenge, we will learn from it, become stronger, and ultimately begin roaring like a goddess.

Knowing that the goddess and I are separated only by the form we take and that our essence is one elevates how I look at myself:

with new divine eyes. Knowing that the goddess is a higher version of myself, I can simply call upon Her to fill in the gaps for me, carry me when I cannot walk, inspire, and protect me, and lead me through this confusing world.

Perhaps if you listen carefully, Goddess Saraswati wants to tell you this: *O Blessed One, know this: you are not just a person, you are Self. Self is not physical but metaphysical. Self is not personal but transpersonal. Self is not worldly but transcendental consciousness.*

A SARASWATI CONTEMPLATION FOR YOU

I ASK: In what situations do I feel generalized (false) guilt?

I RECOGNIZE: Patriarchy is often at the root of false guilt.

I CONNECT: Sitting quietly, eyes closed, notice
    where and how guilt feels in your body.

I DECIDE: I banish unhealthy guilt from my goddess-blessed life.

I ACT: I renegotiate stifling agreements (formal
    or unspoken) made out of false guilt.

I REMEMBER: I tune in to my divine song with self-valuing
    thoughts (not guilt, shame, or self-criticism).

CHAPTER 16

SARASWATI
The Teacher and Giver of
Lasting Inner Peace

Divine Saraswati, you awaken spiritual memory,
divine trust, scared speech, and knowledge of Self.
Please bestow upon me lasting inner peace.

SHARADA STOTRAM, VERSE 2

Saraswati is playing her lute peacefully inside you. A mesmerizing voice is singing inside your heart calming all agitations. Can you hear your inner Saraswati singing . . . calling your name? Or are you so distracted with the disparaging sounds of the divisive world you live in that you can't hear her roaring peacefully within you?

Most women remain stuck in life, estranged from any kind of peace, outer or inner. But clearly, the very fact that you are reading my words indicates that you are en route to realizing the profound peace earned through facing the asuras of life. You are on a journey to reclaim your inner peace, all right! When you have a peaceful Saraswati-Self within you, how long can you keep her concealed? How long can you avoid her peaceful gaze? How long can you avoid *becoming* her peace, in all your splendid authenticity?

SARASWATI'S ULTIMATE
GIFT IS INNER PEACE

There is a certain peace that can be obtained in the mind by reducing the frequency of thoughts. Your true peaceful nature will shine in the gaps between thoughts.

A second kind of peace can be achieved by intellectually recognizing a distance between your true being and your thoughts. The stepping back from the contents of the mind, simply observing it neutrally or witnessing it as if from a distance, creates freedom from the mind's ups and downs—just like you can watch an intense movie but know that you are a removed spectator, not an actor. This is called exercising witnessing awareness. This method of experiencing peace in the mind is often easier than noticing the gaps between thoughts, and I talk about this at length in my book *Sovereign Self*.

In my experiments with goddess consciousness, there is a third type of instant peace that can be experienced simply by remembering soulfully, heartfully, mindfully (even if merely for an instant) that your true Self is one with Saraswati, the *Embodiment of Divine Peace*. Therefore, nothing must be "done," as such. You simply have to relax into your inborn, ever-present authenticity. Even the need to go away from the noisy nonpeaceful world and take a secluded retreat to find inner peace becomes optional at this stage. You will have awareness of your own peaceful goddess core and begin remembering it and living by it, all the time.

In interactions with others, you can benefit from continually remembering your inner Saraswati, whose nature is peace, tranquility, truthfulness. There's no need to project who you are not, nor be apologetic for who you are right now. In a drama, we play a role, don't we? When we remove the costume demanded by that role, we become what we are underneath, the good old Self. Similarly, a life role presents a temporary reality, but when we remove the role (mother, wife, daughter, daughter-in-law), what remains is our true authentic-goddess Self. And in this authentic living, you shall find Saraswati's greatest gift: abiding peace.

Naturally, once this understanding is internalized, no matter where the mind goes—to a dance club, a busy office, a crowded shopping mall, a wedding, or a funeral—and no matter who you meet (whether they like you or not), you'll have the self-awareness that "I AM a goddess, so I don't have to find peace outside me by becoming someone I am not." Your authenticity can coexist with whatever activity the mind is engaged in (whatever role it has to play) while awake, dreaming, or sleeping, and whether your external circumstances of life are peaceful or agitated. Through this journey—from hiding or pretending for the sake of others to expressing yourself with dignified authenticity for your sake and everyone's sake—you will have achieved that necessary self-growth and ego-transcendence to awaken to lasting inner peace.

CULTIVATING YOUR AUTHENTIC NATURE FOR PEACE

From Durga, you learned to keep asuras—both negative people and your own self-diminishing states of mind—at bay, while choosing dharma in every action, along with courage and fearlessness. From Lakshmi, you learned to experience yourself as a gift and to gift the worthy "devas" in your life positive states of emotions, like love, contentment, and generosity. Finally, from Saraswati, you can learn how to discern between what is true and what is false; between when you should think all is okay and relax, and when you should be sobering up with the recognition that all is not well after all, and that it is time to listen to your inner music, up your game, confront injustice, or walk away with your head held high. But either way, she teaches to never stop being authentic to who you are!

That's right—you can drop the hustle right now and simply be you in this moment, and in the next moment, choose you again. In my experience, this is the fastest route to calming the mind and experiencing the bliss of inner peace. Indeed, peace emerges from a fierce commitment to your own authentic wholeness and truth—never comprising it for any reason. Upholding it leads not only to improved self-esteem, personal power, and self-confidence, but a heart full of peace. You shall experience waves of inner peace when you arrive at the crossroads of authenticity and attachments, and you choose authenticity!

By forgetting your goddess nature, you converted your life into a suffering-engendering hustle, and by recalling your true nature, you can convert your life back into a peaceful garden of authenticity—a personal retreat and a blessing for yourself and this whole universe, no less.

I often contemplate the following to cultivate and maintain my inner peace:

Goddess is my own most authentic nature.
Her peace is my peace.
I AM peace.
No thing and no one can take this peace from me as long as I keep celebrating my true nature. Who I am is enough because my nature is pure peace, and I shall remain that way, unchanged, eternally peaceful.

Here are some steps for cultivating your authentic nature for peace.

Deliberately Cultivate a Private Inner Life

The woman who dares to journey inward always becomes rewarded with inner Saraswati-like qualities. To be more and more authentic with every passing day, tend to your inner life. You belong to you first, before you are someone's daughter, sister, partner, mother, girlfriend, employee, boss, or colleague. It is important to stay alert to your inner life while you play public roles as wife, girlfriend, mother, and so on, because otherwise you can easily get wounded (or at the least, sidetracked) by the demands and trivialities of often patriarchally stained relationships. Therefore, cultivating a relationship with your inner being that is beyond all worldly identities is helpful.

It is my belief that inside each one of us sits a singing Saraswati, waiting for us to recognize her. The goddess must appear sooner or later, or else our everyday lives and being everything to everybody will keep us distracted and occupied in the hustle of living.

If you are a goddess already and you know it, you will value every word of this book and shake your head in agreement at every page. Enjoy your own secret and let your significant other know that you love and respect them, but you love yourself too. And don't just talk about self-love. Show it by prioritizing your inner life. Then you will not merely read about Saraswati's, Durga's, and Lakshmi's heroic lives, but you, too, will live with inner conviction and self-worth—quietly and earnestly, even if only privately.

Adopt Straightforwardness

To activate your authentic self, you must be straightforward or straight as an arrow in your dealings! *No manipulations and passive aggressiveness*. Be forthright! Pay attention to your thoughts, feelings, and desires because they matter. It's important to spend time exploring your own inner landscape so your authenticity comes from greater inner alignment and self-familiarity. Do this by making yourself a priority.

- Keep no hidden agendas. Instead of dropping hints, skirting around issues, or hiding behind the unspoken, try putting your cards on the table, honestly, openly, and firmly. When you begin to communicate your needs, boundaries, and values in relationships without shying away from this important task of expressing your authentic and whole truth, then through the act of owning and expressing and ultimately living your entire truth, your being shall become increasingly tranquil in daily life.

- Like Saraswati, be very clear in nonverbal communication. She does not pretend to be delighted when she is not. Instead of pretending "I'm okay," you could see if it feels right to vocalize, "I am okay with it for now, though I have some questions, but I'm not yet clear about my questions. I'm thinking about them seriously, so I'm okay until next month."

- Being straightforward will make you authentic in your thoughts, communication, and actions. Straightforwardness is a core Saraswati value, and it takes inner work. With the desire to be straightforward informing how you communicate, you will no longer remain split among your conscious, subconscious, and unconscious motivations. You may not yet know everything about yourself, but when you make straightforwardness a priority, you can at least hold an intention to uncover more areas of your mind and bring your thoughts, speech, and actions into alignment too. There will be a greater consistency between your thoughts, words, feelings, and actions for sure.

Thus, I invite you to walk in your authentic truth by speaking up or asking for what you need in a straightforward manner, despite people who challenge your worth, right, or authority to do so. But do it anyway, to overcome your inner demon of self-doubt and to touch the true essence of who you are inside you, rather than all the powerless masks we wear to receive acceptance, to feel loved.

DEALING WITH THE ASURA
OF SELF-DOUBT

While a little self-doubt imparts objectivity, when we habitually doubt ourselves to the point of holding our ideas, creativity, and voice back, it is sheer self-abuse! Self-doubters constantly scold themselves, *You're not good enough. What you do, how you look, who you are— none of it is good enough!* This is nothing but fear.

You can dispense with this unwanted tendency by naming this asura and saying, *Gotcha, Self-Doubt Monster! You have no role or use or purpose or power in my life, thank you very much! I am a sovereign being, an embodied goddess no less. And no matter what you say, I choose to believe in myself. I may make mistakes, but I will learn as I go. My true Self, that is eternally FREE will show me the way. If Saraswati is my own Self, then who am I to doubt myself?*

Gradually as you begin housekeeping your mind and filling it with greater Self-knowledge of who you really are, your increasing aware-ness will allow you to uproot the power- and confidence-sucking inner monster of irrational fear parading as self-doubt. You will regain your freedom to think like a sovereign woman, not as a captive of your own mind's silly phantoms that disappear when you turn on the lights!

You will triumph in every situation, just like Saraswati had the last word, despite being publicly discredited, in one of her myths.

That's right—addressing your annoyances, frustrations, needs, and concerns is almost always harder than simply "keeping the peace" or going along with others. For example, say you need to set a polite boundary with your partner and you are afraid to do that because you are unsure how your partner will respond when you express your emotions and affirm your boundaries. First, remember your inner Saraswati, and repeat the following affirmation.

> *May my speech be established in my mind.*
> *May my mind be established in my heart.*
> *May my heart be established in my Soul/Self.*
> *May my Soul be established in Goddess Saraswati.*

Then, speak anyway. If you don't, and instead give in to your fear and wimp out, you will be filled with guilt and shame that will catapult you into a downward emotional spiral. Losing respect for yourself is the fastest way to lose contact with your inner peaceful goddess.

At such emotionally perilous times, when you know the other human may misunderstand you, reject you, get hurt, make it about themselves, dismiss your feelings or concerns, or simply refuse to acknowledge the merit of what you are saying, again connect with the Saraswati archetype, the goddess of truthful speech, inside you. Employing courage in the face of fear, push yourself to speak up and speak only the truth in a straightforward manner. Express what is bothering you, not for that person's sake but for the sake of your own dharma—for honoring your own truth. As Mark Twain succinctly put it: "Courage is resistance to fear, mastery of fear—not absence of fear."[1]

On the battlefield of intimate relationships, it takes conscious choice and employment of conscious courage to be frank, honest, upfront, vulnerable, open, straightforward, and ultimately in integrity with our own goddess (higher) Self, rather than simply holding our tongue and looking the other way only to later explode without or implode within. Relationships can be volatile, too, even dangerous.

And if you feel that speaking your thoughts in a dignified, emotionally discharged, and straightforward manner will nevertheless jeopardize your safety, then you can make a conscious decision to keep quiet, and not air your thoughts—and discern another way to express and live your truth. But your silence in that moment does not mean you are not aligned like an arrow within. Your clarity about your ideas and how they represent your true feelings should remain intact within you. This will be your "authentic space" inside your heart that will nurture you and guide your next steps from within!

Please understand that when I say that it's necessary to speak up even if we are uncomfortable, I am not suggesting you raise your voice or dominate the conversation or decide it is "my way or the highway," or even risk your safety to have the last word! I am not teaching the art of arguing, nagging, pestering, threatening, manipulating, or fighting foolishly. Saraswati-inspired beings often remain silent or meet their partners halfway and work on themselves to become masterful nonviolent communicators. But they also value a greater Truth of Self over a quick patch up or reaching an "understanding" that is essentially false.

Before you quickly say yes and make relationship agreements you live to regret, I am asking you to first slay your own habits of remaining silent and acquiescing to maintain the status quo. This will open all new lines of communication for expressing your truth and help you forge new pathways toward healthier relationships (either together or separately). At least you will not remain stuck, suffering alone in your ill-chosen and unfulfilling tower of silence and codependency.

Suffering silently is never a healthy option, nor the path to abiding peace and authenticity. It's important that we process our feelings, and when appropriate, air them in a straightforward non-charged manner, just like Saraswati addressed Brahma. Saraswati, the goddess of speech and wisdom, shows us through her own myth how we, too, must make use of our faculties of discernment and (straightforward) speech and not be mere mute spectators in our own life.

PRACTICE YOUR GODDESS-
LIKE DETACHMENT

In relationships, the war is rarely outside us. It reaches courtrooms very late. It first begins inside us, between our attachment to preserve the relational harmony (however superficial) versus overcoming fear and cultivating real harmony through our ability to confront the darkness or dysfunctionality in a peaceful and timely manner. I encourage you to emerge from the shadows of relationship attachments and morbid fears and align with your highest authentic nature. We must remember our invincible divine nature and act like Saraswati did in an objective way, despite fear and familiarity with old attachments.

The journey of awakening to Saraswati-like peaceful and expansive consciousness requires a willingness to examine our own mind, our likes and dislikes, and the quantity and quality of attachments that hold us back from being authentic. Are our attachments necessary? How much neediness is valid?

Sadly, it is due to attachments that far too many women endure ongoing disrespect or domestic violence and yet remain fearful of leaving their abusers or even speaking up. They hang on to a job despite their chances of getting a better job, or they hang on to a partner despite being undervalued. Sometimes, in situations of abuse where there is a real threat to our physical safety, we must wisely avoid speaking up or letting our true feelings show—but we can find other empowered ways to act. We may have to find a way to roar that does not endanger our loved ones, our lives, or our livelihood, and at the same time does not let our goddess flame become extinguished. For example, someone in an abusive situation might keep a calm exterior, but then call the authorities or plan an exit befitting their inner goddess, when it is safe to do so.

The point is that we must consider whether our attachments stand in the way of a new or better life as a self-valuing goddess. Our objects of attachment and bondage to fear can result in a mini mental prison of imagination. Soon, chronic anxiety and unease manifest. Then, instead of specific situational fear, *generalized* fear takes over our mind and paralyzes us with a freezing and inhibiting effect. When this happens to you, you must ask yourself: *What am I attached to that I have been reduced to this state? What am I resisting or not facing? What must I let go? What must I accept and move on? Where did I leave my authentic roar behind?*

I encourage you to cultivate conscious detachment: non-neediness in an emotional sense. Then, your neediness will wane or end. You will no longer become filled with fear. Things and people will come and go in your life, but you will be okay (even more than okay) because at least you will have your authentic roar back! Gradually fear shall be replaced by more appropriate, divine emotions to support you—courage, resolution, creativity, ingenuity, and best of all, authenticity! You'll remember that challenges show up to help you serve your higher purpose, to show you what you need to see.

My Guru Baba used to say, "When in crisis, you can choose to either rest your faith in a goddess outside you or believe that the goddess dwells inside you as your own Higher Self. Believing in inner Saraswati means believing in your own capacities, in your own soul potential to be sovereign and non-attached in times of change and challenge."

If your body hurts from fear, your gut feels like it has been punched, you can't breathe, and your heart sinks every time you think about losing something or someone, it will help to simply sit with your hands in the letting go pose, or mudra, as depicted in the figure below.

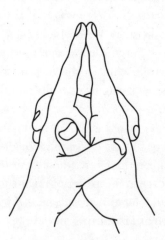 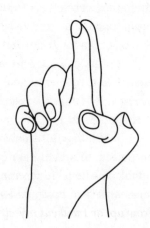

Repeat the following to yourself silently while your hands are in the mudra.

> I am releasing to Divine Mother Saraswati
> the attachments that are pulling me down.
> I am releasing control to her.
> I am trusting her in this time of uncertainty
> and difficulties.
> I am resting in Divine Mother Saraswati's Grace.

Repeat this until you feel less attached. You will notice fear subsiding. The moment you remember your inner Saraswati and ask for help, allow new flowers of detachment borne of wisdom along with feminine courage, fortitude, and ingenuity to blossom in your heart.

This way, your relationships can become your spiritual laboratory. Your growing sense of ease and peace within will radiate out and help everyone relax as you evolve in your own understanding of your authentic goddess nature.

COMMIT TO CONSCIOUS SACRED SELF-NOURISHMENT

A goddess nourishes herself when she exercises regularly; eats nourishing, wholesome food; and even is open to occasional visits to the therapist (if you have access to one). But don't stop here. Continue nourishing yourself with spiritual wisdom from teachers of the Divine Feminine path of soul ascension. Reading this book is a great start. Clearly, self-awareness and wisdom of the goddess archetypes is a great soul balm. This specialized knowledge alone will help women worldwide create an unshakeable foundation of self-respect and self-care because without it, you don't even know what or who you are and what you stand for.

A mind filled with self-abandoning beliefs will experience self-destructive thoughts like, *I will drink until I die, I will stay in this horrible relationship forever, I don't care if I have unsafe sex, I will starve myself to death as long as I can look thin, I will make myself throw up,* or *I will cut myself and watch as I bleed.*

Watch out for the desire to numb your feelings, the desire to not have to take responsibility for your own well-being, the desire to simply follow the impulses of your conditioned mind. Instead, allow yourself to feel. Feel all your feelings, all the way until you feel the love for yourself, deep inside you. This is Saraswati telling you: you matter; you are worth the self-care and self-value.

If goddess lives in all the universes, visible and invisible, then whatever we encounter in the world is meaningful. If not even a speck of dust or a blade of grass is insignificant, then how can you, her own womanly manifestation, be unworthy of your own love and reverence? We often forget that we are goddesses, truly worthy of the highest self-care and self-love, despite our learning curves. We forget that we deserve to give ourselves a few pats on the back and a chance to ascend beyond the darkness that is covering our light. As we discussed before, our thoughts are the mold, and life is the clay. Whichever thoughts take up the most room in your head, so will your life become, so your behaviors will become, so are the friends and professions you will find—and keep. Hence, choose thoughts that are self-nurturing and self-valuing. Try carving out solitude to take a walk alone and to think self-caring thoughts such as:

Today I will please no one but simply rest my being.
Today I will make my happiness a priority.
Today I will gift myself a massage.

You can also meditate, chant, or read this book again and again, or even keep a goddess journal, because writing your inner goddess thoughts will help you listen to them first, and more clearly. Guard your mind fiercely from mind-polluting, gossiping, negativity-spinning, mocking, or shaming relatives or friends or even spending too much time on biased media that mock people who look for the inner or outer goddess. Both paths are valid.

Believe me, when you become ready to nourish your inner-goddess nature, a wealth of self-approval and self-esteem will be revealed from within, along with so many other types of inner gems, spontaneously! Saraswati herself will see to it that you have the wisdom tools you need to pierce your own darkness and awaken to your inner goddess. Perhaps she is looking out for you already?

A student of my goddess teachings shared this with me about mockers and shamers:

> *Now when people drop hints that I am acting kind of weird (just because I am no longer following scripts meekly), I simply smile to myself rather than try to think of witty things to say to them. This battle does not even seem worth engaging in anymore, as I have already won it, inside me. This self-acceptance of my inner goddess at such a deep level is new to me. And it is such a relief.*

Here are some practices that will support the emergence of your authentic self:

- Every day or whenever possible, meditate, chant, and listen to uplifting music or make your own.
- Choose to read a few pages from this book every day or other books that help you feel confident from within.
- Every day in a non-charged manner, exert your opinions every time you must and can do so safely. (Or own them privately in the safety of your heart.)
- Every day do something that is outside your comfort zone. It may be difficult, but it is significant that you push your own self-created barriers.
- Take out time to decide what is important to YOU; set goals and take risks.
- Dare to dream; be creative; be persistent.
- Investigate what it means to live like a goddess would. Plan, act, achieve. Live free by being true to yourself.
- And remember this every day: *I need not become a goddess. I am that already. So I simply must Be who I Already AM.*

Here is what I say to her out loud:

*O Saraswati, when I identify myself with the body, I am
your servant.
When I consider myself as an individual, I am your part.
When I look upon myself as Self, I am one with you.
This is my firm conviction.*

With right knowledge—not only heard or read, but now internalized and lived—all mental delusions will dissolve away, one by one,
slowly but surely. This means Saraswati helps you awaken from the
bondage of wrongly assumed identity and reclaim your true goddess
core. As Durga, she imparts the spiritual courage to look beyond your
darkness and confidently choose a greater life direction. As Lakshmi,
she instills good habits and inner positivity as you make this journey.
Finally, you will be reintroduced to your own inwardly smiling, self-
pleased, deeply peaceful, serene Saraswati goddess Self. Everything
will be influenced by the inner restfulness of your true goddess nature.
Then, even as war, chaos, earthquakes, volcanoes, or violent argu-
ments detonate outside you, you will respond from inner peace. Then
you will be leading a truly authentic life, and roar from the delight of
sheer self-recognition. I am confident that you will begin roaring like
Saraswati, a roar that spreads vibrations of peace, love, and beauty
everywhere in this universe.

Through your peaceful heart, an inner illumination will grow
every day steadily within you, and nine Saraswati qualities will be
revealed from within in your mind:

1 A steady mental state shall emerge where self-
sufficient, self-respecting feelings will dominate.
2 Greater knowledge about your own inner
spiritual nature will emerge spontaneously.
3 You shall feel that a greater presence or intelligence
is available for guidance from within.
4 The ability to generate wealth will be evident. You'll
no longer lose wealth due to a disturbed mind.

5 New abilities or dexterity in leading a life of
   values and wisdom will begin shining.
6 The ability to build teams and collaborate will
   become easeful.
7 The enjoyment of worthy dharmic fame that is the fruit of
   life lived with goddess Self-recognition will become realized.
8 There will be an emergence of inner courage that
   comes from greeting the divine goddess within.
9 An ability to face truth, live with truth, and speak your
   truth, unapologetically and fearlessly, will become evident.

And this is how in my life, through contemplative appreciation of and devotion to Goddess Saraswati, I become peaceful. Through meditation on her, I become inwardly quiet. Through chanting her mantras, I become infinitely inspired. Through vision of her as my own Self and my inherent unity with her, I have become filled with inner light . . . enlightened! May you also discover the blessings of Goddess Saraswati in the spacious chamber of your own heart. This is my wish for you.

YOU ARE THE ONE AND THE MANY

I want to remind you that there are not three goddesses but one. When Saraswati the peaceful one is enraged for a just cause, she becomes Durga, the protector and restorer of the greater truth. And when she is pleased, smiling, and blessing the universe with her light, she becomes Lakshmi, the bestower of joys untold. And when she is silent in divine self-awareness, she is simply being herself, the serenely meditating Saraswati, the ever-flowing one. *She flows because she knows who she is.* Likewise, Durga and Lakshmi, too, become each other from time to time.

This is how the Goddess Shakti is one goddess and many goddesses at the same time. There is none superior to the others. They are all equally and simultaneously *supreme.* They contain each other within their essence and inside us they live in our heart and become activated when we emulate their attitudes and begin to live like bold, beautiful, radiant goddesses ourselves in our daily lives—choosing power, abundance, and peace as our true and absolute expression as goddess-women of the twenty-first century!

Sometimes verses emerging from my soul can express more than prose.

> *The knowledge of who I am, versus who I thought I was,*
> *gives me wings, hitherto, unknown.*
> *I have come to know a magical existence, a Goddess force,*
> *a divine power that dwells within me as Self,*
> *in whose feminine presence . . .*
> *my limitations subside in limitlessness.*
> *my bondages dissolve in boundlessness.*
> *my fears dissolve in fearlessness.*
> *I am powerful, I am fulfilled, I am peaceful, from within,*
> *and I know now, who I am, never to forget again;*
> *that to roar is my destiny, my true voice, my thunder, my*
> *light, my music within.*

May you, too, reclaim your inner goddess, experience your true power, inner fullness, and propensity for radical peace despite going to war if needed, and may you, too, annihilate the asuras of patriarchy, misogyny, sexism, and any form of inequality that still persists in your life and around you . . . this is my prayer for you and all readers of this book.

When you express your true voice and roar like a goddess, no one can burn you because you have become a flame; no one can drown you, for you have become the ocean; no one can imprison you, for you are flowing like the wind. Alive, full, beautiful, a living model of an unending progression of goddess consciousness, you are hard to contain, and yet you fit everywhere, in every heart, reigning like the empress that you are!

A FINAL SARASWATI CONTEMPLATION FOR YOU

I ASK: How peaceful am I, and does that have
any bearing on how authentic I am?

I RECOGNIZE: Inner peace is the ultimate goal. Authenticity is the key.

I CONNECT: Withdrawing from the world a bit, I listen to my goddess voice: What do I want and need? What needs to change?

I DECIDE: Here onwards I will always honor my true voice, in service of authenticity.

I ACT: In every situation, I practice dropping the masks and speaking truthfully.

I REMEMBER: Saraswati dwells within me, in my heart. She is me, I AM peace.

ROAR like the goddess that you are!

ROAR ALONGSIDE YOUR GODDESS COMMUNITY

O Shakti, to those who place their heart in your
heart you restore their true voice.
They begin to roar like you, at last.

ACHARYA SHUNYA

Sometimes, I wonder to myself: What would happen if all the women and beings who identify with the feminine gender in this world knew about Durga's power, Lakshmi's radiance, and Saraswati's peace, and had ways to access their goddess strengths, divine protection, and grace through contemplation of these archetypes?

How would this affect our collective lives, our dreams, our different-gendered goddess children?

Would there be more rejection, wounding, discrimination, and painful abuse of the nondominant genders by the dominant genders, or more compassion, good power, abiding peace, and glorious self- and other-acceptance?

Would our children grow up on a hostile intolerant planet, or be celebrated as radiant goddess sparks? Indeed, a revolution of consciousness may occur when we dare to turn inward to discover our resplendent goddess dimension, a portal to everlasting happiness, power, abundance, and wisdom within!

Therefore, dear reader, ROAR like a goddess for me. ROAR for yourself, for all of us, and for the sake of our planet. ROAR to change unevolved beliefs like patriarchy.

As you continue to ROAR with your true voice, soaring spirit, and free heart, gather with other women and differently gendered beings who were previously suppressing their true voices and ROAR together. Roaring alone and in community will have positive effects in all areas of your life—in your relationships, in your career, in your family, and with yourself—and will manifest in ways big and small. You may find yourself more confident to speak up in a meeting, express a need to your partner, or set a boundary with your family. You may decide to leave an abusive relationship, petition for a raise, or access a new level of personal inner peace and contentment.

As we learn to ROAR together, let's encourage and celebrate each other and help each other along the journey of roaring like a Goddess! Roaring within a community of other modern goddesses— delighting in each other's successes and supporting each other's struggles—amplifies the goddess lifestyle and strengthens the collective Roar. Come join me on RoarLikeaGoddess.com, where we roar together in community. Share with other roaring goddesses how you are ROARing in your life. I will find you in the goddess collective and ROAR alongside you!

My inner goddess is sending her goddess ROAR your way!

Love,
Acharya Shunya

ACKNOWLEDGMENTS

How does one acknowledge the unseen nurturing forces and the guidance of the mystical muses? In writing this book, I am grateful to the realm of the Divine Feminine, which made its presence felt in my heart and intimately revealed my hidden Shakti to me. Deep bows to the Goddess that dwells within all hearts as unbounded creativity and courage to roar with authenticity. HER sacred inspirations became the impetus to write this book.

My gratitude to the students who responded optimistically to my goddess workshops and retreats over the last decade. Your joy and inner growth additionally convinced me to write this book. Many of you shared your journey of transformation through this book. I thank you for your candid contributions.

Ishani Lauren Naidu, a long-time student and now an educator in my lineage, managed all my requests and needs pertaining to the book. Kristen Pope, a relatively new student but definitely an old soul, helped with early proofreading and drafting the contemplation exercises. Thank you both! Gayathri Raman, Aparna Amy Lewis, Janya, Vimala, Lakshmi, Vaidehi, and Aarti, your help with my ongoing work and mission freed up my time to write. At home, my partner Sanjai was a steadying and comforting pillar. Stephany Evans, my literary agent since my first book, was a steadfast captain of my author's ship—I can't thank you enough for being there for me, manifesting this book into a reality!

Deep gratitude to my publisher Tami Simon. You are an original roaring one, Tami! You continue to inspire me with your vision and courage. Thanks to my acquisitions and executive editor, Jennifer Brown, for believing in my manuscript from the get-go, and making valuable editorial suggestions at critical stages. Gretel Hakanson, editor-in-chief, you brought out the shine in my writing, and exactness too! I couldn't have done this without you, Gretel. Thank you, Leslie Brown, production editor, Juniper Stokes, copywriter, and Karen Polaski for designing the book and its gorgeous cover. I also want to acknowledge Christine Day, marketing manager, and Mike Onorato, publicist at Sounds True. Ekabhumi Charles Ellik, you are such a gifted sacred artist and I feel privileged that you have illustrated my book. Your goddess drawings bring life to this book at a totally different level. Thank you from my heart!

I offer deep bows to my teacher and grandfather Baba Ayodhya Nath, for imparting to me the dharma and wisdom of Self. My father, Padmashri Daya Prakash Sinha, gladdens my heart for always nurturing my inner goddess with love and respect. You raised a super confident girl-child by always teaching me to believe in myself.

Finally, I must slow down my writing of this acknowledgment . . . breathe deeply, feel my tender heart, and remember my late mother. Mom, you left me so early. But at least you taught me how to *roar like a goddess*, and now I am teaching others how to roar too. When I roar, all is well in my inner life, and then I am never really far away from you!

ACKNOWLEDGMENTS

NOTES

Prologue: It Is Time to Roar Like a Goddess

1 Charlotte Higgins, "The Age of Patriarchy: How an
Unfashionable Idea Become a Rallying Cry for Feminism Today,"
Guardian, June 22, 2018, theguardian.com/news/2018/jun/22/the
-age-of-patriarchy-how-an-unfashionable-idea-became-a-rallying
-cry-for-feminism-today.

Introduction: The Search for the Hidden Goddess

1 *Shvetashvatara Upanishad* 5.10.
2 Sally Kempton, *Awakening Shakti* (Boulder, CO: Sounds True,
2013), 12.
3 This is not a book of scholarship in the classical sense, and
therefore does not detail the Purana-based source of each myth
exhaustively. However, readers who wish to explore mythology
sources further can look up the *Devi Bhagavata Purana*, also
known as *Bhagavata Purana*, *Srimad Bhagavatam*, and *Srimad
Devi Bhagavatam*. This text enjoys a place of prestige among
Puranic literature, because while all the major Puranas mention
and revere the goddess, the *Devi Bhagavata Purana* focuses
upon her as the primary divinity that is portrayed in its stories.
Another important and perhaps older Purana is the *Markandeya
Purana*, which contains a subsection known as the *Devi
Mahatmya*, glorifying the goddess legends and victories over
the asuras, which is organized in 700 uplifting verses. The other
names for *Devi Mahatmya* are *Durga Saptashati* and *Shri Chandi
Paath*. A Hindu sub-denomination that exclusively reveres
Goddess Shakti (and her avatars), known as the *Shaktas*, consider

the *Devi Mahatmya* as their holiest scripture. Other Puranas that contain similar or different goddess legends include *Matsya Purana, Shiva Purana,* and *Kalika Purana.*

4 Vedic scriptures made no social prohibitions against women's secular or spiritual advancement, as that would go against their very spirit of inclusivity and unity of spirit. But the liberal society gradually morphed toward less inclusivity during medieval times, due to the intermixing of Islamic ideals that were brought to India by invaders in the twelfth century and onward; these invaders later established monarchies that ruled India for almost six hundred years and made Islam the official religion. The self-confident Hindu women who once lived carefree lives had to pay a steep price for their freedom over the next 700 years, including mass rape and public shaming by invaders who later set up feudal establishments and monarchies by the power of the sword and forced religious conversion too. Hindu temples were demolished, and study of the Vedas was obstructed or banned. Women were asked to cover their bodies. This influence, over time, led to a cultural brainwashing.

Chapter 1: Durga: The Power Inherent in Every Power

1 *Devi Mahatmya* 1.84.

2 *Devi Mahatmya* 4.3.

3 "Rosa Parks," Biography.com, last updated March 26, 2021, biography.com/activist/rosa-parks?li_source=LI&li_medium= bio-mid-article&li_pl=208&li_tr=bio-mid-article.

4 "Kathrine Switzer: The Woman Behind Those Numbers," 261 Fearless, 261fearless.org/about-261/kv-switzer/.

Chapter 2: When Raging Is a Goddess Thing to Do

1 Harriet Lerner, "Why Men and Women Dread Female Anger," Psychology Today, February 10, 2019, psychologytoday.com/us /blog/the-dance-connection/201902/why-men-and-women -dread-female-anger.

2 Mahabharata 18.116.37–41.

3 David Saul, *The Indian Mutiny: 1857* (London: Penguin, 2003), 367.

4 Sarah Cascone, "Archaeologists Have Discovered the Skeletons of 'Badass' Warrior Women in Mongolia, Dating Back to the Period of Mulan," Artnet News, May 13, 2020, news.artnet.com/art -world/mongolian-warrior-women-skeletons-mulan-1860144.

5 Caroline Goldstein, "Archaeologists Just Discovered the Bones, Weapons, and Headdresses of Four Real-Life Amazon Warriors in Russia," Artnet News, January 23, 2020, news.artnet.com/art -world/amazon-women-burial-russia-1760256.

6 "Queen Mother Nana Yaa Asantewaa of West Africa's Ashanti Empire," Black History Heroes (blog), accessed October 12, 2021, blackhistoryheroes.com/2010/05/queen-mother-nana-yaa -asantewaa.html.

7 A. Moore, "10 Fearless Black Female Warriors Throughout History," Atlanta Black Star, October 29, 2013, atlantablackstar.com/2013/10/29/10-fearless-black-female -warriors-throughout-history/.

8 A. Moore, "10 Fearless Black Female Warriors Throughout History."

9 "Harriet Tubman," History.com, last updated January 27, 2021, history.com/topics/black-history/harriet-tubman; "After the Underground Railroad, Harriet Tubman Led a Brazen Civil War Raid," History.com, last updated January 25, 2021, history.com /news/harriet-tubman-combahee-ferry-raid-civil-war.

Chapter 3: Roar Like a Goddess When Accosted Sexually

1 Hannah K. Griggs, "Indian Women's Uplift Movements and the Dangers of Cultural Imperialism" (Mary Wollstonecraft Writing Award, Augustana College, 2016), 7, digitalcommons .augustana.edu/cgi/viewcontent.cgi?article=1011&context= wollstonecraftaward.

2 Neha Chuahan, "How Gender-Based Violence in India Continues to Rise," SocialStory, September 16, 2019, yourstory.com /socialstory/2019/09/gender-violence-india/amp.

3 Shweta Desai, "Gulabi Gang: India's Women Warriors," Al Jazeera, March 4, 2014, aljazeera.com/features/2014/3/4/gulabi-gang -indias-women-warriors.

Chapter 5: Establish Boundaries to Live Royally Like Durga

1 Acharya Shunya, *Sovereign Self* (Boulder, CO: Sounds True, 2020), 325.

Chapter 7: Goddess Lakshmi and Her Beautiful Symbolism

1 Harvard Health Publishing, "Giving Thanks Can Make You Happier," August 14, 2021, health.harvard.edu/healthbeat/giving -thanks-can-make-you-happier.

2 Lisa Firestone, "The Healing Power of Gratitude," Psychology Today, November 19, 2015, psychologytoday.com/us/blog /compassion-matters/201511/the-healing-power-gratitude.

3 Oprah Winfrey, "Be thankful for what you have; you'll end up having more. If you concentrate on what you don't have, you will never, ever have enough . . ." Facebook, October 3, 2011, m .facebook.com/oprahwinfrey/posts/be-thankful-for-what-you -have-and-youll-end-up-having-more-if-you-concentrate-on /10150372378472220/.

4 The Law of Karma is based on a core belief of the Hindus that death does not end the living entity called *jiva* (reflected consciousness plus ego). You are a continuing entity and you have faced many deaths and many births prior to your current incarnation. At every death, your body is destroyed, as it is made of perishable matter, but the soul or jiva (reflected consciousness plus ego) and leftover desires (*vasanas*) plus the balance of good and bad deeds (karmic bundle)—this entire (invisible) package transmigrates onward, to find a new body in a new womb (could be a human, animal, insect, or plant womb).

Chapter 8: The Greatest Wealth Comes from Valuing Your Self

1 Vishnu is Goddess Lakshmi's well-known consort. However, other parables connect Lakshmi to the Vedic God Indra, prior to Vishnu. Indra is considered the head of the devas and also the king of the heavens. He is associated with enabling rains and leading righteous wars. Perhaps the link between Indra and Lakshmi emerged from the power associated with the office of kings being represented by the Goddess herself. Lakshmi's association with Indra was considered beneficial to people on Earth because it

resulted in fertile rains pouring down from the heavens, thereby allowing crops to grow, and ultimately, all beings on Earth prospered with Lakshmi and Indra's combined blessings.

2 Nichi Hodgson, "If You're In a Bad Marriage, Don't Mend It—End It," *Guardian*, July 19, 2018, theguardian.com/commentisfree/2018 /jul/19/bad-marriage-unhappy-marriages-health.

3 Emma Gray, "'F**king Bitch' and the Everyday Terror Men Feel About Powerful Women," Huffpost, July 23, 2020, huffpost.com /entry/aoc-ted-yoho-bitch-speech_n_5f19d838c5b6296fbf3f7b6d.

4 Gray, "'F**king Bitch.'"

5 Jack Holland, *A Brief History of Misogyny: The World's Oldest Prejudice* (London: Robinson, 2019).

6 Gray, "'F**king Bitch.'"

Chapter 9: The Four Goals of Life and Goddess Lakshmi

1 Porcshe Moran, "How Much Is a Stay-at-Home Parent Worth?" Investopedia, updated September 5, 2021, investopedia.com /financial-edge/0112/how-much-is-a-homemaker-worth.aspx.

Chapter 10: The Value of Discontentment in a Goddess's Life

1 "Eight Garudhammas," Tibetan Buddhist Encyclopedia, last modified March 8, 2016, tibetanbuddhistencyclopedia.com/en /index.php/Eight_Garudhammas.

2 Lama Rod Owens, "How We Can Address Patriarchy," Lion's Roar, August 4, 2017, lionsroar.com/buddhists-ethical-misconduct-we -all-have-patriarchy-work-to-do/.

3 Qur'an 2:228.

4 Qur'an 4:34.

5 Qur'an 4:11.

6 Qur'an 2:282.

7 Genesis 3:16.

8 1 Corinthians 14:34–35.

9 Ephesians 5:22–23.

10 Deuteronomy 22:28–29.

11 Amelia E. Barr, "Discontented Women," The Literature Network, online-literature.com/amelia-barr/maids-wives-bachelors/13/.

12 Devdutt Pattanaik, "The Ancient Story of Goddess Lakshmi—
Bestower of Power, Wealth, and Sovereignty," Quartz India,
November 10, 2015, qz.com/india/545655/the-ancient-story-of
-goddess-lakshmi-bestower-of-power-wealth-and-sovereignty/.
13 Malala Yousafzai, "Nobel Lecture, December 10, 2014," December 10,
2014, nobelprize.org/uploads/2018/06/yousafzai-lecture_en.pdf.

Chapter 11: Lakshmi Shows the Path to Generosity

1 Bhagavad Gita 17.20–22.
2 Bhagavad Gita 17.20.
3 Bhagavad Gita 17.21.
4 Bhagavad Gita 17.22.
5 *Atharva Veda* 14.1.43–44.
6 Mahabharata, Adi Parva, 1.74.50–51.
7 Megan Friedman and Jenny Hollander, "23 Ways Women Still
Aren't Equal to Men," *Marie Claire*, April 27, 2021, marieclaire
.com/politics/news/a15652/gender-inequality-stats/.
8 Charlotte Higgins, "The Age of Patriarchy: How an Unfashionable
Idea Become a Rallying Cry for Feminism Today," *Guardian*,
June 22, 2018, theguardian.com/news/2018/jun/22/the-age-of
-patriarchy-how-an-unfashionable-idea-became-a-rallying-cry
-for-feminism-today.

Chapter 12: Saraswati's Mythology and Awakening Insights

1 Saraswati Stotram, verse 11.
2 Saraswati's appeal has traveled beyond the borders of India. We
find her being revered as Thurathadi in Myanmar, as Benzaiten
in Japan, as Vagishvari (goddess of sacred speech) in Cambodia,
and as Bharati (goddess of spiritual light) in Khmer literature.
In Thailand, she is beloved alongside her consort Brahma and
is called Suratsawadi. People love wearing her embedded in
necklaces and amulets, depicting her along with her vahana, the
swan or peacock. The island of Bali in Indonesia is especially
dotted with ancient Saraswati temples and figurines and an
entire festival dedicated to the goddess is celebrated every six
months, called Saraswati's Day.

3 *Rig Veda* 1.3.12.

4 Saraswati is sometimes portrayed as the daughter of Hindu God Brahma. In fact, some writers have even accused Brahma of incest. Ouch! These observations could not be further from the truth in my opinion. Brahma is the personification of Creator energy of the universe, and Saraswati is the personification of Knowledge of this universe, and as such, they are the masculine (Shiva) and feminine (Shakti) principles of the same Supreme Truth of a divinity that is nondual—beyond gender, form, and name. Saraswati is not Brahma's biological daughter. Besides, everything created by a person does not become his or her offspring. Though manifested from Brahma, just like Durga emerges from all the assembled devas in her myth, Saraswati is not his daughter, nor Durga the daughter of the devas.

5 *Rig Veda* 2.41.16.

Chapter 13: The Goddess Path of Discernment and Sovereignty

1 In some versions of the legend, Indra suggests that Brahma marry Goddess Gayatri in order to go forward with the ritual.

Chapter 14: Saraswati Says Wake Up and Face Your Trauma

1 Valerie Rein, *Patriarchy Stress Disorder: The Invisible Inner Barrier to Women's Happiness and Fulfillment* (Carson City, NV: Lioncrest Publishing, 2019), 8, 20–23.

2 Nachman Ben-Yehuda, "The European Witch Craze of the 14th to 17th Centuries: A Sociologist's Perspective," *American Journal of Sociology* 86, no. 1 (July 1980): 1–31. doi.org/10.1086/227200.

3 Gwynn Guilford, "Germany Was Once the Witch-Burning Capital of the World. Here's Why," Quartz, January 24, 2018, qz.com /1183992/why-europe-was-overrun-by-witch-hunts-in-early -modern-history/.

4 Diana E. H. Russell, "Defining Femicide: The Most Extreme Form of Violence Against Women and Girls," accessed November 29, 2021, labrys.net.br/labrys24/feminicide/diana.htm.

5 Simone de Beauvoir, *The Second Sex* (New York: Vintage Books, 1974), xxii.

6 Maya Salam, "How the Patriarchy Got in Our Heads," *New York Times*, March 19, 2019, nytimes.com/2019/03/19/us/what-is-patriarchy.html.

7 Lisa Mosconi, *The XX Brain: The Groundbreaking Science Empowering Women to Maximize Cognitive Health and Prevent Alzheimer's Disease* (New York: Avery Publishing, 2020).

8 Sean Illing, "What We Get Wrong About Misogyny," Vox, March 7, 2020, vox.com/identities/2017/12/5/16705284/elizabeth-warren-loss-2020-sexism-misogyny-kate-manne.

9 Meera Atkinson, "Patriarchy Perpetuates Trauma. It's Time to Face the Fact," *Guardian*, April 29, 2018, theguardian.com/commentisfree/2018/apr/30/patriarchy-perpetuates-trauma-its-time-to-face-the-fact.

Chapter 16: Saraswati: The Teacher and Giver of Lasting Inner Peace

1 Quote Investigator, "Courage Is Resistance to Fear, Mastery of Fear—Not Absence of Fear," November 26, 2019, quoteinvestigator.com/2019/11/26/courage-fear/.

ABOUT THE AUTHOR

Acharya Shunya is an internationally renowned teacher, author, speaker, and scholar of nondual wisdom (Advaita) and a classically trained master of Yoga and Ayurveda. The first female lineage-holder in her ancient Vedic family that traces its roots to two thousand years ago in India, Acharya Shunya is known for her unique and revolutionary perspectives and art of sacred storytelling that has enlightened tens of thousands of students worldwide.

Acharya Shunya is the Founder of the Awakened Self Foundation and Vedika Global, Inc., platforms that empower, educate, and inspire. An award-winning author of international repute, besides *Roar Like a Goddess*, Acharya Shunya has also authored *Sovereign Self: Claim Your Inner Joy and Freedom with the Empowering Wisdom of the Vedas, Upanishads, and Bhagavad Gita* (Sounds True, 2020) and *Ayurveda Lifestyle Wisdom: A Complete Prescription to Optimize your Health, Prevent Disease, and Live with Vitality and Joy* (Sounds True, 2017). She is also the host of the top-rated podcast *Shadow to Self*.

Through online courses and retreats on Ayurveda, Yoga, Advaita, and interpreting Vedic goddess mythology, the Awakened Self Foundation is focused on the timeless Vedic teachings that enable all humans to attain their full potential as healthy, authentic, and awakened beings. Vedika Global, Inc., is a 501(c)(3) nonprofit dedicated to forwarding the spiritual teachings and philosophical ideals of Acharya Shunya's lineage. Both organizations are headquartered in Northern California and serve a global community of students.

Acharya Shunya's unique gift to humanity is her deeply personal understanding of the ancient Vedic traditions of spiritual knowledge and their classic scriptures. She expertly demystifies and adapts these into contemporary language, and crafts meaningful practices for Western seekers, providing a rare opportunity to receive authentic teachings from a genuine Vedic master—one with a distinctly down-to-earth feminine flavor—who never lets us forget that our humanity is to be embodied and enjoyed.

Acharya Shunya has grown up revering God as Divine Mother, and has conceived empowering and entirely unique goddess archetypes within the laboratory of her own life as daughter, wife, and mother. As someone who has herself walked the path from shadow to light, she is uniquely able to communicate these subtle teachings to modern seekers through her ability to share candidly by personal example, to interpret mythology, to translate esoteric wisdom from sacred Sanskrit texts, and to communicate consciousness-elevating and emboldening practices and insights.

Learn more at AcharyaShunya.com, AwakenedSelf.com, and RoarLikeAGoddess.com.

ABOUT SOUNDS TRUE

S ounds True is a multimedia publisher whose mission is to inspire and support personal transformation and spiritual awakening. Founded in 1985 and located in Boulder, Colorado, we work with many of the leading spiritual teachers, thinkers, healers, and visionary artists of our time. We strive with every title to preserve the essential "living wisdom" of the author or artist. It is our goal to create products that not only provide information to a reader or listener but also embody the quality of a wisdom transmission.

For those seeking genuine transformation, Sounds True is your trusted partner. At SoundsTrue.com you will find a wealth of free resources to support your journey, including exclusive weekly audio interviews, free downloads, interactive learning tools, and other special savings on all our titles.

To learn more, please visit SoundsTrue.com/freegifts or call us toll-free at 800.333.9185.